STUDIES IN PROSE AND VERSE

de Balzac

STUDIES

IN

PROSE AND VERSE

BY

ARTHUR SYMONS

WITH PORTRAITS
IN PHOTOGRAVURE

LONDON
J. M. DENT & CO.
29 AND 30 BEDFORD STREET, W.C.

TO MRS LUDWIG MOND

I DEDICATE this book to you in memory of evenings, now too many to count, in London and in Rome, when we have talked of books together. There are many things in it with which you will not agree; yet in you there is one thing I can count on, a continual sympathy; and another, rarer thing as well, which does not always go with it: a divination which can strike through the words to the meaning; and deeper, to that meaning's meaning.

If there are any names here that do not interest you, disregard them, or read other names in their places. I am interested only in first principles, and it seems to me that to study first principles one must wait for them till they are made flesh and dwell among us. I have rarely contrasted one writer with another, or compared very carefully the various books of any writer among themselves. Criticism is not an examination with marks and prizes. It is a valuation of forces, and it is indifferent to their direction. It is concerned with them only as force, and it is concerned with force only in its kind and degree.

As you will see in reading the book, I have a few principles of criticism, and I apply these few principles to every writer and on every occasion. If, as I hope, there is any essential unity in this collection of essays on contemporary writers, that unity must come wholly from the uniformity of the tests which I have applied to all this varying material. Others may care, possibly, for my opinion on Balzac, my opinion on Tolstoi; you, I know, will see what my real aim has been, and your interest in the matter will be the same as mine.

ARTHUR SYMONS.

Poltescoe, Cornwall,
September 17, 1904.

CONTENTS

CONTENTS

LIST OF ILLUSTRATIONS

INTRODUCTION

FACT IN LITERATURE

The invention of printing helped to destroy literature. Scribes, and memories not yet spoilt by over-cramming, preserved all the literature that was worth preserving. Books that had to be remembered by heart, or copied with slow, elaborate penmanship, were not thrown away on people who did not want them. They remained in the hands of people of taste. The first book pointed the way to the first newspaper, and a newspaper is a thing meant to be not only forgotten but destroyed. With the deliberate destruction of print, the respect for printed literature vanished, and a single term came to be used for the poem and for the "news item." What had once been an art for the few became a trade for the many, and, while in painting, in sculpture, in music, the mere fact of production means, for the most part, an attempt to produce a work of art, the function of written or printed words ceased to be necessarily more than what a Spanish poet has called "the jabber of the human animal." Unfortunately, words can convey facts; unfortunately, people in general have an ill-regulated but insatiable appetite for facts. Now music cannot convey facts at all; painting or sculpture can only convey fact through a medium which necessarily transforms it. But literature is tied by that which gives it wings. It can do, in a measure, all that can be done by the other arts, and it can speak where they can but make beautiful and expressive gestures. But it has this danger, that its paint, or clay, or crotchets and quavers, may be taken for the colour, or form, or sound, and not as the ministrants of these things. Literature, in making its beautiful piece of work, has to use words and facts; these words, these facts, are the common property of all the world, to whom they mean no more than what each individually says, before it has come to take on beautiful form through its adjustment in the pattern. So, while paints are of no use to the man who does not understand the science of their employment, nor clay, nor the notations of musical sound, to any but the trained artist, words may be used at will, and no literature follow, only something which many people will greatly prefer, and which they will all have the misfortune to understand.

There exist, then, under the vague title of literature, or without even the excuse of a stolen title, books which are not books, printed paper which has come from the rag-heap to return to the rag-heap, that nameless thing the newspaper, which can be likened only, and that at its best, to a printed phonograph. It is assumed that there is a reason in nature why the British shopkeeper should sit down after business hours, and read, for the price of a penny or a halfpenny, that a fire broke out at the other end of London at ten o'clock in the morning, and that a young lady of whom he has never heard was burned to death. But the matter is really of no importance to him, and there is no reason in nature why he should ever know anything at all about it. He has but put one more obstacle between himself and any rational conception of the meaning of his life, between himself and any natural happiness, between himself and any possible wisdom. Facts are difficult of digestion, and should be taken diluted, at infrequent intervals. They suit few constitutions when taken whole, and none when taken indiscriminately. The worship of fact is a wholly modern attitude of mind, and it comes together with a worship of what we call science. True science is a kind of poetry, it is a divination, an imaginative reading of the universe. What we call science is an engine of material progress, it teaches us how to get most quickly to the other end of the world, and how to kill the people there in the most precise and economic manner. The function of this kind of science is to extinguish wonder, whereas the true science deepens our sense of wonder as it enlightens every new tract of the enveloping darkness.

What royalties and religions have been, the newspaper is. It is the idol of the hour, the principality and power of the moment; the average man's Bible, friend, teacher, guide, entertainment, and opiate. Because its power is the aggregate of separate feeblenesses, let us not commit the error of denying that power. As well deny the power of folly, which is the voice of the mob; or of the mob, which is the mouthpiece of folly. The newspaper is the fulfilment of the prophecy that the voice of the people shall be the voice of God. It is the perpetual affirmation of the new law which has abolished all other laws: the law of the greatest wisdom of the greatest number.

The newspaper is the plague, or black death, of the modern world. It is an open sewer, running down each side of the street, and displaying the foulness of every day, day by day, morning and evening. Everything that, having once happened, has ceased to exist, the newspaper sets before you, beating the bones of the buried without pity, without shame, and without understanding. Its pride is that it is the record of facts, but it tells you no fact twice in the same way; for it gorges its insatiable appetite upon rumour, which is wind and noise. All the hypocrisies of the State, of the Church, of the market-place, cling together for once in brotherly love, and speak with unanimous voices.

The excuse for existence offered by the newspaper, and by every other form of printed matter which does not aim at some artistic end, is that it conveys fact, and that fact is indispensable. But, after all, what is fact? "For poetry," says Matthew Arnold, "the idea is everything, the rest is a world of illusion, of divine illusion. Poetry attaches its emotions to the idea; the idea is the fact." Let it be granted that some kind of fact is indispensable to every man: to one man one kind of idea is fact, to another man another; and there remain those to whom fact is really the news of the newspaper. But, even to these, it must be this fact and not that, and certainly not a deluge of any.

Reported speech, for that is what literature is when it is not the musical notation of song, has become more and more a marketable product. It is not paid for, as even the worst picture is paid for, on account of some imagined artistic merit (a picture being always "pretty to look at"), but because it satisfies a curiosity. If the artist in literature chooses to throw in beauty when he is asked only to answer a question, the beauty is not always rejected along with the answer. But the answer will be considered, at the best, a little unsatisfactory, because a plain man wants a plain answer.

1902.

BALZAC

I

The first man who has completely understood Balzac is Rodin, and it has taken Rodin ten years to realise his own conception. France has refused the statue in which a novelist is represented as a dreamer, to whom Paris is not so much Paris as Patmos: "the most Parisian of our novelists," Frenchmen assure you. It is more than a hundred years since Balzac was born: a hundred years is a long time in which to be misunderstood with admiration.

In choosing the name of the "Human Comedy" for a series of novels in which, as he says, there is at once "the history and the criticism of society, the analysis of its evils, and the discussion of its principles," Balzac proposed to do for the modern world what Dante, in his "Divine Comedy," had done for the world of the Middle Ages. Condemned to write in prose, and finding his opportunity in that restriction, he created for himself a form which is perhaps the nearest equivalent for the epic or the poetic drama, and the only form in which, at all events, the epic is now possible. The world of Dante was materially simple compared with the world of the nineteenth century; the "visible world" had not yet begun to "exist," in its tyrannical modern sense; the complications of the soul interested only the Schoolmen, and were a part of theology; poetry could still represent an age and yet be poetry. But to-day poetry can no longer represent more than the soul of things; it has taken refuge from the terrible improvements of civilisation in a divine seclusion, where it sings, disregarding the many voices of the street. Prose comes offering its infinite capacity for detail; and it is by the infinity of its detail that the novel, as Balzac created it, has become the modern epic.

There had been great novels, indeed, before Balzac, but no great novelist; and the novels themselves are scarcely what we should to-day call by that name. The interminable "Astrée" and its companions form a link between the *fabliaux* and the novel, and from them developed the characteristic eighteenth-century *conte*, in narrative, letters, or dialogue, as we see it in Marivaux, Laclos, Crebillon *fils*. Crebillon's longer works, including "Le Sopha," with their conventional paraphernalia of Eastern fable, are extremely tedious; but in two short pieces, "La Nuit et le Moment" and "Le Hasard du Coin du Feu," he created a model of witty, naughty, deplorably natural comedy, which to this day is one of the most characteristic French forms of fiction. Properly, however, it is a form of the drama rather than of the novel. Laclos, in "Les Liaisons Dangereuses," a masterpiece which scandalised the society that adored Crebillon, because its naked human truth left no room for sentimental excuses, comes much nearer to prefiguring the novel (as Stendhal, for instance, is afterward to conceive it), but still preserves the awkward traditional form of letters. Marivaux had indeed already seemed to suggest the novel of analysis, but in a style which has christened a whole manner of writing, that precisely which is least suited to the writing of fiction. Voltaire's *contes*, "La Religieuse" of Diderot, are tracts or satires in which the story is only an excuse for the purpose. Rousseau, too, has his purpose, even in "La Nouvelle Héloïse," but it is a humanising purpose; and with that book the novel of passion comes into existence, and along with it the descriptive novel. Yet with Rousseau this result is an accident of genius; we cannot call him a novelist; and we find him abandoning the form he has found, for another, more closely personal, which suits him better. Restif de la Bretonne, who followed Rousseau at a distance, not altogether wisely, developed the form of half-imaginary autobiography in "Monsieur Nicolas," a book of which the most significant part may be compared with Hazlitt's "Liber Amoris." Morbid and even mawkish as it is, it has a certain uneasy, unwholesome humanity in its confessions, which may seem to have set a fashion only too scrupulously followed by modern French novelists. Meanwhile, the Abbé Prévost's one great story, "Manon Lescaut," had brought for once a purely objective study, of an incomparable simplicity, into the midst of these analyses of difficult souls; and then we return to the confession, in the works of others not novelists: Benjamin Constant, Mme. de Staël, Chateaubriand, in "Adolphe," "Corinne," "René." At once we are in the Romantic movement, a movement which begins lyrically among poets, and at first with a curious disregard of the more human part of humanity.

Balzac worked contemporaneously with the Romantic movement, but he worked outside it, and its influence upon him is felt only in an occasional pseudo-romanticism, like the episode of the pirate in "La Femme de Trente Ans." His vision of humanity was essentially a poetic vision, but he was a poet whose dreams were facts. Knowing that, as Mme. Necker has said, "the novel should be the better world," he knew also that "the novel would be nothing if, in that august lie, it were not true in details." And in the "Human Comedy" he proposed to himself to do for society more than Buffon had done for the animal world.

"There is but one animal," he declares, in his *Avant-Propos*, with a confidence which Darwin has not yet come to justify. But "there exists, there will always exist, social species, as there are zoological species." "Thus the work to be done will have a triple form: men, women, and things; that is to say, human beings and the material representation which they give to their thought; in short, man and life." And, studying after nature, "French society will be the historian, I shall need to be no more than the secretary." Thus will be written "the history forgotten by so many historians, the history of manners." But that is not all, for "passion is the whole of humanity." "In realising clearly the drift of the composition, it will be seen that I assign to facts, constant, daily, open, or secret, to the acts of individual life, to their causes and principles, as much importance as historians had formerly attached to the events of the public life of nations." "Facts gathered together and painted as they are, with passion for element," is one of his definitions of the task he has undertaken. And in a letter to Mme. de Hanska he summarises every detail of his scheme.

"The *Études des Mœurs* will represent social effects, without a single situation of life, or a physiognomy, or a character of man or woman, or a manner of life, or a profession, or a social zone, or a district of France, or anything pertaining to childhood, old age, or maturity, politics, justice, or war, having been forgotten.

"That laid down, the history of the human heart traced link by link, the history of society made in all its details, we have the base. . . .

"Then, the second stage is the *Études philosophiques*, for after the *effects* come the *causes*. In the *Études des Mœurs* I shall have painted the sentiments and their action, life and the fashion of life. In the *Études philosophiques* I shall say *why the sentiments, on what the life*. . . .

"Then, after the *effects* and the *causes*, come the *Études analytiques*, to which the *Physiologie du mariage* belongs, for, after the *effects* and the *causes*, one should seek the *principles*. . . .

"After having done the poetry, the demonstration, of a whole system, I shall do the science in the *Essai sur les forces humaines*. And, on the bases of this palace I shall have traced the immense arabesque of the *Cent Contes drolatiques !*"

Quite all that, as we know, was not carried out; but there, in its intention, is the plan; and after twenty years' work the main part of it, certainly, was carried out. Stated with this precise detail, it has something of a scientific air, as of a too deliberate attempt upon the sources of life by one of those systematic French minds which are so much more logical than facts. But there is one little phrase to be noted: "La passion est toute l'humanité." All Balzac is in that phrase.

Another French novelist, following, as he thought, the example of the "Human Comedy," has endeavoured to build up a history of his own time with even greater minuteness. But "Les Rougon-Macquart" is no more than system; Zola has never understood that detail without life is the wardrobe without the man. Trying to outdo Balzac on his own ground, he has made the fatal mistake of taking him only on his systematic side, which in Balzac is subordinate to a great creative intellect, an incessant, burning thought about men and women, a passionate human curiosity for which even his own system has no limits. "The misfortunes of the *Birotteaus*, the priest and the perfumer," he says, in his *Avant-Propos*, taking an example at random, "are, for me, those of humanity." To Balzac manners are but the vestment of life; it is life that he seeks; and life, to him (it is his own word) is but the vestment of thought. Thought is at the root of all his work, a whole system of thought, in which philosophy is but another form of poetry; and it is from this root of idea that the "Human Comedy" springs.

II

The two books into which Balzac has put his deepest thought, the two books which he himself cared for the most, are "Séraphita" and "Louis Lambert." Of "Louis Lambert" he said: "I write it for myself and a few others"; of "Séraphita": "My life is in it." "One could write 'Goriot' any day," he adds; "'Séraphita' only once in a lifetime." I have never been able to feel that "Séraphita" is altogether a success. It lacks the breath of life; it is glacial. True, he aimed at producing very much such an effect; and it is, indeed, full of a strange, glittering beauty, the beauty of its own snows. But I find in it at the same time something a little factitious, a sort of romanesque, not altogether unlike the sentimental romanesque of Novalis; it has not done the impossible, in humanising abstract speculation, in fusing mysticism and the novel. But for the student of Balzac it has extraordinary interest; for it is at once the base and the summit of the "Human Comedy." In a letter to Mme. de Hanska, written in 1837, four years after "Séraphita" had been begun, he writes: "I am not orthodox, and I do not believe in the Roman Church. Swedenborgianism, which is but a repetition, in the Christian sense, of ancient ideas, is my religion, with this addition: that I believe in the incomprehensibility of God." "Séraphita" is a prose poem in which the most abstract part of that mystical system, which Swedenborg perhaps materialised too crudely, is presented in a white light, under a single, superhuman image. In "Louis Lambert" the same fundamental conceptions are worked out in the study of a perfectly human intellect, "an intellectual gulf," as he truly calls it; a sober and concise history of ideas in their devouring action upon a too feeble physical nature. In these two books we see directly, and not through the coloured veil of human life, the mind in the abstract of a thinker whose power over humanity was the power of abstract thought. They show this novelist, who has invented the description of society, by whom the visible world has been more powerfully felt than by any other novelist, striving to penetrate the correspondences which exist between the human and the celestial existence. He would pursue the soul to its last resting-place before it takes flight from the body; further, on its disembodied flight; he would find out God, as he comes nearer and nearer to finding out the secret of life. And realising, as he does so profoundly, that there is but one substance, but one ever-changing principle of life, "one vegetable, one animal, but a continual intercourse," the whole world is alive with meaning for him, a more intimate meaning than it has for others. "The least flower is a thought, a life which corresponds to some lineaments of the great whole, of which he has the constant intuition." And so, in his concerns with the world, he will find spirit everywhere; nothing for him will be inert matter, everything will have its particle of the universal life. One of those divine spies, for whom the world has no secrets, he will be neither pessimist nor optimist; he will accept the world as a man accepts the woman whom he loves, as much for her defects as for her virtues. Loving the world for its own sake, he will find it always beautiful, equally beautiful in all its parts. Now let us look at the programme which he traced for the "Human Comedy," let us realise it in the light of this philosophy, and we are at the beginning of a conception of what the "Human Comedy" really is.

III

This visionary, then, who had apprehended for himself an idea of God, set himself to interpret human life more elaborately than any one else. He has been praised for his patient observation; people have thought they praised him in calling him a realist; it has been discussed how far his imitation of life was the literal truth of the photograph. But to Balzac the word realism was an insult. Writing his novels at the rate of eighteen hours a day, in a feverish solitude, he never had the time to observe patiently. It is humanity seen in a mirror, the humanity which comes to the great dreamers, the great poets, humanity as Shakespeare saw it. And so in him, as in all the great artists, there is something more than nature, a divine excess. This something more than nature should be the aim of the artist, not merely the accident which happens to him against his will. We require of him a world like our own, but a world infinitely more vigorous, interesting, profound; more beautiful with that kind of beauty which nature finds of itself for art. It is the quality of great creative art to give us so much life that we are almost overpowered by it, as by an air almost too vigorous to breathe: the exuberance of creation which makes the Sibyls of Michelangelo something more than human, which makes Lear something more than human, in one kind or another of divinity.

Balzac's novels are full of strange problems and great passions. He turned aside from nothing which presented itself in nature; and his mind was always turbulent with the magnificent contrasts and caprices of fate. A devouring passion of thought burned on all the situations by which humanity expresses itself, in its flight from the horror of immobility. To say that the situations which he chose are often romantic is but to say that he followed the soul and the senses faithfully on their strangest errands. Our probable novelists of to-day are afraid of whatever emotion might be misinterpreted in a gentleman. Believing, as we do now, in nerves and a fatalistic heredity, we have left but little room for the dignity and disturbance of violent emotion. To Balzac, humanity had not changed since the days when Œdipus was blind and Philoctetes cried in the cave; and equally great miseries were still possible to mortals, though they were French and of the nineteenth century.

And thus he creates, like the poets, a humanity more logical than average life; more typical, more subdivided among the passions, and having in its veins an energy almost more than human. He realised, as the Greeks did, that human life is made up of elemental passions and necessity; but he was the first to realise that in the modern world the pseudonym of necessity is money. Money and the passions rule the world of his "Human Comedy."

And, at the root of the passions, determining their action, he saw "those nervous fluids, or that unknown substance which, in default of another term, we must call the will." No word returns oftener to his pen. For him the problem is invariable. Man has a given quantity of energy; each man a different quantity: how will he spend it? A novel is the determination in action of that problem. And he is equally interested in every form of energy, in every egoism, so long as it is fiercely itself. This pre-occupation with the force, rather than with any of its manifestations, gives him his singular impartiality, his absolute lack of prejudice; for it gives him the advantage of an abstract point of view, the unchanging fulcrum for a lever which turns in every direction; and as nothing once set vividly in motion by any form of human activity is without interest for him, he makes every point of his vast chronicle of human affairs equally interesting to his readers.

Baudelaire has observed profoundly that every character in the "Human Comedy" has something of Balzac, has genius. To himself, his own genius was entirely expressed in that word "will." It recurs constantly in his letters. "Men of will are rare!" he cries. And, at a time when he had turned night into day for his labour: "I rise every night with a keener will than that of yesterday." "Nothing wearies me," he says, "neither waiting nor happiness." He exhausts the printers, whose fingers can hardly keep pace with his brain; they call him, he reports proudly, "a man-slayer." And he tries to express himself: "I have always had in me something, I know not what, which made me do differently from others; and, with me, fidelity is perhaps no more than pride. Having only myself to rely upon, I have had to strengthen, to build up that self." There is a scene in "La Cousine Bette" which gives precisely Balzac's own sentiment of the supreme value of energy. The Baron Hulot, ruined on every side, and by his own fault, goes to Josépha, a mistress who had cast him off in the time of his prosperity, and asks her to lodge him for a few days in a garret. She laughs, pities, and then questions him.

"'Est-ce vrai, vieux,' reprit-elle, 'que tu as tué ton frère et ton oncle, ruiné ta famille, surhypothéqué la maison de tes enfants et mangé la grenouille du gouvernement en Afrique avec la princesse?'

"Le Baron inclina tristement la tête.

"'Eh bien, j'aime cela!' s'écria Josépha, qui se leva pleine d'enthousiasme. 'C'est un *brûlage* général! c'est sardanapale! c'est grand! c'est complet! On est une canaille, mais on a du cœur.'"

The cry is Balzac's, and it is a characteristic part of his genius to have given it that ironical force by uttering it through the mouth of a Josépha. The joy of the human organism at its highest point of activity: that is what interests him supremely. How passionate, how moving he becomes whenever he has to speak of a real passion, a mania, whether of a lover for his mistress, of a philosopher for his idea, of a miser for his gold, of a Jew dealer for masterpieces! His style clarifies, his words become flesh and blood; he is the lyric poet. And for him every idealism is equal: the gourmandise of Pons is not less serious, not less sympathetic, not less perfectly realised, than the search of Claës after the Absolute. "The great and terrible clamour of egoism" is the voice to which he is always attentive; "those eloquent faces, proclaiming a soul abandoned to an idea as to a remorse," are the faces with whose history he concerns himself. He drags to light the hidden joys of the *amateur*, and with especial delight those that are hidden deepest, under the most deceptive coverings. He deifies them for their energy, he fashions the world of his "Human Comedy" in their service, as the real world exists, all but passive, to be the pasture of these supreme egoists.

IV

In all that he writes of life, Balzac seeks the soul, but it is the soul as nervous fluid, the executive soul, not the contemplative soul, that, with rare exceptions, he seeks. He would surprise the motive force of life: that is his *recherche de l'Absolu;* he figures it to himself as almost a substance, and he is the alchemist on its track. "Can man by thinking find out God?" Or life, he would have added; and he would have answered the question with at least a Perhaps.

And of this visionary, this abstract thinker, it must be said that his thought translates itself always into terms of life. Pose before him a purely mental problem, and he will resolve it by a scene in which the problem literally works itself out. It is the quality proper to the novelist, but no novelist ever employed this quality with such persistent activity, and at the same time subordinated action so constantly to the idea. With him action has always a mental basis, is never suffered to intrude for its own sake. He prefers that an episode should seem in itself tedious rather than it should have an illogical interest.

It may be, for he is a Frenchman, that his episodes are sometimes too logical. There are moments when he becomes unreal because he wishes to be too systematic, that is, to be real by measure. He would never have understood the method of Tolstoi, a very stealthy method of surprising life. To Tolstoi life is always the cunning enemy whom one must lull asleep, or noose by an unexpected lasso. He brings in little detail after little detail, seeming to insist on the insignificance of each, in order that it may pass almost unobserved, and be realised only after it has passed. It is his way of disarming the suspiciousness of life.

But Balzac will make no circuit, aims at an open and an unconditional triumph over nature. Thus, when he triumphs, he triumphs signally; and action, in his books, is perpetually crystallising into some phrase, like the single lines of Dante, or some brief scene, in which a whole entanglement comes sharply and suddenly to a luminous point. I will give no instance, for I should have to quote from every volume. I wish rather to remind myself that there are times when the last fine shade of a situation seems to have escaped. Even then, the failure is often more apparent than real, a slight bungling in the machinery of illusion. Look through the phrase, and you will find the truth there, perfectly explicit on the other side of it.

For, it cannot be denied, Balzac's style, as style, is imperfect. It has life, and it has idea, and it has variety; there are moments when it attains a rare and perfectly individual beauty; as when, in "Le Cousin Pons," we read of "cette prédisposition aux recherches qui fait faire à un savant germanique cent lieues dans ses guêtres pour trouver une vérité qui le regard en riant, assise à la marge du puits, sous le jasmin de la cour." But I am far less sure that a student of Balzac would recognise him in this sentence than that he would recognise the writer of this other: "Des larmes de pudeur, qui roulèrent entre les beaux cils de Madame Hulot, arrêtèrent net le garde national." It is in such passages that the failure in style is equivalent to a failure in psychology. That his style should lack symmetry, subordination, the formal virtues of form, is, in my eyes, a less serious fault. I have often considered whether, in the novel, perfect form is a good, or even a possible thing, if the novel is to be what Balzac made it, history added to poetry. A novelist with style will not look at life with an entirely naked vision. He sees through coloured glasses. Human life and human manners are too various, too moving, to be brought into the fixity of a quite formal order. There will come a moment, constantly, when style must suffer, or the closeness and clearness of narration must be sacrificed, some minute exception of action or psychology must lose its natural place, or its full emphasis. Balzac, with his rapid and accumulating mind, without the patience of selection, and without the desire to select where selection means leaving out something good in itself, if not good in its place, never hesitates, and his parenthesis comes in. And often it is into these parentheses that he puts the profoundest part of his thought.

Yet, ready as Balzac is to neglect the story for the philosophy, whenever it seems to him necessary to do so, he would never have admitted that a form of the novel is possible in which the story shall be no more than an excuse for the philosophy. That was because he was a great creator, and not merely a philosophical thinker; because he dealt in flesh and blood, and knew that the passions in action can teach more to the philosopher, and can justify the artist more fully, than all the unacting intellect in the world. He knew that though life without thought was no more than the portion of a dog, yet thoughtful life was more than lifeless thought, and the dramatist more than the commentator. And I cannot help feeling assured that the latest novelists without a story, whatever other merits they certainly have, are lacking in the power to create characters, to express a philosophy in action; and that the form which they have found, however valuable it may be, is the result of this failure, and not either a great refusal or a new vision.

V

The novel as Balzac conceived it has created the modern novel, but no modern novelist has followed, for none has been able to follow, Balzac on his own lines. Even those who have tried to follow him most closely have, sooner or later, branched off in one direction or another, most in the direction indicated by Stendhal. Stendhal has written one book which is a masterpiece, unique in its kind, "Le Rouge et le Noir"; a second, which is full of admirable things, "La Chartreuse de Parme"; a book of profound criticism, "Racine et Shakspeare"; and a cold and penetrating study of the physiology of love, "De l'Amour," by the side of which Balzac's "Physiologie du Mariage" is a mere *jeu d'esprit*. He discovered for himself, and for others after him, a method of unemotional, minute, slightly ironical analysis, which has fascinated modern minds, partly because it has seemed to dispense with those difficulties of creation, of creation in the block, which the triumphs of Balzac have only accentuated. Goriot, Valérie Marneffe, Pons, Grandet, Madame de Mortsauf even, are called up before us after the same manner as Othello or Don Quixote; their actions express them so significantly that they seem to be independent of their creator; Balzac stakes all upon each creation, and leaves us no choice but to accept or reject each as a whole, precisely as we should a human being. We do not know all the secrets of their consciousness, any more than we know all the secrets of the consciousness of our friends. But we have only to say "Valérie!" and the woman is before us. Stendhal, on the contrary, undresses Julien's soul in public with a deliberate and fascinating effrontery. There is not a vein of which he does not trace the course, not a wrinkle to which he does not point, not a nerve which he does not touch to the quick. We know everything that passed through his mind, to result probably in some significant inaction. And at the end of the book we know as much about that particular intelligence as the anatomist knows about the body which he has dissected. But meanwhile the life has gone out of the body; and have we, after all, captured a living soul?

I should be the last to say that Julien Sorel is not a creation, but he is not a creation after the order of Balzac; it is a difference of kind; and if we look carefully at Frédéric Moreau, and Madame Gervaisais, and the Abbé Mouret, we shall see that these also, profoundly different as Flaubert and Goncourt and Zola are from Stendhal, are yet more profoundly, more radically, different from the creations of Balzac. Balzac takes a primary passion, puts it into a human body, and sets it to work itself out in visible action. But, since Stendhal, novelists have persuaded themselves that the primary passions are a little common, or noisy, or a little heavy to handle, and they have concerned themselves with passions tempered by reflection, and the sensations of elaborate brains. It was Stendhal who substituted the brain for the heart, as the battle-place of the novel; not the brain as Balzac conceived it, a motive-force of action, the main-spring of passion, the force by which a nature directs its accumulated energy; but a sterile sort of brain, set at a great distance from the heart, whose rhythm is too faint to disturb it. We have been intellectualising upon Stendhal ever since, until the persons of the modern novel have come to resemble those diaphanous jelly-fish, with balloon-like heads and the merest tufts of bodies, which float up and down in the Aquarium at Naples.

Thus, coming closer, as it seems, to what is called

reality, in this banishment of great emotions, and this attention upon the sensations, modern analytic novelists are really getting further and further from that life which is the one certain thing in the world. Balzac employs all his detail to call up a tangible world about his men and women, not, perhaps, understanding the full power of detail as psychology, as Flaubert is to understand it; but, after all, his detail is only the background of the picture; and there, stepping out of the canvas, as the sombre people of Velazquez step out of their canvases at the Prado, is the living figure, looking into your eyes with eyes that respond to you like a mirror.

The novels of Balzac are full of electric fluid. To take up one of them is to feel the shock of life, as one feels it on touching certain magnetic hands. To turn over volume after volume is like wandering through the streets of a great city, at that hour of the night when human activity is at its full. There is a particular kind of excitement inherent in the very aspect of a modern city, of London or Paris; in the mere sensation of being in its midst, in the sight of all those active and fatigued faces which pass so rapidly; of those long and endless streets, full of houses, each of which is like the body of a multiform soul, looking out through the eyes of many windows. There is something intoxicating in the lights, the movement of shadows under the lights, the vast and billowy sound of that shadowy movement. And there is something more than this mere unconscious action upon the nerves. Every step in a great city is a step into an unknown world. A new future is possible at every street corner. I never know, when I go out into one of those crowded streets, but that the whole course of my life may be changed before I return to the house I have quitted.

I am writing these lines in Madrid, to which I have

come suddenly, after a long quiet in Andalusia; and I feel already a new pulse in my blood, a keener consciousness of life, and a sharper human curiosity. Even in Seville I knew that I should see to-morrow, in the same streets, hardly changed since the Middle Ages, the same people that I had seen to-day. But here there are new possibilities, all the exciting accidents of the modern world, of a population always changing, of a city into which civilisation has brought all its unrest. And as I walk in these broad, windy streets and see these people, whom I hardly recognise for Spaniards, so awake and so hybrid are they, I have felt the sense of Balzac coming back into my veins. At Cordova he was unthinkable; at Cadiz I could realise only his large, universal outlines, vague as the murmur of the sea; here I feel him, he speaks the language I am talking, he sums up the life in whose midst I find myself.

For Balzac is the equivalent of great cities. He is bad reading for solitude, for he fills the mind with the nostalgia of cities. When a man speaks to me familiarly of Balzac I know already something of the man with whom I have to do. "The physiognomy of women does not begin before the age of thirty," he has said; and perhaps before that age no one can really understand Balzac. Few young people care for him, for there is nothing in him that appeals to the senses except through the intellect. Not many women care for him supremely, for it is part of his method to express sentiments through facts, and not facts through sentiments. But it is natural that he should be the favourite reading of men of the world, of those men of the world who have the distinction of their kind; for he supplies the key of the enigma which they are studying.

VI

The life of Balzac was one long labour, in which time, money, and circumstances were all against him. In 1835 he writes: "I have lately spent twenty-six days in my study without leaving it. I took the air only at that window which dominates Paris, which I mean to dominate." And he exults in the labour: "If there is any glory in that, I alone could accomplish such a feat." He symbolises the course of his life in comparing it to the sea beating against a rock: "To-day one flood, to-morrow another, bears me along with it. I am dashed against a rock, I recover myself and go on to another reef." "Sometimes it seems to me that my brain is on fire. I shall die in the trenches of the intellect."

Balzac, like Scott, died under the weight of his debts; and it would seem, if one took him at his word, that the whole of the "Human Comedy" was written for money. In the modern world, as he himself realised more clearly than any one, money is more often a symbol than an entity, and it can be the symbol of every desire. For Balzac money was the key of his only earthly paradise. It meant leisure to visit the woman whom he loved, and at the end it meant the possibility of marrying her.

There were only two women in Balzac's life: one, a woman much older than himself, of whom he wrote, on her death, to the other: "She was a mother, a friend, a family, a companion, a counsel, she made the writer, she consoled the young man, she formed his taste, she wept like a sister, she laughed, she came every day, like a healing slumber, to put sorrow to sleep." The other was Mme. de Hanska, whom he married in 1850, three months before his death. He had loved her for twenty years; she was married, and lived in Poland: it was only at rare intervals that he was able to see her, and then very briefly; but his letters to her, published since his death, are a simple, perfectly individual, daily record of a great passion. For twenty years he existed on a divine certainty without a future, and almost without a present. But we see the force of that sentiment passing into his work; "Séraphita" is its ecstasy, everywhere is its human shadow; it refines his strength, it gives him surprising intuitions, it gives him all that was wanting to his genius. Mme. de Hanska is the heroine of the "Human Comedy," as Beatrice is the heroine of the "Divine Comedy."

A great lover, to whom love, as well as every other passion and the whole visible world, was an idea, a flaming spiritual perception, Balzac enjoyed the vast happiness of the idealist. Contentedly, joyously, he sacrificed every petty enjoyment to the idea of love, the idea of fame, and to that need of the organism to exercise its forces, which is the only definition of genius. I do not know, among the lives of men of letters, a life better filled, or more appropriate. A young man who, for a short time, was his secretary, declared: "I would not live your life for the fame of Napoleon and of Byron combined!" The Comte de Gramont did not realise, as the world in general does not realise, that, to the man of creative energy, creation is at once a necessity and a joy, and, to the lover, hope in absence is the elixir of life. Balzac tasted more than all earthly pleasures as he sat there in his attic, creating the world over again, that he might lay it at the feet of a woman. Certainly to him there was no tedium in life, for there was no hour without its vivid employment, and no moment in which to perceive the most desolate of all certainties, that hope is in the past. His death was as fortunate as his life; he died at the height of his powers, at the height of his fame, at the moment of the fulfilment of his happiness, and perhaps of the too sudden relief of that delicate burden.

1899.

PROSPER MÉRIMÉE

I

Stendhal has left us a picture of Mérimée as "a young man in a grey frock-coat, very ugly, and with a turned-up nose. . . . This young man had something insolent and extremely unpleasant about him. His eyes, small and without expression, had always the same look, and this look was ill-natured. . . . Such was my first impression of the best of my present friends. I am not too sure of his heart, but I am sure of his talents. It is M. le Comte Gazul, now so well known; a letter from him, which came to me last week, made me happy for two days. His mother has a good deal of French wit and a superior intelligence. Like her son, it seems to me that she might give way to emotion once a year." There, painted by a clear-sighted and disinterested friend, is a picture of Mérimée almost from his own point of view, or at least as he would himself have painted the picture. How far is it, in its insistence on the *attendrissement une fois par an*, on the subordination of natural feeling to a somewhat disdainful aloofness, the real Mérimée?

Early in life, Mérimée adopted his theory, fixed his attitude, and to the end of his life he seemed, to those about him, to have walked along the path he had chosen, almost without a deviation. He went to England at the age of twenty-three, to Spain four years later, and might seem to have been drawn naturally to those two countries, to which he was to return so often, by natural affinities of temper and manner. It was the

English manner that he liked, that came naturally to him; the correct, unmoved exterior, which is a kind of positive strength, not to be broken by any onslaught of events or emotions; and in Spain he found an equally positive animal acceptance of things as they are, which satisfied his profound, restrained, really Pagan sensuality, Pagan in the hard, eighteenth-century sense. From the beginning he was a student, of art, of history, of human nature, and we find him enjoying, in his deliberate, keen way, the studied diversions of the student; body and soul each kept exactly in its place, each provided for without partiality. He entered upon literature by a mystification, "Le Théâtre de Clara Gazul," a book of plays supposed to be translated from a living Spanish dramatist; and he followed it by "La Guzla," another mystification, a book of prose ballads supposed to be translated from the Illyrian. And these mystifications, like the forgeries of Chatterton, contain perhaps the most sincere, the most undisguised emotion which he ever permitted himself to express; so secure did he feel of the heart behind the pearl necklace of the *décolletée* Spanish actress, who travesties his own face in the frontispiece to the one, and so remote from himself did he feel the bearded gentleman to be, who sits cross-legged on the ground, holding his lyre or *guzla*, in the frontispiece to the other. Then came a historical novel, the "Chronique du Règne de Charles IX.," before he discovered, as if by accident, precisely what it was he was meant to do: the short story. Then he drifted into history, became Inspector of Ancient Monuments, and helped to save Vézelay, among other good deeds toward art, done in his cold, systematic, after all satisfactory manner. He travelled at almost regular intervals, not only in Spain and England, but in Corsica, in Greece and Asia Minor, in Italy, in Hungary, in Bohemia, usually with a definite, scholarly object, and always with an alert attention to everything that came in his way, to the manners of people, their national characters, their differences from one another. An intimate friend of the Countess de Montijo, the mother of the Empress Eugénie, he was a friend, not a courtier, at the court of the Third Empire. He was elected to the Academy, mainly for his "Études sur l'Histoire Romaine," a piece of dry history, and immediately scandalised his supporters by publishing a story, "Arsène Guillot," which was taken for a veiled attack on religion and on morals. Soon after, his imagination seemed to flag; he abandoned himself, perhaps a little wearily, more and more to facts, to the facts of history and learning; learned Russian, and translated Poushkin and Tourguenieff; and died in 1870, at Cannes, perhaps less satisfied with himself than most men who have done, in their lives, far less exactly what they have intended to do.

"I have theories about the very smallest things—gloves, boots, and the like," says Mérimée in one of his letters; *des idées très-arrêtées*, as he adds with emphasis in another. Precise opinions lead easily to prejudices, and Mérimée, who prided himself on the really very logical quality of his mind, put himself somewhat deliberately into the hands of his prejudices. Thus he hated religion, distrusted priests, would not let himself be carried away by any instinct of admiration, would not let himself do the things which he had the power to do, because his other, critical self came mockingly behind him, suggesting that very few things were altogether worth doing. "There is nothing that I despise and even detest so much as humanity in general," he confesses in a letter; and it is with a certain self-complacency that he defines the only kind of society in which he found himself at home: "(1) With unpretentious people whom I have known a long time; (2) in a Spanish *venta*, with muleteers and peasant women of Andalusia." One day, as he finds himself in a pensive mood, dreaming of a woman, he translates for her some lines of Sophocles, into verse, "English verse, you understand, for I abhor French verse." The carefulness with which he avoids received opinions shows a certain consciousness of those opinions, which in a more imaginatively independent mind would scarcely have found a place. It is not only for an effect, but more and more genuinely, that he sets his acquirements as a scholar above his accomplishments as an artist. Clearing away, as it seemed to him, every illusion from before his eyes, he forgot the last illusion of positive people: the possibility that one's eyes may be short-sighted.

Mérimée realises a type which we are accustomed to associate almost exclusively with the eighteenth century, but of which our own time can offer us many obscure examples. It is the type of the *esprit fort*: the learned man, the choice, narrow artist, who is at the same time the cultivated sensualist. To such a man the pursuit of women is part of his constant pursuit of human experience, and of the document, which is the summing up of human experience. To Mérimée history itself was a matter of detail. "In history I care only for anecdotes," he says in the preface to the "Chronique du Règne de Charles IX." And he adds: "It is not a very noble taste; but, I confess to my shame, I would willingly give Thucydides for the authentic memoirs of Aspasia or of a slave of Pericles; for only memoirs, which are the familiar talk of an author with his reader, afford those portraits of *man* which amuse and interest me." This curiosity of mankind above all things, and of mankind at home, or in private actions, not necessarily of any import to the general course of the world, leads the curious searcher naturally to the more privately interesting and the less publicly important half of mankind. Not scrupulous in arriving at any end by the most adaptable means, not disturbed by any illusions as to the physical facts of the universe, a sincere and grateful lover of variety, doubtless an amusing companion with those who amused him, Mérimée found much of his entertainment and instruction, at all events in his younger years, in that "half world" which he tells us he frequented "very much out of curiosity, living in it always as in a foreign country." Here, as elsewhere, Mérimée played the part of the amateur. He liked anecdotes, not great events, in his history; and he was careful to avoid any too serious passions in his search for sensations. There, no doubt, for the sensualist, is happiness, if he can resign himself to it. It is only serious passions which make anybody unhappy; and Mérimée was carefully on the lookout against a possible unhappiness. I can imagine him ending every day with satisfaction, and beginning every fresh day with just enough expectancy to be agreeable, at that period of his life when he was writing the finest of his stories, and dividing the rest of his leisure between the drawing-rooms and the pursuit of uneventful adventures.

Only, though we are *automates autant qu'esprit*, as Pascal tells us, it is useless to expect that what is automatic in us should remain invariable and unconditioned. If life could be lived on a plan, and for such men on such a plan, if first impulses and profound passions could be kept entirely out of one's own experience, and studied only at a safe distance, then, no doubt, one could go on being happy, in a not too heroic way. But, with Mérimée as with all the rest of the world, the scheme breaks down one day, just when a reasonable solution to things seems to have been arrived at. Mérimée had already entered on a peaceable enough *liaison* when the first letter came to him from the *Inconnue* to whom he was to write so many letters, for nine years without seeing her, and then for thirty years more after he had met her, the last letter being written but two hours before his death. These letters, which we can now read in two volumes, have a delicately insincere sincerity which makes every letter a work of art, not because he tried to make it so, but because he could not help seeing the form simultaneously with the feeling, and writing genuine love-letters with an excellence almost as impersonal as that of his stories. He begins with curiosity, which passes with singular rapidity into a kind of self-willed passion; already in the eighth letter, long before he has seen her, he is speculating which of the two will know best how to torture the other: that is, as he views it, love best. "We shall never love one another really," he tells her, as he begins to hope for the contrary. Then he discovers, for the first time, and without practical result, "that it is better to have illusions than to have none at all." He confesses himself to her, sometimes reminding her: "You will never know either all the good or all the evil that I have in me. I have spent my life in being praised for qualities which I do not possess, and calumniated for defects which are not mine." And, with a strange, weary humility, which is the other side of his contempt for most things and people, he admits: "To you I am like an old opera, which you are obliged to forget, in order to see it again with any pleasure." He, who has always distrusted first impulses, finds himself telling her (was she really so like him, or was he arguing with himself?): "You always fear first impulses; do you not see that they are the only ones which are worth anything and which always succeed?" Does he realise, unable to change the temperament which he has partly made for himself, that just there has been his own failure?

Perhaps of all love-letters, these of Mérimée show us love triumphing over the most carefully guarded personality. Here the obstacle is not duty, nor circumstance, nor a rival; but (on her side as on his, it would seem) a carefully trained natural coldness, in which action, and even for the most part feeling, are relinquished to the control of second thoughts. A habit of repressive irony goes deep: Mérimée might well have thought himself secure against the outbreak of an unconditional passion. Yet here we find passion betraying itself, often only by bitterness, together with a shy, surprising tenderness, in this curious lovers' itinerary, marked out with all the customary sign-posts, and leading, for all its wilful deviations, along the inevitable road.

It is commonly supposed that the artist, by the habit of his profession, has made for himself a sort of cuirass of phrases against the direct attack of emotion, and so will suffer less than most people if he should fall into love, and things should not go altogether well with him. Rather, he is the more laid open to attack, the more helplessly entangled when once the net has been cast over him. He lives through every passionate trouble, not merely with the daily emotions of the crowd, but with the whole of his imagination. Pain is multiplied to him by the force of that faculty by which he conceives delight. What is most torturing in every not quite fortunate love is memory, and the artist becomes an artist by his intensification of memory. Mérimée has himself defined art as exaggeration *à propos*.

Well, to the artist his own life is an exaggeration not *à propos*, and every hour dramatises for him its own pain and pleasure, in a tragic comedy of which he is the author and actor and spectator. The practice of art is a sharpening of the sensations, and, the knife once sharpened, does it cut into one's hand less deeply because one is in the act of using it to carve wood?

And so we find Mérimée, the most impersonal of artists, and one of those most critical of the caprices and violences of fate, giving in to an almost obvious temptation, an anonymous correspondence, a mysterious unknown woman, and passing from stage to stage of a finally very genuine love-affair, which kept him in a fluttering agitation for more than thirty years. It is curious to note that the little which we know of this *Inconnue* seems to mark her out as the realisation of a type which had always been Mérimée's type of woman. She has the "wicked eyes" of all his heroines, from the Mariquita of his first attempt in literature, who haunts the Inquisitor with "her great black eyes, like the eyes of a young cat, soft and wicked at once." He finds her at the end of his life, in a novel of Tourguenieff, "one of those diabolical creatures whose coquetry is the more dangerous because it is capable of passion." Like so many artists, he has invented his ideal before he meets it, and must have seemed almost to have fallen in love with his own creation. It is one of the privileges of art to create nature, as, according to a certain mystical doctrine, you can actualise, by sheer fixity of contemplation, your mental image of a thing into the thing itself. The *Inconnue* was one of a series, the rest imaginary; and her power over Mérimée, we can hardly doubt, came not only from her queer likeness of temperament to his, but from the singular, flattering pleasure which it must have given him to find that he had invented with so much truth to nature.

II

Mérimée as a writer belongs to the race of Laclos and of Stendhal, a race essentially French; and we find him representing, a little coldly, as it seemed, the claims of mere unimpassioned intellect, at work on passionate problems, among those people of the Romantic period to whom emotion, evident emotion, was everything. In his subjects he is as "Romantic" as Victor Hugo or Gautier; he adds, even, a peculiar flavour of cruelty to the Romantic ingredients. But he distinguishes sharply, as French writers before him had so well known how to do, between the passion one is recounting and the moved or unmoved way in which one chooses to tell it. To Mérimée art was a very formal thing, almost a part of learning; it was a thing to be done with a clear head, reflectively, with a calm mastery of even the most vivid material. While others, at that time, were intoxicating themselves with strange sensations, hoping that "nature would take the pen out of their hands and write," just at the moment when their own thoughts became least coherent, Mérimée went quietly to work over something a little abnormal which he had found in nature, with as disinterested, as scholarly, as mentally reserved an interest as if it were one of those Gothic monuments which he inspected to such good purpose, and, as it has seemed to his biographer, with so little sympathy. His own emotion, so far as it is roused, seems to him an extraneous thing, a thing to be concealed, if not a little ashamed of. It is the thing itself he wishes to give you, not his feelings about it; and his theory is that if the thing itself can only be made to stand and speak before the reader, the reader will supply for himself all the feeling that is needed, all the feeling that would be called out in nature by a perfectly clear sight of just such passions in action. It seems to him bad art to paint the picture, and to write a description of the picture as well.

And his method serves him wonderfully up to a certain point, and then leaves him, without his being well aware of it, at the moment even when he has convinced himself that he has realised the utmost of his aim. At a time when he had come to consider scholarly dexterity as the most important part of art, Mérimée tells us that "La Vénus d'Ille" seemed to him the best story he had ever written. He has often been taken at his word, but to take him at his word is to do him an injustice. "La Vénus d'Ille" is a modern setting of the old story of the Ring given to Venus, and Mérimée has been praised for the ingenuity with which he has obtained an effect of supernatural terror, while leaving the way open for a material explanation of the supernatural. What he has really done is to materialise a myth, by accepting in it precisely what might be a mere superstition, the form of the thing, and leaving out the spiritual meaning of which that form was no more than a temporary expression. The ring which the bridegroom sets on the finger of Venus, and which the statue's finger closes upon, accepting it, symbolises the pact between love and sensuality, the lover's abdication of all but the physical part of love; and the statue taking its place between husband and wife on the marriage-night, and crushing life out of him in an inexorable embrace, symbolises the merely natural destruction which that granted prayer brings with it, as a merely human Messalina takes her lover on his own terms, in his abandonment of all to Venus. Mérimée sees a cruel and fantastic superstition, which he is afraid of seeming to take too seriously, which he prefers to leave as a story of ghosts or bogies, a thing at which we are to shiver as at a mere twitch on the nerves, while our mental confidence in the impossibility of what we cannot explain is preserved for us by a hint at a muleteer's vengeance. "Have I frightened you?" says the man of the world, with a reassuring smile. "Think about it no more; I really meant nothing."

And yet, does he after all mean nothing? The devil, the old pagan gods, the spirits of evil incarnated under every form, fascinated him; it gave him a malign pleasure to set them at their evil work among men, while, all the time, he mocks them and the men who believed in them. He is a materialist, and yet he believes in at least a something evil, outside the world, or in the heart of it, which sets humanity at its strange games, relentlessly. Even then he will not surrender his doubts, his ironies, his negations. Is he, perhaps, at times, the atheist who fears that, after all, God may exist, or at least who realises how much he would fear him if he did exist?

Mérimée had always delighted in mystifications; he was always on his guard against being mystified himself, either by nature or by his fellow-creatures. In the early "Romantic" days he had had a genuine passion for various things: "local colour," for instance. But even then he had invented it by a kind of trick, and, later on, he explains what a poor thing "local colour" is, since it can so easily be invented without leaving one's study. He is full of curiosity, and will go far to satisfy it, regretting "the decadence," in our times, "of energetic passions, in favour of tranquillity and perhaps of happiness." These energetic passions he will find, indeed, in our own times, in Corsica, in Spain, in Lithuania, really in the midst of a very genuine and profoundly studied "local colour," and also, under many disguises, in Parisian drawing-rooms. Mérimée prized happiness, material comfort, the satisfaction of one's immediate desires, very highly, and it was his keen sense of life, of the pleasures of living, that gave him some of his keenness in the realisation of violent death, physical pain, whatever disturbs the equilibrium of things with unusual emphasis. Himself really selfish, he can distinguish the unhappiness of others with a kind of intuition which is not sympathy, but which selfish people often have: a dramatic consciousness of how painful pain must be, whoever feels it. It is not pity, though it communicates itself to us, often enough, as pity. It is the clear-sighted sensitiveness of a man who watches human things closely, bringing them home to himself with the deliberate, essaying art of an actor who has to represent a particular passion in movement.

And always in Mérimée there is this union of curiosity with indifference: the curiosity of the student, the indifference of the man of the world. Indifference, in him, as in the man of the world, is partly an attitude, adopted for its form, and influencing the temperament just so much as gesture always influences emotion. The man who forces himself to appear calm under excitement teaches his nerves to follow instinctively the way he has shown them. In time he will not merely seem calm but will be calm, at the moment when he learns that a great disaster has befallen him. But, in Mérimée, was the indifference even as external as it must always be when there is restraint, when, therefore, there is something to restrain? Was there not in him a certain drying up of the sources of emotion, as the man of the world came to accept almost the point of view of society, reading his stories to a little circle of court ladies, when, once in a while, he permitted himself to write a story? And was not this increase of well-bred indifference, now more than ever characteristic, almost the man himself, the chief reason why he abandoned art so early, writing only two or three short stories during the last twenty-five years of his life, and writing these with a labour which by no means conceals itself?

Mérimée had an abstract interest in, almost an enthusiasm for, facts; facts for their meaning, the light they throw on psychology. He declines to consider psychology except through its expression in facts, with an impersonality far more real than that of Flaubert. The document, historical or social, must translate itself into sharp action before he can use it; not that he does not see, and appreciate better than most others, all there is of significance in the document itself; but his theory of art is inexorable. He never allowed himself to write as he pleased, but he wrote always as he considered the artist should write. Thus he made for himself a kind of formula, confining himself, as some thought, within too narrow limits, but, to himself, doing exactly what he set himself to do, with all the satisfaction of one who is convinced of the justice of his aim and confident of his power to attain it.

Look, for instance, at his longest, far from his best work, "La Chronique du Règne de Charles IX." Like so much of his work, it has something of the air of a *tour de force*, not taken up entirely for its own sake. Mérimée drops into a fashion, half deprecatingly, as if he sees through it, and yet, as with merely mundane elegance, with a resolve to be more scrupulously exact than its devotees. "Belief," says some one in this book, as if speaking for Mérimée, "is a precious gift which has been denied me." Well, he will do better, without belief, than those who believe. Written under a title which suggests a work of actual history, it is more than possible that the first suggestion of this book really came, as he tells us in the preface, from the reading of "a large number of memoirs and pamphlets relating to the end of the sixteenth century." "I wished to make an epitome of my reading," he tells us, "and here is the epitome." The historical problem attracted him, that never quite explicable Massacre of St Bartholomew, in which there was precisely the violence of action and uncertainty of motive which he liked to set before him at the beginning of a task in literature. Probable, clearly defined people, in the dress of the period, grew up naturally about this central motive; humour and irony have their part; there are adventures, told with a sword's point of sharpness, and in the fewest possible words; there is one of his cruel and loving women, in whom every sentiment becomes action, by some twisted feminine logic of their own. It is the most artistic, the most clean-cut, of historical novels; and yet this perfect neatness of method suggests a certain indifference on the part of the writer, as if he were more interested in doing the thing well than in doing it.

And that, in all but the very best of his stories (even, perhaps, in "Arsène Guillot," only not in such perfect things as "Carmen," as "Mateo Falcone"), is what Mérimée just lets us see, underneath an almost faultless skill of narrative. An incident told by Mérimée at his best gathers about it something of the gravity of history, the composed way in which it is told helping to give it the equivalent of remoteness, allowing it not merely to be, but, what is more difficult, to seem, classic in its own time. "Magnificent things, things after my own heart—that is to say, Greek in their truth and simplicity," he writes in a letter, referring to the tales of Poushkin. The phrase is scarcely too strong to apply to what is best in his own work. Made out of elemental passions, hard, cruel, detached as it were from their own sentiments, the stories that he tells might in other hands become melodramas: "Carmen," taken thoughtlessly out of his hands, has supplied the libretto to the most popular of modern light operas. And yet, in his severe method of telling, mere outlines, it seems, told with an even stricter watch over what is significantly left out than over what is briefly allowed to be said in words, these stories sum up little separate pieces of the world, each a little world in itself. And each is a little world which he has made his own, with a labour at last its own reward, and taking life partly because he has put into it more of himself than the mere intention of doing it well. Mérimée loved Spain, and "Carmen," which by some caprice of popularity is the symbol of Spain to people in general, is really, to those who know Spain well, the most Spanish thing that has been written since "Gil Blas." All the little parade of local colour and philology, the appendix on the *Calo* of the gipsies, done to heighten the illusion, has more significance than people sometimes think. In this story all the qualities of Mérimée come into agreement; the student of human passions, the traveller, the observer, the learned man, meet in harmony; and, in addition, there is the *aficionado*, the true *amateur*, in love with Spain and the Spaniards.

It is significant that at the reception of Mérimée at the Académie Française in 1845, M. Étienne thought it already needful to say: "Do not pause in the midst of your career; rest is not permitted to your talent."

Already Mérimée was giving way to facts, to facts in themselves, as they come into history, into records of scholarship. We find him writing, a little dryly, on Catiline, on Cæsar, on Don Pedro the Cruel, learning Russian, and translating from it (yet, while studying the Russians before all the world, never discovering the mystical Russian soul), writing learned articles, writing reports. He looked around on contemporary literature, and found nothing that he could care for. Stendhal was gone, and who else was there to admire? Flaubert, it seemed to him, was "wasting his talent under the pretence of realism." Victor Hugo was "a fellow with the most beautiful figures of speech at his disposal," who did not take the trouble to think, but intoxicated himself with his own words. Baudelaire made him furious, Renan filled him with pitying scorn. In the midst of his contempt, he may perhaps have imagined that he was being left behind. For whatever reason, weakness or strength, he could not persuade himself that it was worth while to strive for anything any more. He died probably at the moment when he was no longer a fashion, and had not yet become a classic.

1901.

THÉOPHILE GAUTIER

GAUTIER has spoken for himself in a famous passage of "Mademoiselle de Maupin": "I am a man of the Homeric age; the world in which I live is not my world, and I understand nothing of the society which surrounds me. For me Christ did not come; I am as much a pagan as Alcibiades or Phidias. I have never plucked on Golgotha the flowers of the Passion, and the deep stream that flows from the side of the Crucified, and sets a crimson girdle about the world, has never washed me in its flood; my rebellious body will not acknowledge the supremacy of the soul, and my flesh will not endure to be mortified. I find the earth as beautiful as the sky, and I think that perfection of form is virtue. I have no gift for spirituality; I prefer a statue to a ghost, full noon to twilight. Three things delight me: gold, marble, and purple; brilliance, solidity, colour. . . . I have looked on love in the light of antiquity, and as a piece of sculpture more or less perfect. . . . All my life I have been concerned with the form of the flagon, never with the quality of its contents." That is part of a confession of faith, and it is spoken with absolute sincerity. Gautier knew himself, and could tell the truth about himself as simply, as impartially, as if he had been describing a work of art. Or is he not, indeed, describing a work of art? Was not that very state of mind, that finished and limited temperament, a thing which he had collaborated with nature in making, with an effective heightening of what was most natural to him, in the spirit of art?

Gautier saw the world as mineral, as metal, as pigment, as rock, tree, water, as architecture, costume, under sunlight, gas, in all the colours that light can bring out of built or growing things; he saw it as contour, movement; he saw all that a painter sees, when the painter sets himself to copy, not to create. He was the finest copyist who ever used paint with a pen. Nothing that can be expressed in technical terms escaped him; there were no technical terms which he could not reduce to an orderly beauty. But he absorbed all this visible world with the hardly discriminating impartiality of the retina; he had no moods, was not to be distracted by a sentiment, heard no voices, saw nothing but darkness, the negation of day, in night. He was tirelessly attentive, he had no secrets of his own and could keep none of nature's. He could describe every ray of the nine thousand precious stones in the throne of Ivan the Terrible, in the Treasury of the Kremlin; but he could tell you nothing of one of Maeterlinck's bees.

The five senses made Gautier for themselves, that they might become articulate. He speaks for them all with a dreadful unconcern. All his words are in love with matter, and they enjoy their lust and have no recollection. If the body did not dwindle and expand to some ignoble physical conclusion; if wrinkles did not creep yellowing up women's necks, and the fire in a man's blood did not lose its heat; he would always be content. Everything that he cared for in the world was to be had, except, perhaps, rest from striving after it; only, everything would one day come to an end, after a slow spoiling. Decrepit, colourless, uneager things shocked him, and it was with an acute, almost disinterested pity that he watched himself die.

All his life Gautier adored life, and all the processes and forms of life. A pagan, a young Roman, hard and delicate, with something of cruelty in his sympathy with things that could be seen and handled, he would have hated the soul, if he had ever really apprehended it, for its qualifying and disturbing power upon the body. No other modern writer, no writer perhaps, has described nakedness with so abstract a heat of rapture: like d'Albert when he sees Mlle. de Maupin for the first and last time, he is the artist before he is the lover, and he is the lover while he is the artist. It was above all things the human body whose contours and colours he wished to fix for eternity, in the "robust art" of "verse, marble, onyx, enamel." And it was not the body as a frail, perishable thing, and a thing to be pitied, that he wanted to perpetuate; it was the beauty of life itself, imperishable at least in its recurrence.

He loved imperishable things: the body, as generation after generation refashions it, the world, as it is restored and rebuilt, and then gems, and hewn stone, and carved ivory, and woven tapestry. He loved verse for its solid, strictly limited, resistant form, which, while prose melts and drifts about it, remains unalterable, indestructible. Words, he knew, can build as strongly as stones, and not merely rise to music, like the walls of Troy, but be themselves music as well as structure. Yet, as in visible things he cared only for hard outline and rich colour, so in words too he had no love of half-tints, and was content to do without that softening of atmosphere which was to be prized by those who came after him as the thing most worth seeking. Even his verse is without mystery; if he meditates, his meditation has all the fixity of a kind of sharp, precise criticism.

What Gautier saw he saw with unparalleled exactitude: he allows himself no poetic license or room for fine phrases; has his eye always on the object, and really uses the words which best describe it, whatever they may be. So his books of travel are guide-books, in addition to being other things; and not by any means "states of soul" or states of nerves. He is willing to give you information, and able to give it to you without deranging his periods. The little essay on Leonardo is an admirable piece of artistic divination, and it is also a clear, simple, sufficient account of the man, his temperament, and his way of work. The study of Baudelaire, reprinted in the *édition définitive* of the "Fleurs du Mal," remains the one satisfactory summing up, it is not a solution, of the enigma which Baudelaire personified; and it is almost the most coloured and perfumed thing in words which he ever wrote. He wrote equally well about cities, poets, novelists, painters, or sculptors; he did not understand one better than the other, or feel less sympathy for one than for another. He, the "parfait magicien ès lettres françaises," to whom faultless words came in faultlessly beautiful order, could realise, against Balzac himself, that Balzac had a style: "he possesses, though he did not think so, a style, and a very beautiful style, the necessary, inevitable, mathematical style of his ideas." He appreciated Ingres as justly as he appreciated El Greco; he went through the Louvre, room by room, saying the right thing about each painter in turn. He did not say the final thing; he said nothing which we have to pause and think over before we see the whole of its truth or apprehend the whole of its beauty. Truth, in him, comes to us almost literally through the eyesight, and with the same beautiful clearness as if it were one of those visible things which delighted him most: gold, marble, and purple; brilliance, solidity, colour.

1902.

A WORD ON DE QUINCEY

THE work of De Quincey must be read tolerantly, rarely, and in fragments. Not even Coleridge is so uneven as De Quincey, for with Coleridge there is always an alert intellectual subtlety, troubling itself very little about the words in which it is to express itself; an unsteady, but incessant, inner illumination. De Quincey, always experimentalising with his form, forgetting and remembering it with equal persistence, has no fixed mind underneath the swaying surface of his digressions, and holds our interest, when he has once captured it, in a kind of unquiet expectancy. He will write about anything, making what he chooses of his subject, as in the fantasias around the mail-coach; he writes, certainly, for the sake of writing, and also to rid himself of all the cobwebs that are darkening his brain. His mind is subtle, yet without direction; his nerves are morbidly sensitive, and they speak through all his work; he is a scholar outside life, to whom his own mind is interesting, not in the least because it is his own; and he has the scholar's ideal of a style which is a separate thing from the thing which it expresses.

"My mother," he says in a significant passage, "was predisposed to think ill of all causes that required many words: I, predisposed to subtleties of all sorts and degrees, had naturally become acquainted with cases that could not unrobe their apparellings down to that degree of simplicity. . . . I sank away in a hopelessness that was immeasurable from all effort at explanation."

And he defines "the one misery having no relief," as "the burden of the incommunicable." That burden, thus desperately realised, was always his, and the whole of his work is a tangled attempt to communicate the incommunicable. He has a morbid kind of conscience, an abstract, almost literary conscience, which drives him to the very edge and last gulf of language, in his endeavour to express every fine shade of fact and sensation. At times this search is rewarded with miraculous findings, and all the colours seem to fade down to him out of the sunset when he would put purple into speech, words turn into solemn music when he would have them chant, and sensations become embodied fear or pain or wonder when he evokes them upon the page. But, in its restlessness, its discontent with the best service that words can render, it heaps parenthesis on parenthesis, drags down paragraphs with leaden foot-notes, and pulls up the reader at every other moment to remind him of something which he has forgotten or does not wish to know. De Quincey never knows when to stop, because his own mind never stops. He turns upon himself, like a nervous man trying to get out of a room full of people; apologises, interrupts his own apologies, leaving you at last a sharer of his own fluster. And in all this search for exactitude there is a certain pedantry, and also a certain mental haze. His imagination was pictorial, but it was not always precise enough in its outlines. Rhetoric comes into even the finest of his "dream-scenery," and rhetoric, in a picture, is colour making up for absence of form. He believed in words too much and too little.

De Quincey's "Confessions" are among the most fascinating of autobiographies, but they have an air of unreality because they are written round such experiences as only a very unreal kind of man could have known. However sincere he may mean to be, De Quincey must always make a deliberate arrangement of what he has to tell us; things fall into attitudes as he looks at them; he hears them in long and winding sentences. To an opium-smoker time and space lose even that sort of reality which normal people are accustomed to assign to them. Under the influence of such a drug it is somewhat perilous to cross the street, for it is impossible to realise the distance between oneself and the hansom which is coming towards one, or the length of time which it will require to get from pavement to pavement. It is this disturbed sense of proportion, this broken equilibrium of the mind, which gave De Quincey so faint and variable a hold on fact, even mental fact. He saw everything on the same plane, one thing not more important than another; at the moment when it engaged his interest anything was of supreme importance. But interest drove out interest, or came and went, with the disturbance of an obsession. In writing he wants to tell us everything about everything; he takes up first one subject, handling it elaborately; then handles another subject elaborately; then goes back to the first; and so the narrative moves onward, like a worm, turning back upon itself as it moves.

When people praise the style of De Quincey, they praise isolated outbursts, and there are outbursts in his work which have almost every quality of external splendour. But it was De Quincey's error to seek splendour for its own sake, to cultivate eloquence in rhetoric, to write prose loudly, as if it were to be delivered from a pulpit. Listen to the first sentence of his famous "dream-fugue": "Passion of sudden death! that once in youth I read and interpreted by the shadows of thy averted signs!—rapture of panic taking the shape (which amongst tombs in churches I have seen) of woman bursting her sepulchral bonds—of woman's Ionic form bending forward from the ruins of her grave with arching foot, with eyes upraised, with clasped adoring hands—waiting, watching, trembling, praying for the trumpet's call to rise from dust for ever." Now if prose is something said, as poetry is something sung, that is not good prose, any more than it is even bad poetry. It is oratory, and oratory has qualities quite different from literature; qualities which fit it to impress a multitude when spoken aloud, in a voice artificially heightened in order to be heard by that multitude. De Quincey's prose is artificially heightened; it cannot be spoken naturally, but must be spoken with an emphasis quite unlike that of even the most emotional speech. Perhaps the most perfect prose in the English language is the prose of Shakespeare: take a single sentence from "Love's Labour's Lost": "The sweet war-man is dead and rotten; sweet chucks, beat not the bones of the buried: when he breathed, he was a man!" There you have every merit of prose, in form and substance, and it may be spoken as easily as the expression of one's own thought. Hamlet's "What a piece of work is man!" with its elaborate splendour, can be spoken on the conversational level of the voice. Now De Quincey thinks it a mean thing to write as if he were but talking, and, whenever he rises with his subject, seems to get on a platform. It is a wonderful thing, undoubtedly, that he gives us, but a thing structurally unsatisfactory.

Carried further, used with less imagination but with a finer sense for the colour of words, it becomes the style of Ruskin, and is what is frankly called prose poetry, a lucky bastard, glorying in the illegitimacy of its origin.

1901.

NATHANIEL HAWTHORNE

All Hawthorne's work is one form or another of "handling sin." He had the Puritan sense of it in the blood, and the power to use it artistically in the brain. With Tolstoi, he is the only novelist of the soul, and he is haunted by what is obscure, dangerous, and on the confines of good and evil; by what is abnormal, indeed, if we are to accept human nature as a thing set within responsible limits, and conscious of social relations. Of one of his women he says that she "was plucked up out of a mystery, and had its roots still clinging to her." It is what is mysterious, really, in the soul that attracts him. "When we find ourselves fading into shadows and unrealities": that is when he cares to concern himself with humanity. And, finding the soul, in its essence, so intangible, so mistlike, so unfamiliar with the earth, he lays hold of what to him is the one great reality, sin, in order that he may find out something definite about the soul, in its most active, its most interesting, manifestations.

To Hawthorne what we call real life was never very real, and he has given, as no other novelist has given, a picture of life as a dream, in which the dreamers themselves are, at intervals, conscious that they are dreaming. At a moment of spiritual crisis, as at that moment when Hester Prynne and Arthur Dimmesdale meet in the forest, he can render their mental state only through one of his ghostly images: "It was no wonder that they thus questioned one another's actual bodily existence, and even doubted of their own. So strangely did they meet, in the dim wood, that it was like the first encounter, in the world beyond the grave, of two spirits who had been intimately connected in their former life, but now stood coldly shuddering, in mutual dread, as not wonted to this companionship of disembodied spirits." To Hawthorne, by a strange caprice or farsightedness of temperament, the supreme emotion comes only under the aspect of an illusion, for the first time recognised as being real, that is, really an illusion. "He himself, as was perceptible by many symptoms," he says of Clifford, "lay darkly behind his pleasure and knew it to be a baby-play, which he was to toy and trifle with, instead of thoroughly believing." To Clifford, it is mental ruin, a kind of exquisite imbecility, which brings this consciousness; to Hester Prynne, to Arthur Dimmesdale, to Donatello, to Miriam, it is sin. Each, through sin, becomes real, and perceives something of the truth.

In this strange pilgrim's progress, the first step is a step outside the bounds of some moral or social law, by which the soul is isolated, for its own torture and benefit, from the rest of the world. All Hawthorne's stories are those of persons whom some crime, or misunderstood virtue, or misfortune, has set by themselves, or in a worse companionship of solitude. Hester Prynne "stood apart from moral interests, yet close beside them, like a ghost that revisits the familiar fireside, and can no longer make itself seen or felt." The link between Hester and Arthur Dimmesdale, between Miriam and Donatello, was "the iron link of mutual crime, which neither he nor she could break. Like all other sins, it brought along with it its obligations." Note how curious the obsession by which Hawthorne can express the force of the moral law, the soul's bond with itself, only through the consequences of the breaking of that law! And note, also, with how perfect a sympathy he can render the sensation itself, what is exultant, liberating, in a strong sin, not yet become one's companion and accuser. "For, guilt has its rapture, too. The foremost result of a broken law is ever an ecstatic sense of freedom."

"I tremble at my own thoughts," he says somewhere, "yet must needs probe them to their depths." His people are always, like Miriam, "hinting at an intangible confession, such as persons with overburdened hearts often make to children and dumb animals, or to holes in the earth, where they think their secrets may be at once revealed and buried." All his work is such a confession, which he seems to make shyly, and, at the end, to have only half made. He wonders, speculates, plays around a dreadful idea, like a moth around the flame of a candle ; and then draws back, partly with the artist's satisfaction, partly with a slight natural shiver. In the preface to the "Mosses from an Old Manse" he dwells on the story of the boy who wanders upon the battle-field, axe in hand, out of the woods where he has been felling trees, and, by a sort of fierce unconscious instinct, kills the wounded British soldier. "Oftentimes, as an intellectual and moral exercise, I have sought to follow that poor youth through his subsequent career, and observe how his soul was tortured by the bloodstain." He is always searching for these bloodstains on the conscience, delicately weighing the soul's burden of sin; and it is his "intellectual and moral exercise."

Though Hawthorne has said, not without truth, "so far as I am a man of really individual attributes, I veil my face," there never was a more sincere or a more personal writer. Everything in his work is a growth out of his own soil, and we must be careful not to attribute any too deliberate intentions to what may seem most conscious or persistent in his work. The qualities which we prize most in it seem to have been those against which he tried hardest to be on his guard. We find him wishing for some contact with the "small, familiar, gentle interests of life," that they may "carry off what would otherwise be a dangerous accumulation of morbid sensibility." He is interested only in those beings, of exceptional temperament or destiny, who are alone in the world; and yet what he represents is the necessity and the awfulness, not the pride or the choice, of isolation. "This perception of an infinite shivering solitude, amid which we cannot come close enough to human beings to be warmed by them, and where they turn to cold, chilly shapes of mist," brings with it no sense of even consciously perverse pleasure. His men and women are no egoists, to whom isolation is a delight; they suffer from it, they try in vain to come out of the shadow and sit down with the rest of the world in the sunshine. Something ghostly in their blood sets them wandering among shadows, but they long to be merely human, they would come back if they could, and their tragedy is to find some invisible and impenetrable door shut against them.

It had always been the destiny of Hawthorne to watch life from a corner, as he watched the experimental life at Brook Farm, sitting silent among the talkers in the hall, "himself almost always holding a book before him, but seldom turning the pages." In all his novels, there is some such spectator of life, whom indeed he usually represents as a cold or malevolent person, intent for his own ends on the tragic climax which he will not actually precipitate. Hawthorne's attitude was rather that of a sensitive but morbidly clear-sighted friend, or of a physician, affectionately observant of the disease which he cannot cure. It was his sympathy with the soul that made him so watchful of its uneasy moods, its strange adventures, especially those which remove it furthest from the daylight and perhaps nearest to its true nature and proper abode.

"Not supernatural, but just on the verge of nature, and yet within it:" that is where he sets himself to surprise the soul's last secrets. What Hawthorne aimed at doing was to suggest that mystery, which is the most definite thing which we know about human life. "It annoys me very much," says Hilda, in "Transformation," "this inclination, which most people have, to explain away the wonder and the mystery out of everything." To Hawthorne it was the wonder and the mystery which gave its meaning to life, and to paint life without them was like painting nature without atmosphere. Only, in his endeavour to evoke this atmosphere, he did not always remember that, if it had any meaning at all, it was itself a deeper reality. And so his weakness is seen in a persistent desire to give an air of miracle to ordinary things, which gain nothing by becoming improbable; as in the sentence which describes Hester's return to her cottage, at the end of "The Scarlet Letter": "In all these years it had never once been unlocked; but either she unlocked it, or the decaying wood and iron yielded to her hand, or she glided shadowlike through these impediments—and, at all events, went in." His books are full of this futile buzzing of fancy; and it is not only in the matter of style that he too often substitutes fancy for imagination.

Hawthorne never quite fully realised the distinction between symbol and allegory, or was never long able to resist the allegorising temptation. Many of his shorter stories are frankly allegories, and are among the best of their kind, such as "Young Goodman Brown," or "The Minister's Black Veil." But, in all his work, there is an attempt to write two meanings at once, to turn what should be a great spiritual reality into a literal and barren figure of speech. He must always broider a visible badge on every personage: Hester's "A," Miss Hepzibah's scowl, the birthmark, the furry ears of the Faun. In all this there is charm, surprise, ingenuity; but is it quite imagination, which is truth, and not a decoration rather than a symbol? He passes, indeed, continually from one to the other, and is now crude and childish, as in the prattle about the Faun's furry ears, and now subtly creative, as in the figure of the child Pearl, who is in the true sense a living symbol. Nor does he insist less that every coincidence shall be as obedient as a wizard's phantom, nature and circumstance always in attendance to complete the emotion or the picture. He has used the belief in witchcraft with admirable effect, the dim mystery which clings about haunted houses, the fantastic gambols of the soul itself, under what seem like the devil's own promptings. But he must direct his imps as if they were marionettes, and, as he lets us see the wires jerking, is often at the pains to destroy his own illusion.

Hawthorne is the most sensitive of those novelists who have concerned themselves with the soul's problems; and he concerns himself, though all in hints and reticences, with the great spiritual realities. The subject of "The Scarlet Letter" is the most poignant in the world. In "Transformation" Hawthorne asks himself, seriously enough: "The story of the Fall of Man! Is it not repeated in our romance of Monte Beni?" He is at home in all those cloudy tracts of the soul's regions in which most other novelists go astray; he finds his way there, not by sight, but by feeling, like the blind. He responds to every sensation of the soul; morbidly, as people say: that is, with a consciousness of how little anything else matters.

Yet is there not some astringent quality lacking in Hawthorne, the masculine counterpart of what was sensitively feminine in him? Is he not like one of his characters "whose sensibility of nerves often produced the effect of spiritual intuition?" No one has ever rendered subtler sensations with a more delicate precision. When he speaks of flowers, we can say of him, as he says of Clifford: "His feeling for flowers was very exquisite, and seemed not so much a taste as an emotion." Speaking of a rare wine he says: "The wine demanded so deliberate a pause in order to detect the hidden peculiarities and subtle exquisiteness of its flavor that to drink it was really more a moral than a physical enjoyment." Of all natural delights and horrors, of every sensation in which the soul may be thought to have a part, he can write as if he wrote literally with his nerves. And he is full of wise discretion, he knows what not to say, he will never dissect, with most surgical analysts, the corpse of a sensation. Yet there is much in his sentiment and in his reflection which is the more feminine part of sensitiveness, and which is no more than a diluted and prettily coloured commonplace. That geniality of reflection, of which we find so much in "The House of the Seven Gables," is really a lack of intellectual backbone, a way of disguising any too austere truth from his sensibilities. The two chapters, in that often beautiful and delightful book, written around Judge Pyncheon, as he sits dead in his chair, show how lamentable a gap existed in the intellectual taste of Hawthorne. They need only be compared with the treatment of Maeterlinck of a not unsimilar situation in the little dramatic masterpiece, "Intérieur," to see all the difference between the work of the complete artist and the work of one in whom there remained always something of the amateur.

Mr Henry James has, very unjustly, as I think, accused Hawthorne of provincialism. There was nothing provincial in the temperament or intelligence of this shy and brooding spectator of human affairs, but he was not without some of the graces and limitations of the amateur. His style, at its best so delicately woven, so subdued and harmonious in colour, has gone threadbare in patches; something in its gentlemanly ease has become old-fashioned, has become genteel. There are moments when he reminds us of Charles Lamb, but in Lamb nothing has faded, or at most a few too insistent pleasantries: the salt in the style has preserved it. There is no salt in the style of Hawthorne. Read that charming preface to the "Mosses from an Old Manse," so full of country quiet, with a music in it like the gentle, monotonous murmur of a country stream. Well, at every few pages the amateur peeps out, anxiously trying to knit together his straying substance with a kind of arch simplicity. In the stories, there is rarely a narrative which has not drifted somewhere a little out of his control; and of the novels, only "The Scarlet Letter" has any sort of firmness of texture; and we have only to set it beside a really well-constructed novel, beside "Madame Bovary," for instance, to see how loosely, after all, it is woven. Even that taste, which for growing things and for all the strange growths of the soul is so fine, so sensitive, passes into a vague, moralising sentimentality whenever he speaks, as he does so often in "Transformation," of painting or of sculpture. He seems incapable of looking at either without thinking of something else, some fancy or moral, which he must fit into the frame or the cube, or else drape around it, in the form of a veil meant for ornament. Yet, in all this, and sometimes by a felicity in some actual weakness, turned, like a woman's, into a fragile and pathetic grace, there is a continual weaving of intricate mental cobwebs, and an actual creation of that dim and luminous atmosphere in which they are best seen. And, in the end, all that is finest in Hawthorne seems to unite in the creation of atmosphere.

In the preface to "Transformation," Hawthorne admits that he "designed the story and the characters to bear, of course, a certain relation to human nature and human life, but still to be so artfully and airily removed from our mundane sphere, that some laws and proportions of their own should be implicitly and insensibly acknowledged." And he defends himself, on the ground of reality, by saying: "The actual experience of even the most ordinary life is full of events that never explain themselves, either as regards their origin or their tendency." Is it not the novelist's business, it may be objected, to explain precisely what would not, in real life, explain itself, to those most closely concerned in it? But to Hawthorne, perhaps rightly, even the clearest explanation is no more than a deepening of the illusion, as the poor ghosts, like Feathertop in the story, see themselves for what they are. Something unsubstantial, evasive, but also something intellectually dissatisfied, always inquiring, in his mind, set Hawthorne spinning these arabesques of the soul, in which the fantastic element may be taken as a note of interrogation. Seeing always "a grim identity between gay things and sorrowful ones," he sets a masquerade before us, telling us many of the secrets hidden behind the black velvet, but letting us see no more than the glimmer of eyes, and the silent or ambiguous lips.

Hawthorne's romances are not exactly (he never

wished them to be) novels, but they are very nearly poems. And they are made, for the most part, out of material which seems to lend itself singularly ill to poetic treatment. In the preface to "Transformation" he says: "No author, without a trial, can be conscious of the difficulty of writing a romance about a country where there is no shadow, no antiquity, no mystery, no picturesque and gloomy wrong." Yet this shadow, this antiquity, this mystery, this picturesque and gloomy wrong, is what he has found or created in America. Already in the "Twice-Told Tales" ("these fitful sketches," as he called them, "with so little of external life about them, yet claiming no profundity of purpose—so reserved, even while they sometimes seem so frank—often but half in earnest, and never, even when most so, expressing satisfactorily the thoughts which they propose to image") there is a kind of ghostly America growing older and older as one looks at it, as if some wizard had set ivy climbing over new walls. In "The House of the Seven Gables," and in his masterpiece, "The Scarlet Letter," we have, without any undue loss of reality, a more admirably prepared atmosphere, which I imagine to be quite recognisably American, and which is at least as much the atmosphere proper to romance as the Italian atmosphere of "Transformation." Each is not so much a narrative which advances, as a canvas which is covered; or, in his own figure, a tapestry "into which are woven some airy and unsubstantial threads, intermixed with others twisted out of the commonest stuff of human existence." A Puritan in fancy dress, he himself passes silently through the masquerade, as it startles some quiet street in New England. Where what is fantastic in Poe remains geometrical, in Hawthorne it is always, for good and evil, moral. It decorates, sometimes plays pranks with, a fixed belief, a fundamental religious seriousness; and has thus at least an immovable centre to whirl from. And, where fancy passes into imagination, and a world, not quite what seems to us the real world, grows up about us with a new, mental kind of reality, it is as if that arrangement or transposition of actual things with which poetry begins had taken place already. I do not know any novelist who has brought into prose fiction so much of the atmosphere of poetry, with so much of the actual art of composition of the poet. It is a kind of poetry singularly pure, delicate, and subtle, and, at its best, it has an almost incalculable fascination, and some not quite realised, but insensibly compelling, white magic.

1904.

Walter Pater.

WALTER PATER

Walter Pater was a man in whom fineness and subtlety of emotion were united with an exact and profound scholarship; in whom a personality singularly unconventional, and singularly full of charm, found for its expression an absolutely personal and an absolutely novel style, which was the most carefully and curiously beautiful of all English styles. The man and his style, to those who knew him, were identical; for, as his style was unlike that of other men, concentrated upon a kind of perfection which, for the most part, they could not even distinguish, so his inner life was peculiarly his own, centred within a circle beyond which he refused to wander; his mind, to quote some words of his own, "keeping as a solitary prisoner its own dream of a world." And he was the most lovable of men; to those who rightly apprehended him, the most fascinating; the most generous and helpful of private friends, and in literature a living counsel of perfection, whose removal seems to leave modern English prose without a contemporary standard of values.

"For it is with the delicacies of fine literature especially, its gradations of expression, its fine judgment, its pure sense of words, of vocabulary—things, alas! dying out in the English literature of the present, together with the appreciation of them in our literature of the past—that his literary mission is chiefly concerned." These words, applied by Pater to Charles Lamb, might reasonably enough have been applied to himself; especially in that earlier part of his work, which remains to me, as I doubt not it remains to many others, the most entirely delightful. As a critic, he selected for analysis only those types of artistic character in which delicacy, an exquisite fineness, is the principal attraction; or if, as with Michelangelo, he was drawn towards some more rugged personality, some more massive, less finished art, it was not so much from sympathy with these more obvious qualities of ruggedness and strength, but because he had divined the sweetness lying at the heart of the strength: "ex forti dulcedo." Leonardo da Vinci, Joachim du Bellay, Coleridge, Botticelli: we find always something a little exotic, or subtle, or sought out, a certain rarity, which it requires an effort to disengage, and which appeals for its perfect appreciation to a public within the public; those fine students of what is fine in art, who take their artistic pleasures consciously, deliberately, critically, with the learned love of the amateur.

And not as a critic only, judging others, but in his own person as a writer, both of critical and of imaginative work, Pater showed his preoccupation with the "delicacies of fine literature." His prose was from the first conscious, and it was from the first perfect. That earliest book of his, "Studies in the History of the Renaissance," as it was then called, entirely individual, the revelation of a rare and special temperament, though it was, had many affinities with the poetic and pictorial art of Rossetti, Swinburne, and Burne Jones, and seems, on its appearance in 1873, to have been taken as the manifesto of the so-called "æsthetic" school. And, indeed, it may well be compared, as artistic prose, with the poetry of Rossetti; as fine, as careful, as new a thing as that, and with something of the same exotic odour about it: a savour in this case of French soil, a

Watteau grace and delicacy. Here was criticism as a fine art, written in prose which the reader lingered over as over poetry; modulated prose which made the splendour of Ruskin seem gaudy, the neatness of Matthew Arnold a mincing neatness, and the brass sound strident in the orchestra of Carlyle.

That book of "Studies in the Renaissance," even with the rest of Pater to choose from, seems to me sometimes to be the most beautiful book of prose in our literature. Nothing in it is left to inspiration; but it is all inspired. Here is a writer who, like Baudelaire, would better nature; and in this goldsmith's work of his prose he too has "rêvé le miracle d'une prose poétique, musicale sans rhythme et sans rime." An almost oppressive quiet, a quiet which seems to exhale an atmosphere heavy with the odour of tropical flowers, broods over these pages; a subdued light shadows them. The most felicitous touches come we know not whence, "a breath, a flame in the doorway, a feather in the wind"; here are the simplest words, but they take colour from each other by the cunning accident of their placing in the sentence, "the subtle spiritual fire kindling from word to word."

In this book prose seemed to have conquered a new province; and further, along this direction, prose could not go. Twelve years later, when "Marius the Epicurean" appeared, it was in a less coloured manner of writing that the "sensations and ideas" of that reticent, wise, and human soul were given to the world. Here and there, perhaps, the goldsmith, adding more value, as he thought, for every trace of gold that he removed, might seem to have scraped a little too assiduously. But the style of "Marius," in its more arduous self-repression, has a graver note, and brings with it a severer kind of beauty. Writers who have paid particular attention to style have often been accused of caring little *what* they say, knowing how beautifully they can say anything. The accusation has generally been unjust: as if any fine beauty could be but skin-deep! The merit which, more than any other, distinguishes Pater's prose, though it is not the merit most on the surface, is the attention to, the perfection of, the ensemble. Under the soft and musical phrases an inexorable logic hides itself, sometimes only too well. Link is added silently, but faultlessly, to link; the argument marches, carrying you with it, while you fancy you are only listening to the music with which it keeps step. Take an essay to pieces, and you will find that it is constructed with mathematical precision; every piece can be taken out and replaced in order. I do not know any contemporary writer who observes the logical requirements so scrupulously, who conducts an argument so steadily from deliberate point to point towards a determined goal. And here, in "Marius," though the story is indeed but a sequence of scenes, woven around a sequence of moods, there is a scarcely less rigorous care for the ensemble, as that had been intended, the story being properly speaking no story, but the philosophy of a soul. And thus it is mainly by a kind of very individual atmosphere, mental and physical, that the sense of unity is conveyed. It is a book to read slowly, to meditate over; more than any of Pater's books, it is a personal confession and the scheme of a doctrine.

In this book, and in the "Imaginary Portraits" of three years later, which seems to me to show his imaginative and artistic faculties at their point of most perfect fusion, Pater has not endeavoured to create characters, in whom the flesh and blood should seem to be that of life itself; he had not the energy of creation, and he was content with a more shadowy life than theirs for the children of his dreams. What he has done is to give a concrete form to abstract ideas; to represent certain types of character, to trace certain developments, in the picturesque form of narrative; to which, indeed, the term portrait is very happily applied; for the method is that of a very patient and elaborate brush-work, in which the touches that go to form the likeness are so fine that it is difficult to see quite their individual value, until, the end being reached, the whole picture starts out before you. Each, with perhaps one exception, is the study of a soul, or rather of a consciousness; such a study as might be made by simply looking within, and projecting now this now that side of oneself on an exterior plane. I do not mean to say that I attribute to Pater himself the philosophical theories of Sebastian van Storck, or the artistic ideals of Duke Carl of Rosenmold. I mean that the attitude of mind, the outlook, in the most general sense, is always limited and directed in a certain way, giving one always the picture of a delicate, subtle, aspiring, unsatisfied personality, open to all impressions, living chiefly by sensations, little anxious to reap any of the rich harvest of its intangible but keenly possessed gains; a personality withdrawn from action, which it despises or dreads, solitary with its ideals, in the circle of its "exquisite moments," in the Palace of Art, where it is never quite at rest. It is somewhat such a soul, I have thought, as that which Browning has traced in "Sordello"; indeed, when reading for the first time "Marius the Epicurean," I was struck by a certain resemblance between the record of the sensations and ideas of Marius of White-Nights and that of the sensations and events of Sordello of Goito.

The style of the "Imaginary Portraits" is the ripest, the most varied and flawless, their art the most assured and masterly, of any of Pater's books: it was the book that he himself preferred in his work, thinking it, to use his own phrase, more "natural" than any other. And of the four portraits the most wonderful seems to me the poem, for it is really a poem, named "Denys l'Auxerrois." For once, it is not the study of a soul, but of a myth; a transposition (in which one hardly knows whether to admire most the learning, the ingenuity, or the subtle imagination) of that strangest myth of the Greeks, the "Pagan after-thought" of Dionysus Zagreus, into the conditions of mediæval life. Here is prose so coloured, so modulated, as to have captured, along with almost every sort of poetic richness, and in a rhythm which is essentially the rhythm of prose, even the suggestiveness of poetry, that most volatile and unseizable property, of which prose has so rarely been able to possess itself. The style of "Denys l'Auxerrois" has a subdued heat, a veiled richness of colour, which contrasts curiously with the silver-grey coolness of "A Prince of Court Painters," the chill, more leaden grey of "Sebastian van Storck," though it has a certain affinity, perhaps, with the more variously-tinted canvas of "Duke Carl of Rosenmold." Watteau, Sebastian, Carl: unsatisfied seekers, all of them, this after an artistic ideal of impossible perfection, that after a chill and barren ideal of philosophical thinking and living, that other after yet another ideal, unattainable to him in his period, of life "im Ganzen, Guten, Schönen," a beautiful and effective culture. The story of each, like that of "Marius," is a vague tragedy, ending abruptly, after so many uncertainties, and always with some subtly ironic effect in the accident of its conclusion. The mirror is held up to Watteau while he struggles desperately or hesitatingly forward, snatching from art one after another of her reticent secrets;

then, with a stroke, it is broken, and this artist in immortal things sinks out of sight, into a narrow grave of red earth. The mirror is held up to Sebastian as he moves deliberately, coldly, onward in the midst of a warm life which has so little attraction for him, freeing himself one by one from all obstructions to a clear philosophic equilibrium; and the mirror is broken, with a like suddenness, and the seeker disappears from our sight, to find, perhaps, what he had sought. It is held up to Duke Carl, the seeker after the satisfying things of art and experience, the dilettante in material and spiritual enjoyment, the experimenter on life; and again it is broken, with an almost terrifying shock, just as he has come to a certain rash crisis: is it a step upward or downward? a step, certainly, towards the concrete, towards a possible material felicity.

We see Pater as an imaginative writer, pure and simple, only in these two books, "Marius" and the "Imaginary Portraits," in the unfinished romance of "Gaston de Latour" (in which detail had already begun to obscure the outlines of the central figure), and in those "Imaginary Portraits" reprinted in various volumes, but originally intended to form a second series under that title: "Hippolytus Veiled," "Apollo in Picardy," "Emerald Uthwart"; and that early first chapter of an unwritten story of modern English life, "The Child in the House." For the rest, he was content to be a critic: a critic of poetry and painting in the "Studies in the Renaissance" and the "Appreciations," of sculpture and the arts of life in the "Greek Studies," of philosophy in the volume on "Plato and Platonism." But he was a critic as no one else ever was a critic. He had made a fine art of criticism. His criticism, abounding in the close and strenuous qualities of really earnest judgment, grappling with his subject as if there were nothing to do but that, the "fine writing" in it being largely mere conscientiousness in providing a subtle and delicate thought with words as subtle and delicate, was, in effect, written with as scrupulous a care, with as much artistic finish, as much artistic purpose, as any imaginative work whatever; being indeed, in a sense in which, perhaps, no other critical work is, imaginative work itself.

"The æsthetic critic," we are told in the preface to the "Studies in the Renaissance," "regards all the objects with which he has to do, all works of art, and the fairer forms of nature and human life, as powers or forces producing pleasurable sensations, each of a more or less peculiar and unique kind. This influence he feels, and wishes to explain, analysing it, and reducing it to its elements. To him, the picture, the landscape, the engaging personality in life or in a book, *La Gioconda*, the hills of Carrara, Pico of Mirandola, are valuable for their virtues, as we say in speaking of a herb, a wine, a gem; for the property each has of affecting one with a special, a unique, impression of pleasure." To this statement of what was always the aim of Pater in criticism, I would add, from the later essay on Wordsworth, a further statement, applying it, as he there does, to the criticism of literature. "What special sense," he asks, "does Wordsworth exercise, and what instincts does he satisfy? What are the subjects which in him excite the imaginative faculty? What are the qualities in things and persons which he values, the impression and sense of which he can convey to others, in an extraordinary way?" How far is this ideal from that old theory, not yet extinct, which has been briefly stated, thus, by Edgar Poe: "While the critic is *permitted* to play, at times, the part of the mere commentator—while he is *allowed*, by way of merely *interesting* his readers, to put in the fairest light the merits of his author—his *legitimate* task is still, in pointing out and analysing defects, and showing how the work might have been improved, to aid the cause of letters, without undue heed of the individual literary men." And Poe goes on to protest, energetically, against the more merciful (and how infinitely more fruitful!) principles of Goethe, who held that what it concerns us to know about a work or a writer are the merits, not the defects, of the writer and the work. Pater certainly carried this theory to its furthest possible limits, and may almost be said never, except by implication, to condemn anything. But then the force of this implication testifies to a fastidiousness infinitely greater than that of the most destructive of the destructive critics. Is it necessary to *say* that one dislikes a thing? It need but be ignored; and Pater ignored whatever did not come up to his very exacting standard, finding quite enough to write about in that small residue which remained over.

Nor did he merely ignore what was imperfect, he took the further step, the taking of which was what made him a creative artist in criticism. "It was thus," we are told of Gaston de Latour, in one of the chapters of the unfinished romance, "it was thus Gaston understood the poetry of Ronsard, *generously expanding it to the full measure of its intention.*" That is precisely what Pater does in his criticisms, in which criticism is a divining-rod over hidden springs. He has a unique faculty of seeing, through every imperfection, the perfect work, the work as the artist saw it, as he strove to make it, as he failed, in his measure, quite adequately to achieve it. He goes straight to what is fundamental, to the root of the matter, leaving all the rest out of the question. The essay on Wordsworth is perhaps the best example of this, for it has fallen to the lot of Wordsworth to suffer more than most at the hands of interpreters. Here, at last, is a critic who can see in him "a poet somewhat bolder and more passionate than might at first sight be supposed, but not too bold for true poetical taste; an unimpassioned writer, you might sometimes fancy, yet thinking the chief aim, in life and art alike, to be a certain deep emotion"; one whose "words are themselves thought and feeling"; "a master, an expert, in the art of impassioned contemplation." Reading such essays as these, it is difficult not to feel that if Lamb and Wordsworth, if Shakespeare, if Sir Thomas Browne, could but come to life again for the pleasure of reading them, that pleasure would be the sensation: "Here is some one who understands just what I meant to do, what was almost too deep in me for expression, and would have, I knew, to be divined; that something, scarcely expressed in any of my words, without which no word I ever wrote would have been written."

Turning from the criticisms of literature to the studies in painting, we see precisely the same qualities, but not, I think, precisely the same results. In a sentence of the essay on "The School of Giorgione," which is perhaps the most nicely balanced of all his essays on painting, he defines, with great precision: "In its primary aspect, a great picture has no more definite message for us than an accidental play of sunlight and shadow for a moment on the floor: is itself in truth a space of such fallen light, caught as the colours are caught in an Eastern carpet, but refined upon, and dealt with more subtly and exquisitely than by nature itself." But for the most part it was not in this spirit that he wrote of pictures. His criticism of pictures is indeed creative, in a fuller sense than his criticism of books; and, in the necessity of things, dealing with an art which, as he admitted, has, in its primary aspect, no more definite message for us than the sunlight on the floor, he not merely divined, but also added, out of the most sympathetic knowledge, certainly. It is one thing to interpret the meaning of a book; quite another to interpret the meaning of a picture. Take, for instance the essay on Botticelli. That was the first sympathetic study which had appeared in English of a painter at that time but little known; and it contains some of Pater's most exquisite writing. All that he writes, of those Madonnas "who are neither for Jehovah nor for his enemies," of that sense in the painter of "the wistfulness of exiles," represents, certainly, the impression made upon his own mind by these pictures, and, as such, has an interpretative value, apart from its beauty as a piece of writing. But it is after all a speculation before a canvas, a literary fantasy; a possible interpretation, if you will, of one mood in the painter, a single side of his intention; it is not a criticism, inevitable as that criticism of Wordsworth's art, of the art of Botticelli.

This once understood, we must admit that Pater did more than any one of our time to bring about a more intimate sympathy with some of the subtler aspects of art; that his influence did much to rescue us from the dangerous moralities, the uncritical enthusiasms and prejudices, of Ruskin; that of no other art-critic it could be said that his taste was flawless. In some of the "Greek Studies" in the essays on "The Beginnings of Greek Sculpture," and the rest, he has made sculpture a living, intimate thing; and, with no addition of his fancy, but in a minute, learned, intuitive piecing together of little fact by little fact, has shown its growth, its relation to life, its meaning in art. I find much of the same quality in his studies in Greek myths: that coloured, yet so scrupulous "Study of Dionysus," the patient disentanglings of the myth of Demeter and Persephone. And, in what is the latest work, practically, that we have from his hand, the lectures on "Plato and Platonism," we see a like scrupulous and discriminating judgment brought to bear, as upon an artistic problem, upon the problems of Greek ethics, Greek philosophy.

"Philosophy itself indeed, as he conceives it," Pater tells us, speaking of Plato (he might be speaking of himself), "is but the systematic appreciation of a kind of music in the very nature of things." And philosophy, as he conceives it, is a living, dramatic thing, among personalities, and the strife of temperaments; a doctrine being seen as a vivid fragment of some very human mind, not a dry matter of words and disembodied reason. "In the discussion even of abstract truth," he reminds us, "it is not so much what he thinks as the person who is thinking, that after all really tells." Thus, the student's duty, in reading Plato, "is not to take his side in a controversy, to adopt or refute Plato's opinions, to modify, or make apology for what may seem erratic or impossible in him; still less, to furnish himself with arguments on behalf of some theory or conviction of his own. His duty is rather to follow intelligently, but with strict indifference, the mental process there, as he might witness a game of skill; better still, as in reading *Hamlet* or *The Divine Comedy*, so in reading *The Republic*, to watch, for its dramatic interest, the spectacle of a powerful, of a sovereign intellect, translating itself, amid a complex group of conditions which can never in the nature of things occur again, at once pliant and resistant to them, into a great literary monument." It is thus that Pater studies his subject, with an extraordinary patience and precision; a patience with ideas, not, at first sight, so clear or so interesting as he induces them to become; a precision of thinking, on his part, in which no licence is ever permitted to the fantastic side-issues of things. Here again we have criticism which, in its divination, its arrangement, its building up of many materials into a living organism, is itself creation, becomes imaginative work itself.

We may seem to be far now, but are not in reality so far as it may seem, from those "delicacies of fine literature," with which I began by showing Pater to be so greatly concerned. And, in considering the development by which a writer who had begun with the "Studies in the Renaissance" ended with "Plato and Platonism," we must remember, as Mr Gosse has so acutely pointed out in his valuable study of Pater's personal characteristics, that, after all, it was philosophy which attracted him before either literature or art, and that his first published essay was an essay on Coleridge, in which Coleridge the metaphysician, and not Coleridge the poet, was the interesting person to him. In his return to an early, and one might think, in a certain sense, immature interest, it need not surprise us to find a development, which I cannot but consider as technically something of a return to a primitive lengthiness and involution, towards a style which came to lose many of the rarer qualities of its perfect achievement. I remember that when he once said to me that the "Imaginary Portraits" seemed to him the best written of his books, he qualified that very just appreciation by adding: "It seems to me the most *natural.*" I think he was even then beginning to forget that it was not natural to him to be natural. There are many kinds of beauty in the world, and of these what is called natural beauty is but one. Pater's temperament was at once shy and complex, languid and ascetic, sensuous and spiritual. He did not permit life to come to him without a certain ceremony; he was on his guard against the abrupt indiscretion of events; and if his whole life was a service of art, he arranged his life so that, as far as possible, it might be served by that very dedication. With this conscious ordering of things, it became a last sophistication to aim at an effect in style which should bring the touch of unpremeditation, which we seem to find in nature, into a faultlessly combined arrangement of art. The lectures on Plato, really spoken, show traces of their actual delivery in certain new, vocal effects, which had begun already to interest him as matters of style; and which we may find, more finely, here and there in "Gaston de Latour." Perhaps all this was but a pausing-place in a progress. That it would not have been the final stage, we may be sure. But it is idle to speculate what further development awaited, at its own leisure, so incalculable a life.

1896.

ROBERT LOUIS STEVENSON

The death of Robert Louis Stevenson deprived English literature of the most charming and sympathetic writer of the present day. He was a fastidious craftsman, caring, we might almost say pre-eminently, for style; yet he was popular. He was most widely known as the writer of boys' books of adventure; yet he was the favourite reading of those who care only for the most literary aspects of literature. Within a few days after the news of his death reached England, English newspapers vied with each other in comparing him with Montaigne, with Lamb, with Scott, with Defoe; and he has been not merely compared, but preferred. Uncritical praise is the most unfriendly service a man can render to his friend; but here, where so much praise is due, may one not try to examine a little closely just what those qualities are which call for praise, and just what measure of praise they seem to call for?

Stevenson somewhere describes certain of his own essays as being "but the readings of a literary vagrant." And, in truth, he was always that, a literary vagrant; it is the secret of much of his charm, and of much of his weakness. He wandered, a literary vagrant, over the world, across life, and across literature, an adventurous figure, with all the irresponsible and irresistible charm of the vagabond. To read him is to be for ever setting out on a fresh journey, along a white, beckoning road, on a blithe spring morning. Anything may happen, or nothing; the air is full of the gaiety of possible chances. And in this exhilaration of the blood, unreasoning, unreasonable, as it is, all the philosophies merge themselves into those two narrow lines which the "Child's Garden of Verses" piously encloses for us:

> "The world is so full of a number of things,
> I am sure we should all be as happy as kings."

It is the holiday mood of life that Stevenson expresses, and no one has ever expressed it with a happier abandonment to the charm of natural things. In its exquisite exaggeration, it is the optimism of the invalid, due to his painful consciousness that health, and the delights of health, are what really matter in life. Most of those who have written captivatingly of the open air, of what are called natural, healthy things, have been invalids: Thoreau, Richard Jefferies, Stevenson. The strong man has leisure to occupy his thoughts with other things; he can indulge in abstract thinking without a twinge of the brain, can pursue the moral issues of conduct impersonally; he is not condemned to the bare elements of existence. And, in his calm acceptance of the privileges of ordinary health, he finds no place for that lyric rapture of thanksgiving which a bright day, a restful night, wakens in the invalid. The actual fever and languor in the blood: that counts for something in Stevenson's work, and lies at the root of some of its fascination.

His art, in all those essays and extravagant tales into which he put his real self, is a romantic art, alike in the essay on "Walking Tours" and in the "Story of the Young Man with the Cream Tarts." Stevenson was passionately interested in people; but there was something a trifle elvish and uncanny about him, as of a bewitched being who was not actually human, had not actually a human soul, and whose keen interest in the fortunes of his fellows was really a vivid curiosity, from one not quite of the same nature as those about him. He saw life as the most absorbing, the most amusing, game; or, as a masquerade, in which he liked to glance behind a mask, now and again, on the winding and coloured way he made for himself through the midst of the pageant. It was only in his latest period that he came to think about truth to human nature; and even then it was with the picturesqueness of character, with its adaptability to the humorous freaks of incident, that he was chiefly concerned.

He was never really himself except when he was in some fantastic disguise. From "The Pavilion on the Links" to "Dr Jekyll and Mr Hyde," he played with men and women as a child plays with a kaleidoscope; using them freakishly, wantonly, as colours, sometimes as symbols. In some wonderful, artificial way, like a wizard who raises, not living men from the dead, but the shadows of men who had once died, he calls up certain terrifying, but not ungracious, phantoms, who frisk it among the mere beings of flesh and blood, bringing with them the strangest "airs from heaven or blasts from hell." No; in the phrase of Beddoes, Stevenson was "tired of being merely human." Thus there are no women in his books, no lovers; only the lure of hidden treasures and the passion of adventure. It was for the accidents and curiosities of life that he cared, for life as a strange picture, for its fortunate confusions, its whimsical distresses, its unlikely strokes of luck, its cruelties, sometimes, and the touch of madness that comes into it at moments. For reality, for the endeavour to see things as they are, to represent them as they are, he had an impatient disregard. These matters did not interest him.

But it is by style, largely, we are told, that Stevenson is to live, and the names of Lamb and of Montaigne are called up on equal terms. Style, with Stevenson, was certainly a constant preoccupation, and he has told us how, as a lad, he trained himself in the use of language; how, in his significant phrase, he "lived with words"; by "playing the sedulous ape to Hazlitt, to Lamb, to Wordsworth, to Sir Thomas Browne, to Defoe, to Hawthorne, to Montaigne, to Baudelaire, and to Obermann." He was resolved from the first to reject the ready-made in language, to combine words for himself, as if no one had ever used them before; and, with labour and luck, he formed for his use a singularly engaging manner of writing, full of charm, freshness, and flexibility, and with a certain human warmth in the words. But it is impossible to consider style in the abstract without taking into account also what it expresses; for true style is not the dress, but the very flesh, of the informing thought. Stevenson's tendency, like that of his admirers, was rather to the forgetfulness of this plain and sometimes uncongenial fact. But, in comparing him with the great names of literature, we cannot but feel all the difference, and all the meaning of the difference, between a great intellect and a bright intelligence. The lofty and familiar homeliness of Montaigne, the subtle and tragic humour of Lamb, are both on a far higher plane than the gentle and attractive and whimsical confidences of Stevenson. And, underlying what may seem trifling in both, there is a large intellectual force, a breadth of wisdom, which makes these two charming writers not merely charming, but great. Stevenson remains charming; his personality, individual and exquisite as it was, had not the strength and depth of greatness. And, such as it was, it gave itself to us completely; there was no sense, as there is with the really great writers, of reserve power, of infinite riches to draw upon. Quite by himself in a certain seductiveness of manner, he ranks, really, with Borrow and Thoreau, with the men of secondary order in literature, who appeal to us with more instinctive fascination than the very greatest; as a certain wayward and gipsy grace in a woman thrills to the blood, often enough, more intimately and immediately than the august perfection of classic beauty. He is one of those writers who speak to us on easy terms, with whom we may exchange affections. We cannot lose our heart to Shakespeare, to Balzac; nay, even to Montaigne, because of the height and depth, the ardour and dignity, of the wisdom in his "smiling" pages (to use Stevenson's own word). But George Borrow makes every one who comes under his charm a little unfit for civilisation, a little discontented with drawing-rooms; Thoreau leads his willing victim into the ardent austerity of the woods; and Stevenson awakens something of the eternal romance in the bosom even of the conventional. It is a surprising, a marvellous thing to have done; and to afford such delights, to call forth such responsive emotions, is a boon that we accept with warmer rejoicing than many more solid gifts. But to be wine and song to us for a festive evening is, after all, not the highest form of service or the noblest ministration of joy. It is needful to discriminate in these generous and perilous enthusiasms, as it is in judging fairly of the character of a friend. Let us love our friend, with all his shortcomings; let him be the more lovable for them, if chance wills it; but it is better to be aware of the truth, before we proceed to act with affectionate disregard of it. Stevenson captivates the heart: that is why he is in such danger of being wronged by indiscriminate eulogy. Let us do him justice: he would have wished only for justice. It is a dishonour to the dead if we strive to honour their memory with anything less absolute than truth.

1894.

JA Symonds

JOHN ADDINGTON SYMONDS

Mr Horatio Brown's Life of John Addington Symonds is composed with so careful and so successful a reticence on the part of the author, that it is not at first sight obvious how much its concealment of art is a conscious subtlety in art. These two volumes, containing, for the most part, extracts from an autobiography, from diaries and from letters, woven together so as to make an almost consecutive narrative (a plan which recalls a little the admirable and unusual method of Mason's "Gray") present a most carefully arranged portrait, which, in one sense, is absolutely the creation of the biographer. All this material, ready-made as it may seem to be, has really been fitted together, according to a well-defined scheme, with immense ingenuity and diligence, and with a remarkable subtlety and insight into the very complex nature of the man whose portrait is here presented to the world. It is a painful, a tragic book, this record of what Symonds calls "my chequered, confused, and morally perturbed existence," and yet at the same time an inspiring, an exhilarating book, which quickens one with a sense of the possibilities of life by its revelation of the charm, the courage, the nobility, the fixed aim, the endlessly thwarted and undaunted endeavour of a human spirit "to live resolvedly in the Whole, the Good, the Beautiful." To those who knew and loved the man, it calls up, not merely the blithe companion of any hour's adventure, but the real, suffering, and sympathetic individuality that lay deeper; and it recalls that memory with almost intolerable vividness.

In the early part of 1889 Symonds wrote an Autobiography, which he himself considered the best piece of literary work he had ever done. A good deal, especially of the earlier part, of this Autobiography is incorporated in Mr Brown's volumes, and I am inclined to think that Symonds was right in his estimate of it. It is full of subtle self-analysis of a nature which realises itself to be "impenetrably reserved in the depths of myself, rhetorically candid on the surface." That, indeed, was Symonds' attitude through life; and (strange, contradictory, as the man was in all things) even more so at the beginning than at the end of his career. Early in the Autobiography we find this curious description of a kind of trance which occurred at intervals up to the age of twenty-eight.

"Suddenly, at church or in company, or when I was reading, and always, I think, when my muscles were at rest, I felt the approach of the mood. Irresistibly it took possession of my mind and will, lasted what seemed an eternity, and disappeared in a series of rapid sensations, which resembled the awakening from anæsthetic influence. One reason why I disliked this kind of trance was that I could not describe it to myself. I cannot even now find words to render it intelligible, though it is probable that many readers of these pages will recognise the state in question. It consisted in a gradual but swiftly progressive obliteration of space, time, sensation, and the multitudinous factors of experience which seem to qualify what we are pleased to call ourself. In proportion as these conditions of ordinary consciousness were subtracted, the sense of an underlying or essential consciousness acquired intensity. At last nothing remained but a pure, absolute, abstract self. The universe became without form and void of content. But self persisted, formidable in its vivid keenness, feeling the most poignant doubt about reality, ready, as it seemed, to find existence break as breaks a bubble round about it. And what then? The apprehension of a coming dissolution, the grim conviction that this state was the last state of the conscious self, the sense that I had followed the last thread of being to the verge of the abyss, and had arrived at demonstration of eternal Maya or illusion, stirred or seemed to stir me up again. The return to ordinary conditions of sentient existence began by my first recovering the power of touch, and then by the gradual though rapid influx of familiar impressions and diurnal interests. At last I felt myself once more a human being; and though the riddle of what is meant by life remained unsolved, I was thankful for this return from the abyss—this deliverance from so awful an initiation into the mysteries of scepticism."

The record of this singular experience is but one of many revelations which we get in these pages of that brooding meditativeness which lay at the root of Symonds' nature; that painfully minute introspection which finds more concrete expression in these passages from a Diary, written at the age of twenty-one:

"I may rave, but I shall never rend the heavens: I may sit and sing, but I shall never make earth listen. And I am not strong enough to be good—what is left? I do not feel strong enough to be bad. . . . The sum of intellectual progress I hoped for has been obtained, but how much below my hopes. My character has developed, but in what puny proportions, below my meanest anticipations. I do not feel a man. This book is an evidence of the yearnings without power, and the brooding self-analysis without creation that afflict me."

In all this there was a certain undoubted truth, and

a part of the unhappiness of Symonds' life was certainly due to an only too precise sense of the limit of his own capacities, and an only too acute longing for an absolute achievement. "Women," he writes in a letter at the age of twenty-five, "do not, need not, pose themselves with problems about their own existence; but a man must do it, unless he has a fixed impulse in one definite direction, or an external force compelling him to take an inevitable line." Now, this was just what Symonds, even after the awakening of his ambition, even after the moment when Plato had in a sense revealed him to himself ("as though the voice of my own soul spoke to me through Plato") this was just what Symonds never had. We find him questioning himself:

"If I give myself to literature, and find myself inadequate, can I be content with a fastidious silence? . . . I feel so weak, so unable to do anything, or to take hold of any subject. In the room with me at this moment are five men, all provided with clear brains for business, all talking slang, and all wondering what strange incapable animal I am who have thus come among them."

And, again, in the Diary, we read:

"Why do I say 'Lord, Lord,' and do not? Here is my essential weakness. I wish and cannot will. I feel intensely, I perceive quickly, sympathise with all I see, or hear, or read. To emulate things nobler than myself is my desire. But I cannot get beyond—create, originate, win heaven by prayers and faith, have trust in God, and concentrate myself upon an end of action."

Here, indeed, we seem to be at the root of the great spiritual tragedy of his life, a tragedy of noble ambition, thwarted on every side, physically, morally, mentally. It was quite true that Symonds could create nothing, neither a well-balanced personality nor an achieved work of art. No one ever had a higher ideal of perfection, or strove more earnestly to reach it. But, as he well knew, there was something lacking, a certain disarray of faculties, and the full achievement never came. Those hesitations as to the path to pursue, law or literature, and, if literature, the special form of it, are significant. Every true artist is eternally doubtful of himself, eternally dissatisfied with the result of his best endeavours. But no true artist doubts in his heart of hearts whether the art of his choice is really the art for which he is best fitted. Himself he doubts, not his vocation. Now with Symonds the very impulse towards literature was a half-hearted one. He came to it as to a branch of culture; he toiled at it conscientiously, enthusiastically; but it was, in a certain sense, "work without hope," and it was also work done as a sort of gymnastic, a way of letting off energies. Much of Symonds' writing (most of it being so curiously impersonal, and yet not impersonal in the truly artistic way) was a means of escape, escape from himself. "Neither then nor afterwards," he writes, near the beginning of the Autobiography, "did I fear anything so much as my own self."

Symonds' detailed estimate of his own literary capacities and acquirements, in the Autobiography, is somewhat cruelly just:

"Having an active brain and a lively curiosity, I was always acquiring information, while the defect of my retentive power made me continually lose the larger portion of it. Yet in this way my intellectual furniture grew to be a vague, ill-digested, inaccurate mass, rich in possibilities, but poor in solid stuff. . . . I cannot learn anything systematically. Grammar, logic, political economy, the exact sciences, offered insuperable difficulties to my mind. The result is, that I know nothing thoroughly, and I do not think this is so much due to laziness as to cerebral incapacity. . . . Retentive receptivity is the quality I claim. Combined with a moderate estimate of my own powers and a fair share of common sense, together with an active curiosity, this receptive and retentive susceptibility to various objects and emotions has given a certain breadth, a certain catholicity, a certain commonplaceness, to my æsthetic conclusions.

"My powers of expression were considerable, yet not of first-rate quality. Vaughan, at Harrow, told me the truth when he said that my besetting sin was 'fatal facility.' I struggled long to conquer fluency. Still, I have not succeeded. I find a pleasure in expression for its own sake; but I have not the inevitable touch of the true poet, the unconquerable patience of the conscious artist. As in other matters, so here, I tried to make the best of my defects. Concentration lies beyond my grasp. The right words do not fall into the right places at my bidding. I have written few good paragraphs, and possibly no single perfect line."

Not a word need be added, nor a word altered, in this unsparing self-criticism. In truth, Symonds was neither a scholar nor an artist. He loved literature for its own sake, scholarship for the sake of its gifts to culture. Living always under sentence of death, he filled out that "indefinite reprieve" with the diligence of a fixed endeavour to work while it was day. But it was probably this sense of the shortness as well as the relish of life, this somewhat feverish intentness upon opportunity, which caused him to do many things hastily that would have been done better with more leisure, and to attempt a universal conquest of literature where limitation would have been an act of wisdom. What he possessed, however, was an extraordinarily interesting and unusual personality, which, gradually outgrowing the reserve and speculation of the earlier years, came at last to be intensely vivid, human, and in love with humanity. In 1877 he writes in a letter:

"I, for my part, try to live without asking many questions. I do not want to be indifferent to the great problems of morals, immortality, and the soul; but I want to learn to be as happy as my health and passions will allow me, without raising questions I am convinced no one will ever answer from our human standpoint."

It was a sort of awakening, this more human view of life; and, this sense of reality once firmly apprehended, he could write, as he does in one of his latest letters:

"With me life burns ever more intense as my real strength wanes and my days decrease. It seems to me sometimes awful—the pace at which I live in feeling—inversely to the pace at which myself is ebbing to annihilation."

Gradually, therefore, a new estimate of the value, not merely of such literature as he could write, but of literature itself, formed itself in his mind, and united with that other feeling of powerlessness in still further discouraging him from too keen a following of art and the rewards of art. A passage which I may quote from an unpublished letter gives characteristic expression to this view of things:

"You are quite right to regard art, literature, as the noblest function of your life. What I gently said, and somewhat cynically, perhaps, to the contrary, is very much the result of a long experience in renunciation and patience, the like of which you have not yet had to undergo. I think it best for men to arm themselves with Stoicism as regards success (either external, or in proportion to their own ideals) and to maintain as a guiding principle what is the ultimate fact—namely, that art and literature are and never can be more than functions of human life. Life therefore first."

"Life therefore first." Symonds was right; and it was the life in him, the personality, that gave the man his real interest, his real fascination. But either he did not realise, or realised too late, that where he might have added something vital to literature was precisely in the record of this passionate communion with life. Perhaps, after all, "the right word" would never have "fallen into the right place." But, judging by the few personal things that he did, and by what we are allowed to read of that Autobiography, which is not likely at present to be published in its entirety, he might have done much; he would certainly have done something more essentially valuable than the never quite satisfying contributions to general culture, to which the main part of his life was devoted. But, as I have said, all this work was in part an escape, an escape from himself; and the "life" which he placed before "literature" was in part also an escape in another direction. Never "truly reconciled either with life or with himself," he chose the simpler task of writing the History of the Renaissance, rather than the perhaps impossible one of writing the history of his own soul.

1893.

WILLIAM MORRIS'S PROSE

THE later work of William Morris is mostly in prose, and it consists in a series of prose romances, "News from Nowhere," "The Roots of the Mountains," "The Wood beyond the World," "The Sundering Flood," and others, into which he put the same placid and passionate love of beauty, the same sense of life and of nature, as into his verse. In their simple remoteness, their cunningly woven pattern, their open-heartedness, so absolute that it seems to be itself the concealment of a secret, they have commonly been taken to be not so much romances as allegories, and many fruitless attempts have been made to find out what meaning is hidden away under so much mere decoration. Morris has set this question finally at rest in a letter to the *Spectator*, dated July 16, 1895, where the statement made in reference to a single one of the prose romances holds good in reference to them all. "I had not," he wrote, "the least intention of thrusting an allegory into 'The Wood beyond the World': it is meant for a tale pure and simple, with nothing didactic about it. If I have to write or speak on social problems, I always try to be as direct as I possibly can be. On the other hand, I should consider it bad art in any one writing an allegory not to make it clear from the first that that was his intention, and not to take care throughout that the allegory and the story should interpenetrate, as does the great master of allegory, Bunyan."

Morris was a poet, never more truly a poet than when he wrote in prose; and it was because he was a poet that he resented the imputation of writing allegories. Allegory is the prose writer's substitute for symbol; and, in its distressing ingenuity, it resembles what it aims at as closely as the marionette resembles his less methodical brother, man. Without the indwelling symbol, art is no more than a beautiful body without breath; but this breath, this flame, this indestructible and fragile thing, need be no more visible in the work of art than the actual breath of our nostrils, which needs the frost before it shows us its essential heat. To Morris art was a peculiar, absorbing, quite serious kind of play, in which the stanza of a poem, an acanthus on a wall-paper, a square of stitches in tapestry, a paragraph of prose, were all of precisely equal importance, and, in a way, equal lack of importance. He was in love with the beauty of the world, and he loved the beauty of the world joyously, as no one of our time has been simple enough and pure enough and strong enough to do. And he loved all visible beauty indifferently, as a child does, not preferring the grass to the emerald, nor the lake to the leaf. His many activities, in which it seemed to some of his friends that he scattered his energy too liberally, were but so many expressions of his unbounded delight in beauty, in the unbounded beauty of all the forms of life. He was not a thinker; the time-woven garment of the unseen was too satisfying to him that he should ever have cared to look behind it; but wisdom came to him out of his love of the earth, and a curious pathos, touching one like the sight of wet blossoms or a child's smile, from his apprehension of what is passing, and subject to the dishonour of age, in earthly beauty. His work, then, is a tender refashioning of his own vision of the world, of the world as it was to him; that is to say, as it never was, and never will be, in any past or future golden age, to any one who is not a poet, and something of a child, at heart. He takes one "morsel of the world" after another, and it is to him as to Birdalone, in the book, when she awakes: "And it was an early morning of later spring, and the sky was clear blue, and the sun shining bright, and the birds singing in the garden of the house, and in the street was the sound of the early market-folk passing through the streets with their wares; and all was fresh and lovely." He knows that there are "dragons" to be slain; but, knowing that Perseus or St George is even now coming through the woods or to the sea-shore, he is content, when it is not his turn to strike, merely to pass on, through ways which are none the less beautiful, weaving all these things into pictures, whereby joy may come into the hearts of weary people whose eyes are dim with sorrow and much labour.

"The Water of the Wondrous Isles," like all Morris's prose, is written in that elaborately simple language, in which the Latin element of English is drawn on as little as possible, and the Saxon element as largely as possible, a language which it has pleased some persons to call a bastard tongue. Artificial, indeed, to a certain extent, it undoubtedly, and very properly, is. Every writer of good prose is a conscious artificer; and to write without deliberately changing the sequence of words as they come into the mind is to write badly. There is no such thing, properly speaking, as a "natural" style; and it is merely ignorance of the mental processes of writing which sometimes leads us to say that the style of Swift, for instance, is more natural than the style of Ruskin. To write so that it may seem as if the words were unpremeditated is at least as artificial a process, and at least as difficult, as to write picturesquely, allowing more liberty to words, in their somewhat unreasonable desire to sparkle and shoot many colours, and become little unruly orchestras of their own. And so, in regard to Morris's choice of language, it is merely to be noted that he writes a purer English than most people, obtaining an effect of almost unparalleled simplicity, together with a certain monotony, perhaps even greater than that required by style, though without monotony there can be no style. If he occasionally uses a word now obsolete, such as "hight," or a combination now unfamiliar, such as "speech-friend," how numberless are the words of hurried modern coinage from which he refrains! seeming to have read the dictionary, as Pater used to advise young writers to read it, in order to find out the words *not* to use. It is sufficient justification of his style to say that it is perfectly suited to his own requirements, and that it could not possibly suit the requirements of any other writer; being, as it is, so intimate a part of his own personality, of his own vision of things.

And here, as elsewhere, it must be remembered that art, to Morris, was always conventional art, in which the external shape, so carefully seen in nature and so carefully copied, was realised always as line or colour in a pattern, which it was the business of the artist to disentangle from the lovely confusions of growth. Morris was passionate only in his impersonality; in deep passion he was as lacking as he was lacking in profound thought. He loved nature, as I have said, joyously; and nature, apprehended without passion, becomes a kind of decoration. He beheld a golden and green and blue earth, in which the fashion of the world is like that coloured, flat-surfaced thing which the painters before perspective made into pictures. A craftsman's term comes naturally to him when he is speaking of "the green earth and its well-wrought little blossoms and leaves and grass." The beautiful description of Birdalone's body has almost the reflecting coldness of a mirror, so purely is the living beauty of woman seen as a piece of decoration, a tapestried figure in a "well-wrought" green wood. Here and there, tenderness, which is never absent, rises, in the intensity of its pity, into a kind of grave passion, as in these words: "and tender was she of her body as of that which should one day be so sorely loved." And once more, in the accomplishment of love foreseen:

"And she murmured over him: O friend, my dear, think not that I had will to hide me from thee. All that is here of me is thine, and thine, and thine.

"And she took his hand, and they arose together, and she said: O friend, I fled from thee once and left thee lonely of me because I deemed need drave me to it; and I feared the strife of friends, and confusion and tangle. Now if thou wilt avenge thee on me thou mayst, for I am in thy power. Yet will I ask thee what need will drive thee to leave me lonely?

"He said: The need of death. But she said: Mayhappen we shall lie together then, as here to-night we shall lie."

But, for the rest, this book, like the others, is of an equable sweetness, a continual going on, like running water in pale sunlight, never rising or falling, nor varying in colour, nor changing in sound. It is a story, which takes place at a time without a date, in a country without a name, among persons who have the simple, elementary qualities of humanity, the qualities which are older than civilisation, and yet who are shown to us only in conventionalised attitudes and in decorative costumes. Never was anything so close to nature and so far from it. I had no notion, when I had finished the book, whether the story had been well told, as the phrase is, or ill told. Meeting, immediately afterwards, a friend and admirer of Morris, I learnt from him that Morris's romances were "rambling." To me it was as if he had said that a pattern of scroll-work was rambling. Within its limits the art of the thing had seemed to me flawless. I was in a world which indeed you may refuse to enter, but where, having entered, you have no choice; you can impose no limit but the limits of the design. I find stories, as a rule, difficult to read; but I read these five hundred pages of prose as easily as if they had been verse, and with the same kind of pleasure. To read such a book is to receive an actual gift of happiness, in this quickened sense of the beauty of life and of the visible world, without that after-sense of the worm at the fruit's heart, which is left with us by most histories of the doings of humanity.

1897.

GUY DE MAUPASSANT

I

THE first aim of art, no doubt, is the representation of things as they are. But, then, things are as our eyes see them and as our minds make them, and it is thus of primary importance for the critic to distinguish the precise qualities of those eyes and minds which make the world into imaginative literature. Reality may be so definite and so false, just as it may be so fantastic and so true; and, among work which we can apprehend as dealing justly with reality, there may be quite as much difference in all that constitutes outward form and likeness as there is between a Dutch interior by Peter van der Hooch, the portrait of a king by Velazquez, and the image of a woman smiling by Leonardo da Vinci. The soul, for instance, is as real as the body; but, as we hear it only through the body speaking, and see it only through bodily eyes, and measure it, often enough, only in the insignificant moment of its action, it may come to seem to us, at all events, less realisable; and thus it is that we speak of those who have vividly painted exterior things as realists. Properly speaking, Maupassant is no more a realist than Maeterlinck. He paints a kind of reality which it is easier for us to recognise; that is all.

Every artist has his own vision of the world. Maupassant's vision was of solid superficies, of texture which his hands could touch, of action which his mind could comprehend from the mere sight of its incidents. He saw the world as the Dutch painters saw it, and he was as great a master of form, of rich and sober colour, of the imitation of the outward gestures of life, and of the fashion of external things. He had the same view of humanity, and shows us, with the same indifference, the same violent ferment of life, the life of full-blooded people who have to elbow their way through the world. His sense of desire, of greed, of all the baser passions, was profound; he had the terrible logic of animalism. Love-making, drunkenness, cheating, quarrelling, the mere idleness of sitting drowsily in a chair, the gross life of the farmyard and the fields, civic dissensions, the sordid provincial dance of the seven deadly sins, he saw in the same direct, unilluminating way as the Dutch painters; finding, indeed, no beauty in any of these things, but getting his beauty in the deft arrangement of them, in the mere act of placing them in a picture. The world existed for him as something formless which could be cut up into little pictures. He saw no further than the lines of his frame. The interest of the thing began inside that frame, and what remained outside was merely material.

As a writer, Maupassant was *de race*, as the French say; he was the lineal descendant of the early *conteurs*. Trained under the severe eye of the impeccable Flaubert, he owed infinitely, no doubt, to that training, and much to the actual influence of the great novelist, who, in "L'Education Sentimentale," has given us the type of the modern novel. But his style is quite different from that of Flaubert, of which it has none of the splendid, subdued richness, the harmonious movement; it is clear, precise, sharply cut, without ornament or elaboration; with much art, certainly, in its deliberate plainness, and with the admirable skill of an art which conceals art. M. Halévy has aptly applied to him the saying of Vauvenargues: "La netteté est le vernis des maîtres." Not Swift himself had a surer eye or hand for the exact, brief, malicious notation of things and ideas. He seems to use the first words that come to hand, in the order in which they naturally fall; and when he has reached this point he stops, not conceiving that there is anything more to be done. "Maupassant," writes Goncourt in his Journal, with that acuteness which the touch of malice only sharpened, "is a very remarkable *novelliere*, a very charming writer of short stories, but a stylist, a great writer, no, no!"

A story of Maupassant, more than almost anything in the world, gives you the impression of manual dexterity. It is adequately thought out, but it does not impress you by its thought; it is clearly seen, but it does not impress you specially by the fidelity of its detail; it has just enough of ordinary human feeling for the limits it has imposed on itself. What impresses you is the extreme ingenuity of its handling; the way in which this juggler keeps his billiard-balls harmoniously rising and falling in the air. Often, indeed, you cannot help noticing the conscious smile which precedes the trick, and the confident bow which concludes it. He does not let you into the secret of the trick, but he prevents you from ignoring that it is after all only a trick which you have been watching.

There is a philosophy of one kind or another behind the work of every artist. Maupassant's was a simple one, sufficient for his needs as he understood them, though perhaps really consequent upon his artistic methods, rather than at the root of them. It was the philosophy of cynicism, the most effectual means of limiting one's outlook, of concentrating all one's energies on the task in hand. Maupassant wrote for men of the world, and men of the world are content with the wisdom of their counting-houses. The man of the world is perfectly willing to admit that he is no better than you, because he takes it for granted that you will admit yourself to be no better than he. It is a way of avoiding comparisons. To Maupassant this cynical point of view was invaluable for his purpose. He wanted to tell stories just for the pleasure of telling them; he wanted to concern himself with his story simply as a story; incidents interested him, not ideas, nor even characters, and he wanted every incident to be immediately effective. Now cynicism in France supplied a sufficient basis for all these requirements; it is the equivalent, for popular purposes, of that appeal to the average which in England is sentimentality. Compare, for instance, the first and perhaps the best story which Maupassant ever wrote, "Boule de Suif," with a story of somewhat similar motive, Bret Harte's "Outcasts of Poker Flat." Both stories are pathetic, but the pathos of the American (who had formed himself upon Dickens, and in the English tradition) becomes sentimental, and gets its success by being sentimental; while the pathos of the Frenchman (who has formed himself on Flaubert, and in the French tradition) gets its success precisely by being cynical.

And then this particular variety of Maupassant's cynicism was just that variation of the artistic idea upon the temperament which puts the best finish upon work necessarily so limited, obliged to be so clenching, as the short story. Flaubert's gigantic dissatisfaction with life, his really philosophic sense of its vanity, would have overweighted a writer so thoroughly equipped for his work as the writer of "Boule de Suif" and "La Maison Tellier." Maupassant had no time, he allowed himself no space, to reason about life; the need was upon him to tell story after story, each with its crisis, its thrill, the summing up of a single existence or a single action. The sharp, telling thrust that this conception of art demanded could be given only by a very specious, not very profound, very forth-right kind of cynicism, like the half-kindly, half-contemptuous laugh of the man who tells a good story at his club. For him it was the point of the epigram.

II

Maupassant in his work gives us the will to live, and with him it is the will of the body to be always happy, always conscious of happiness, not too conscious of itself, the body's desire of light, heat, comfort, the pleasure of all the senses, and sound sleep without dreams. His work is the confession of the average sensual man, in whom an extravagance of health turns to fever, that there is something in the world, or not in it, which sets a term to enjoyment even while one has both will and strength to enjoy. Here is one of the most intimate of his confessions: "How gladly, at times, I would think no more, feel no more, live the life of a brute, in a warm, bright country, in a yellow country, without crude and brutal verdure, in one of those Eastern countries in which one falls asleep without sadness, awakens without concern, is active and has no cares, loves and has no distress, and is scarcely aware that one is going on living." It is in "Sur l'Eau" that he says that, the book in which he has "thought simply" and written down his thoughts as they came to him. It is love of life which drives him to this fear even of living, this desire of a vegetable warmth and growth, which seems to promise continuance. Goncourt notes in his "Journal," in 1889, how Mirbeau "speaks curiously of the fear of death which haunts Maupassant, and which is the cause of his life of perpetual wandering over land and sea, in the effort to escape from that fixed idea." In "Sur l'Eau" he speaks, in terrified words, of this fear of death, this fear of an invisible monster, hidden in some corner, spying on men's lives, and breathing a slow pestilence upon them. The soul hardly comes at all into this hatred of the earth on which men suffer so much before dying; it is the body which cries out against age, wrinkles, and the sure tardiness of decay. It is the body which will not be satisfied with what it can gather to itself under the sun, nor with any of the fruits of the earth into which it is to relapse, in the end.

Maupassant loved and hated life, and he hated it because he loved it. Tolstoi has pointed out how he becomes unconsciously a moralist by the mere force and clear-sightedness of his talent, his fidelity to what he has seen and to what he has felt. Caring for nothing in the world so much as for women, setting the monotonous and various drama of sex in motion through all his stories, he comes in the end to find all this amusing and absorbing comedy turning tragic. "He would have exalted love, but the more he knew it the more he cursed it." He cannot endure solitude, and he finds only a more ignoble solitude where it has been his pleasure to seek distraction. "I was at home and alone, and I felt that if I remained there I should fall into a horrible fit of melancholy, the sort of melancholy that must drive men to suicide if it returns too often." That is how he presents to us the state of mind of the man who is going out to "a night of pleasure"; and, at the end of that typical story, "L'Armoire," we see the man, overcome by horror and pity, hurrying home in the middle of the night, that he may escape from a more poignant sense of the wretchedness of things.

Maupassant saw life with his senses, and he reflected on it in a purely animal revolt, the recoil of the hurt animal. His observation is not, as it has been hastily assumed to be, cold; it is as superficially emotional as that of the average sensual man, and its cynicism is only another, not less superficial, kind of feeling. He saw life in all its details, and his soul was entangled in the details. He saw it without order, without recompense, without pity; he saw too clearly to be duped by appearances, and too narrowly to distinguish any light beyond what seemed to him the enclosing bounds of darkness. And so he settled down, with a kind of violent indifference, which was almost despair, to live his life and to accomplish his task. Goncourt reports a conversation in which Céard "declares that, in him, literature was a matter wholly of instinct, not of reflection; and affirms that, of all the men whom he has known, he was the most absolutely indifferent to everything, and that, at the very moment in which he seemed most keenly set on a thing, he was already aloof from it." In ten years he wrote thirty volumes; he wrote well or ill, but he wrote always, not for love of art nor for love of money, but out of the need of his organism to spend its force after its kind, after all kinds.

In that famous chapter on the novel, which Maupassant put as a preface to "Pierre et Jean," he summarises for us those counsels of Flaubert under which he worked for seven years, before the publication of "Boule de Suif" in the "Soirées de Médan" of 1880, presented him to the public as a finished artist. "'Talent is a long patience.' The thing is to look at what one wishes to express, long enough and carefully enough to discover in it an aspect which no one has ever seen or said. In everything there is something undiscovered, because we are only accustomed to use our eyes with the recollection of what people have thought before us about the thing at which we are looking. There is a certain unknown quantity in the smallest thing. Find it." This unknown quantity in familiar things Maupassant knew how to find. He sought for it chiefly in that part of human nature which interested him most and which was most familiar to him. Being professedly not a psychologist, being content to leave the soul out of the question, he found that the animal passions were at the root of our nature, that they gave rise to the most vivid and interesting kinds of action, and he persisted in rendering mainly the animal side of life. Probably no writer has ever done so more convincingly, with a more thorough knowledge of his subject, and a more perfect mastery of his knowledge. At his best he gives us, as in "Une Vie," "the humble truth," or, in "La Petite Roque," the horrible truth, or, in "Le Horla," the truth which destroys. It was the fear of death that wrung imagination out of him: "Le Horla," the invisible spectre of the mind. "Le Horla" is the soul of the materialist vindicating itself against the self-confidence of the body.

III

Everything which Maupassant wrote is interesting, it is more exclusively and merely interesting than the work of any writer of fiction who has been called great, it is too exclusively and merely interesting to be really great work. Really great work, in fiction as in every other form of art, requires too close and too constant an attention to be quite easy reading. When we read Balzac we seem to have been plunged suddenly into the midst of so great a turbulence of life that the effort to absorb this new, irresistible, hurrying, and mysterious world makes us pause; we try to withdraw into ourselves, as one might step aside into a doorway out of a great crowd, in the streets of a city. We look up from the page, we half-close the book, that we may think a little, that we may rest from this fatiguing demand on all our faculties. When we read Flaubert, we are delightfully delayed by the completeness and the beauty of every detail; we linger over this prose as we linger over verse. When we read Mérimée, even, in those stories which may be so well compared with Maupassant's for their economy and precision of effect, we are conscious of some hard, intellectual quality which takes hold of us, not only through the mere events of the story. But we read Maupassant for nothing but the story; we read him hurriedly, without lifting our eyes from the page; we are only anxious to get to the end, to see what happens. One should never read stories for the story. However absorbing may be the interest of the plot, of the working out of a given situation, the plot and the situation should never be taken as more than the means to an end. In great art they are never more than the means to an end, to the interpretation, the new creation, of life; and no great artist allows himself to become so amusing, in his treatment of what is not essential, as to withdraw the attention of the reader from what is essential. That is why no great writer has ever been immediately popular. The books that pass away are the books that have too easily, too feverishly, interested a generation.

Maupassant is the best of the popular novelists, of the novelists who have not had to wait for admiration. His appeal is genuine, and his skill, of its kind, incontestable. He attracts, as certain men do, by a warm and blunt plausibility. He is so frank, and seems so broad; and is so skilful, and seems so living. All the exterior heat of life is in his work; and this exterior heat gives a more immediate illusion of what we call real life than the profound inner vitality of, let us say, Hawthorne. He comes to us, saying impressively: "Certain meetings, certain inexplicable combinations of things, contain undoubtedly, however insignificant they may seem to be, a larger quantity of the secret quintessence of life than that dispersed in the ordinary course of events." He promises us this secret quintessence of life, and he tells us anecdote after anecdote, full of moving facts, and the obvious emotion of every fact. He is eager and unabashed, and, he assures us, this is life, and these amusing and horrible and ordinary things are the things that really happen. He assures us: "Blind and intoxicated with foolish pride must he be who believes himself more than an animal a little better than the others." And the others? "I seem to see in them the horror of their souls as one sees a monstrous fœtus in spirits of wine, in a glass jar." And his scornful conclusion is: "Happy are they whom life satisfies, who can amuse themselves, and be content. . . . Happy are they who have not discovered, with a vast disgust, that nothing changes, that nothing passes, and that all things are a weariness."

Is that a philosophy or is it an outcry? Is it not the unprofitable anger of the craftsman with his material? Is it not the helpless anger of the child with the toys which he has broken?

1899, 1903.

ALPHONSE DAUDET

The novels of Daudet are distinguished from the average popular novel not in kind, but in degree. The study of manners, the novel of sensation, the pathetic novel, the novel of satire, the novel of humour, he has done them all, and he has done them all with an admirable skill, a controlling sense of art. But he has brought nothing new into fiction, or, if he has brought anything, it is the particular variety of his humour, a Southern blend, which seems to unite American humour with Irish humour. "Tartarin" should be compared with the work of Mark Twain and with the work of Carleton, not, certainly, with anything greater than the work of these admirable writers. "Tartarin" is an heroical farce, full of comic observation, of comic invention, but, after all, how little more than the froth on the wine as it bubbles over! Daudet is himself rash enough to challenge comparison with "Don Quixote," and the comparison has been extended to Falstaff. But here the difference is a difference in kind. Daudet is a genuine humourist, but he is a humourist for his time, not for all time. He deals, not with that humour of fundamental ideas which is one of the voices of wisdom, but rather with a humour of shining accidents, which is at its best but the consecration of folly. There are men of science, men who deserve well of science, who have spent their lives in classifying a single species of beetle. That is what Daudet has done in "Tartarin," into which he has packed all the exterior qualities of the

South, "les gestes, frénésies et ébullitions de notre soleil," as he says.

And so with his serious studies in life. He is a quick observer, but never a disinterested observer, for he is a sentimentalist among realists. All his power comes from the immediateness of his appeal to the heart: to the intellect he never appeals. He appeals, certainly, to the average human sympathies, and he appeals to them with his power of writing a story which shall absorb the interest as an English novel absorbs the interest, by its comedy, using that word in its broadest sense. Even "Sapho" is essentially comedy, and Daudet is not far from being at his best in that brief, emphatic tale of a dull and disenchanted Bohemia. Others before Daudet had studied the life of a woman professionally "gay." Huysmans had studied it brutally, with a deliberate lack of sympathy, in "Marthe." Zola had studied it, with his exuberant method of representing, not the living woman, but the pattern of her trade. Goncourt had studied it, delicately, but with a subtlety which digresses into merely humanitarian considerations, in "La Fille Elisa." Daudet gives us neither vice nor romance, but the average dreariness of *le collage*. Yet he is not content with painting his picture: he must moralise, arrange, with an appeal to the sympathies as definitely sentimental, for all its disguises, as that of "La Dame aux Camélias." He cannot be as indifferently just to his Sapho as Flaubert in "L'Éducation Sentimentale" is indifferently and supremely just to Rosanette. And, partly for this very reason, it is only the external semblance of life which he gives; rarely the heart, never the soul.

In his vivid, passionate, tragically pathetic studies of "that exciting Paris" (it is his own word), "where the very dolls talk," Daudet is as entertaining as the writer of a fairy tale, and he writes fairy tales, in which J. Tom Lévis, the pseudo-Englishman of the confidential agency, Jansoulet, the Nabob, Delobelle the actor, Sidonie (a new Sidonia the Sorceress), Bompard, Tartarin, are all inhabitants of a world certainly more amusing than real life. That they should "o'erstep the modesty of nature" at every movement is partly his intention, partly he is indifferent to it, and partly unaware of it.

No gift with which a man can be cursed is more fatal than a thin vein of poetry. Daudet had a thin vein of poetry, not enough to make him a poet, but enough to distort the focus of his vision of truth. When he looked at external objects he saw something a little different from their shape as it appears to people in general, but he did not see them transfigured into the celestial images of themselves, as the poet sees them. He saw the face of Joy a little more laughing than it is, the face of Sorrow a little more distressed, and just that half-poetical exaggeration, missing all that is essential in poetry, was enough to leave him somewhere between the realists and the properly imaginative writers, artistically insincere, though, in his intention, of an almost touching sincerity.

He was a novelist as men are ceasing to be novelists, a novelist for the story's sake. He professes frankly to amuse you, and his absence of affectation in regard to his own art is itself almost an affectation. And his stories first of all amuse, excite, distress himself; "and then one loves them, these books, these novels, sorrowful fruits of your entrails, made of your very flesh and blood; how can one look on them disinterestedly?" He never could, indeed, look on them disinterestedly, either while they were making or when they were made. He made them with actual tears and laughter;

and they are read with actual tears and laughter by the crowd. May it not, therefore, be said that he achieved his end, that he gained the reward he had proposed to himself, and that a more lofty, a more lonely, fame would have left one who was always so eager after present happiness, after what is companionable in praise, a little cold and unsatisfied?

"It is all very well to put oneself outside the crowd and above it; it always comes, in the end, to be the crowd for which one writes." That sentence, written by Daudet in an article on Goncourt, does something to show why the writer of "Sapho," "Froment Jeune et Risler Aîné," and "Les Aventures Prodigieuses de Tartarin de Tarascon" was a popular writer, but not a great writer. Daudet wrote for the crowd. He wrote also, certainly, for his own pleasure; he wrote as he might have talked; and it would have been easier to imagine Zola not writing than Daudet not writing. It amused him supremely to tell stories; but he had to be listened to. Feverish as his method of writing was, he took endless pains to write well, writing every MS. three times over from beginning to end. But he had no philosophy behind his fantastic and yet only too probable creations. Caring, as he thought, supremely for life, he cared really for that surprising, bewildering pantomime which life seems to be to those who watch its coloured movement, its flickering lights, its changing costumes, its powdered faces, without looking through the eyes into the hearts of the dancers. He wrote from the very midst of the human comedy; and it is for this that he seems at times to have caught the bodily warmth and the taste of the tears and the very ring of the laughter of men and women. He was too much the comrade of his own characters; there are times when he seems actually to judge them from their own point of view, to be deceived by the speciousness of their protestations, to descend to their own level.

To the great artist life is indeed a comedy, but it is a comedy in which his own part is to stand silently in the wings, occasionally ringing down the curtain. Every joy and sorrow which he gives to his characters he has indeed felt, in his own heart, or in his own imagination; but, his characters once in motion, he surveys them with the controlling indifference of Fate. He will render the pity of love and death, but he will not say, with Daudet: "Quel coup terrible pour la jeune fille!" He will feel the whole intimacy of the contact between nature and humanity, but he will not say with Daudet: "A passionate sob, so profound, so rending, that it would have touched any heart, especially in the presence of nature, splendid and pitiless in the soft, odorous heat." He will render the sensation of, for instance, the happiness of a loving family, but he will not, with Daudet, bless the Paris Sunday, "especially because of all the happiness that thou givest, over and above other days, on that day, in the large new house at the end of the old suburb." He will write tragedy, not melodrama; comedy, not farce.

By the very superficiality with which he has entered into the sentiment of his creations, Daudet has obtained an impression of life which cannot be obtained by a more careful, a more truly successful artist. We praise a photograph for its likeness, and we please ourselves and the photographer if we say that it is a flattering likeness; that is to say, if, in the average or accidental expression which the camera has caught for us, we have removed precisely those lines, wrinkles, idiosyncratic defects, which indicate character. But when we come to look at a portrait, painted by a great painter, we consider, indeed, the question of the likeness, and at its full value ; but we consider, besides, how many qualities, purely of art, which have nothing to do with the exactitude of the reflection, but whose presence or absence gives the picture its worth or defect. Daudet shows us, for the most part, exceptional people, grimacing with the exterior violence of life with which he has animated them, seeming to be wonderfully close to us, but at the best as close to us as the people we pass in the street, not as the friend whose soul is in our hands. It might almost be said that his human curiosity was as great as Balzac's ; but what a different kind of curiosity ! It is never fundamental, it is often for no more than the bric-à-brac of humanity. "Le Nabab," "Les Rois en Exil" : he is as filled with wonderment before these fantastic and misplaced people as any Provençal from Avignon or Arles. "Ah !" he cries, "c'était le bon temps alors. Paris bondé d'étrangers, et non pas d'étrangers de passage, mais une installation de fortunes exotiques ne demandant que noces et ripailles." Even in his satire you feel the *naïveté* of a certain surprise. In "Le Nabab," for instance, which is a satire of the manifold hypocrisies of modern society, the indignation which thrills through all the satire is really the recoil of a shock which has come heavily upon an ingenuous nature ; and one of the finest chapters of that book, "Un Début dans le Monde," a masterpiece of the satirical observation of small meannesses, has all the pungency, with all the limitation, of the young débutant himself, to whom these things are personally irritating. And his pathos has the same quality as his satire.

The pathos of Daudet, a very genuine pathos, as melting as that of Dickens or Bret Harte, is a pathos of things which are also laughable, a grotesque, a fantastic pathos, made of the antithesis of unhappiness and its surroundings. Delobelle the actor in "Froment Jeune," the Nabob, the kings in exile, are studies of "humours," in Ben Jonson's sense; they are not studies of character. And so, in their pathos, they are either traps to catch tears, or part of the rhetoric of situation. Daudet's pathos is the pathos of the sentimentalist; it dwells on grief where grief is picturesque, touching, immediately telling; it has no reserve, no transfusion into other substances. The sovereign pathos of Lear, the noble pathos of Antigone, do not make you cry; the pathos of Jack makes you cry. And this easy tribute of tears is but the return of sentiment to sentiment, a wholly physical sensation, in which the intellect is for nothing. Pathos which can touch the intellect becomes so transfigured that its tears shine: you can see by their light. But we cry over melodrama because a single appeal is made to a single sense, an appeal, from the point of view of the finest art, almost as illegitimate as the appeal of obscenity. Pathos such as Daudet's comes from the man to whom life is an entertainment absolutely entertaining: he dreads only its ending, or an accident which may interrupt it. The supreme pathos can come only from one to whom the very fact of life is itself more pathetic than any sorrow; to whom the happiness which goes contentedly, with bandaged eyes, through the mystery of things, is a sadder wonder than the narrow grief which measures itself by the four sides of a grave; to whom love, death, joy, sorrow, are words equally mournful in our unbounded ignorance of them.

Daudet is really neither more nor less than "l'homme du Midi," but the one "homme du Midi" who, feeling always as a Southerner, has been able to look at himself almost as objectively as a Parisian. In the

"Souvenirs d'un Homme de Lettres," Daudet tells us that he has a little green note-book, entitled "Le Midi," in which he has noted down, for years and years, everything that might help to sum up his country. "All noted down in the green note-book, from the country songs, the proverbs and phrases in which the instinct of the people comes out, to the cries of water-carriers, of the lollipop and fruit sellers of our fairs, and to the very whimperings of our sicknesses, heightened and re-echoed by the imagination, almost all nervous, rheumatic, caused by the sky of wind and flame which eats into our marrow, and sets the whole being in fusion, like a sugar-cane; all noted down, to the crimes of the South, explosions of passion, of drunken violence, drunken without drink, which bewilder and appal the conscience of judges, who have come from another climate, and are lost in the midst of these exaggerations, these extravagances of witnesses, which they do not know how to 'bring to a point.'" From this book have come "Numa Roumestan" ("which seems to me," he tells us, "the least incomplete of my books, the one into which I have put the best of myself, into which I have put the most invention, in the aristocratic sense of the word") and all the chronicles of "Tartarin," certainly his greatest achievement as a humourist, and containing his one type, the type of the braggart by imagination. It is his Southern blood which has given him that vivacity of temperament by which a long novel, written with the most conscientious labour, appears to be an improvisation, comes to us with such engaging heat, such a breathing aspect. It is from the South that he has taken those honeyed and delicate short stories, which have brought into French certain naïve and subtly humorous and quaintly poetical qualities, which, to those who know Provence or can read

Provençal, have the very taste of the soil. It is directly from the Provençal that he has taken the vocal and gesticulating quality of his style, in which everything must give way to the search after the sound of the spoken word. His epithets, when they are fine, are sudden ("le geste tutoyeur," for instance, said of Gambetta), epithets of a good talker. In the South every one talks, and Daudet aims always at giving you the sensation of one who talks. When Goncourt desires to give you the sensation of talking, with what an elaborate, minute, almost painful effort he produces his effects, never more artificial than in these moments; succeeding indeed, but with all the labour of one who has not only an impression to convey, but an idea at the back of the sensation. Daudet aims at the immediate sensation and gets it, as if it were the easiest thing in the world. It was, to him; and he trained a natural aptitude to the finest uses of which it was capable. It did not make him a great artist, but it made him the best writer, next to Maupassant, among the novelists who are not great artists.

1898.

Hubert Crackanthorpe

HUBERT CRACKANTHORPE

THE "Last Studies" of Hubert Crackanthorpe, published after his death, with an introduction, a little hesitating, by Mr Henry James, contain three stories, two of them, "Anthony Garstin's Courtship" and "Trevor Perkins," ranking among his good, his characteristic work. The stories, perhaps, tell us nothing new about their author, though I seemed to feel in "Anthony Garstin," when it came into my hands in the summer of 1896, for publication in the *Savoy*, something almost like a reaching out in more or less a new direction. In any case, they are well worth adding to the work contained in those few, small books which are all that a writer cut off so early had time to leave us: "Wreckage," published in 1893; "Sentimental Studies," in 1895; and "Vignettes," in 1896. A life's work so narrow in compass, so limited, indeed, in range, may seem to require a certain explanation from those who consider it to have been of importance. A few dreary stories, a few pages of impressionistic writing about moods and landscapes, that is all we have to set over against the brilliant productiveness of such scarcely older men as Mr Kipling. Is there a place anywhere, we can imagine many people asking, for even a present memory of this young man and his depressing work?

No one in England, with the single exception of Mr Frank Harris, has gone further in the direction of bare, hard, persistent realism, the deliberately unsympathetic record of sordid things which have really happened because they have really happened. With Crackanthorpe there was always a revolt, the revolt of the impersonal artist, to whom evil things had certainly no attraction but a cold, intellectual one, against those English conventions which make it difficult to be quite frank in English. His courage was absolute, Quixotic on behalf of an idea. All his stories were written with the one intention of being true to his artistic conception of life, and with no more cherished hope than that of vindicating the claims and possibilities of art, of removing perhaps some restriction, of at least making way for liberty.

And, in his measure, he succeeded. When "Wreckage" was published, nothing so audacious had been seen in English prose fiction for a long time. And it must, I think, have seemed evident that this audacity was an audacity without fever (as with George Egerton) or special pleading (as with Sarah Grand). Probably, indeed, the impartiality of the manner may have seemed a very vice of vice to persons, very numerous in England, who condone sensuality if it is sentimental, and condemn the philosophic recognition that evil is merely evil. But I speak of those who are really capable of forming an honest and intelligent opinion on these matters. To them, surely, it must have been evident that here was a writer of proud sincerity, to whom any baseness would have been an impossibility. He seemed to come forward, saying: "I am going to try to show you some of the things I have seen in life, pitiable things, in whose sorrows I have sorrowed, out of whose despair I see no way, but which I shall tell you as calmly as I can, for I do not wish to prejudice you with what may be my own prejudices. I shall draw no moral from what I have seen; there may be more morals to draw than one; I leave you to do that, each for himself. Other people have shown you what they take to be life, and it has been for the most part the story of courtships, ending with marriage, though indeed marriage is properly a beginning and not an ending. In this world of theirs there have been heroical and pathetic adventures, villains who have been very black, and saints who have been very white. For myself I see another kind of world, in which no one is quite good or quite bad, in which nothing extraordinary happens, but which is full of mean troubles, and sordid cares, and too heedless and too passionate people, and in which love, and death, and pity, and wrong-doing come and go under dim masks and soiling disguises. Who knows if there is any such thing as 'real life'? To each of us there appears his own image of the world; art is the shadowing of that perhaps illusory image."

Such writers as these are not popular writers; but they are salutary. It is well that there should be those who have these stern things to say to us; they save us from the dominion of smoothness and the dominion of untruth, and they hinder us from growing contented with our life or with our art. For the most part, we reward them by making them martyrs, martyrs for art.

By a curious, yet easily explicable paradox, it is the impersonal artist who is most commonly in revolt; for he has to fight for his idea. The world is lenient towards the sinner, even if he does not repent; for his outcry is the subtlest of tributes to that morality of which the world is the guardian, and which is the guardian of the conventions of the world. The impersonal artist, whose only duty is towards a higher law, smites suddenly on the satisfaction of things as they are, and with the sword of the idea. It is the world's turn to cry out, for here is a new assaying of its accepted currency, a trying over again of its leading cases, a judging of itself, and not by its own laws. The world does well to hate abstract ideas, for it is at the sound of the crying (scarce above a whisper) of the voice of abstract ideas that the walls of its fools' paradise come clattering about its ears.

To say that Crackanthorpe's view of life was limited, to say that it was youthful (and both may with some truth be said), is after all to disprove nothing that I have said in his honour. Force, and especially directing force, comes from limitation, and wisdom has the folly of its courage only when it is young. There is a certain *naïveté*, even, in Crackanthorpe's disregard of the fair colours which are on the other and outer side of the garment, just as real as the seams and the grey lining. And the hardest thing that can be said of him is that he misses beauty in his desire to come closer than beauty will let men come to truth. It is possible, indeed, to think the whole direction of his talent not the best one; to think that in following Maupassant he had mistaken his leader; that the part of life which can be rendered by that somewhat dusty method is not even the most interesting part of life. After all has been said, what I call Crackanthorpe's heroism remains, a personal quality, which, if he had lived, would have led him to do perhaps quite different, perhaps more lasting, things. As it is, he has done something not inconsiderable. It is no slight thing to have merely written the story, in "Wreckage," called "A Dead Woman." But, above all, he was of those who fight well, who fight unselfishly, the knights errant of the idea.

1897.

ROBERT BUCHANAN

ROBERT BUCHANAN was a soldier of fortune who fought under any leader or against any cause so long as there was heavy fighting to be done. After a battle or two, he left the camp and enlisted elsewhere, usually with the enemy. He was, or aimed at being, a poet, a critic, a novelist, a playwright; he was above all a controversialist; he also tried being his own publisher. As a poet he wrote ballads, lyrics, epics, dramas, was realist and transcendentalist, was idyllic, tragic, pathetic, comic, religious, objective, subjective, descriptive, reflective, narrative, polemic, and journalistic. He wrote rhetorical and "Christian" romances before Mr Hall Caine; his plays were done entirely for the market, some of them in collaboration with Mr G. R. Sims; his criticism was all a kind of fighting journalism. "Lacking the pride of intellect," he has said of himself, "I have by superabundant activity tried to prove myself a man among men, not a mere *littérateur*." And, indeed, his career shows an activity not less surprising than superabundant. He took himself so seriously that he considered it legitimate to "stoop to hodman's work"; thinking, he tells us, "no work undignified which did not convert him into a Specialist or a Prig." He never doubted that he might have been "sitting empty-stomached on Parnassus," if he had cared for the position. He defended himself, perhaps unnecessarily, for not having done so. "I have written," he said, "for all men and in all moods." He took the day's wages for the day's work, but was not satisfied. From the first his books were received with serious attention; they were considered, often praised greatly, often read largely. Whenever he had anything to say, people listened. When he hit other men, the other men usually paid him the compliment of hitting back. "For nearly a generation," he lamented, ten years ago, "I have suffered a constant literary persecution." Well, it is difficult to do justice to one who has never done justice to another. But persecution is hardly the word to be used for even a hard hit, when the hit is received by a fighter of all work.

Like most fighters, Buchanan fought because he could not think, and his changing sides after the fight was neither loss nor gain to either cause. It was at most the loss or gain of a weapon, and the weapon was often more dangerous to friends than foes. He liked playing with big names, as childen play with dolls and call them after their dreams. He took God and the devil into his confidence, very publicly, and with a kind of lofty patronage. He used the name of God to checkmate the devil, and the devil's name to checkmate God. "And absolutely," he tells us, "I don't know whether there are gods or not. I know only that there is Love and Lofty Hope and Divine Compassion." There are more big names to play with, and he wrote them, even their adjectives, in capital letters. The capital letters were meant for emphasis, they also indicated defiance. He gave many definitions of what he meant by God, the devil, Love, Hope, and Compassion. The definitions varied, and were often interchangeable. I find some of them in a book written in his honour, called "Robert Buchanan, the Poet of Modern Revolt." From this book I gather that Buchanan was himself an example of the "divine" and the "lofty" virtues. His weakness, he admits, was too much brotherly love. "With a heart overflowing with love, I have gathered to myself only hate and misconception." Whatever he attacked, he attacked in all the sincerity of anger, and anger no doubt is the beginning of all avenging justice. He has said (so Mr Stodart-Walker's book tells me, and though I gather that it was said in verse, I am unable to reconstruct the lines in metrical form) "I've popt at vultures circling skyward, I've made the carrion hawks a byword, but never caused a sigh or sob in the breast of mavis or cockrobin, nay, many such have fed out of my hand and blest me." There is hardly a contemporary writer whom he did not attack, but it is true that he recanted with not less vehemence, and with a zest in the double function which suggests the swinging impartiality of the pendulum. When he insulted an idea, it was with the best intentions and on behalf of another idea. If he spoke blasphemously of God, it has only been, he assures us, in his zeal for religion, and when he "lifted his hat to the Magdalen," in a famous phrase, it was all in the cause of chastity. With infinite poetic ambition, he had a certain prose force, which gave his verse, at times, the vehemence of telling oratory. He attempted in verse many things which were not worth attempting and some which were. In all he aimed at effect, sometimes getting it. He was indifferent to the quality of the effect, so long as the effect was there, and the mere fact of his aiming at it disqualified him, at his best, from a place among genuine, that is to say disinterested artists.

1901.

AN ARTIST IN ATTITUDES:

OSCAR WILDE

When the "Ballad of Reading Gaol" was published, it seemed to some people that such a return to, or so startling a first acquaintance with, real things, was precisely what was most required to bring into relation, both with life and art, an extraordinary talent, so little in relation with matters of common experience, so fantastically alone in a region of intellectual abstractions. In this poem, where a style formed on other lines seems startled at finding itself used for such new purposes, we see a great spectacular intellect, to which, at last, pity and terror have come in their own person, and no longer as puppets in a play. In its sight, human life has always been something acted on the stage; a comedy in which it is the wise man's part to sit aside and laugh, but in which he may also disdainfully take part, as in a carnival, under any mask. The unbiassed, scornful intellect, to which humanity has never been a burden, comes now to be unable to sit aside and laugh, and it has worn and looked behind so many masks that there is nothing left desirable in illusion. Having seen, as the artist sees, further than morality, but with so partial an eyesight as to have overlooked it on the way, it has come at length to discover morality in the only way left possible, for itself. And, like most of those who, having "thought themselves weary," have made the adventure of putting thought into action, it has had to discover it sorrowfully, at its own incalculable expense. And now, having become so newly acquainted with what is pitiful, and what seems most unjust, in the arrangement of human affairs, it has gone, not unnaturally, to an extreme, and taken, on the one hand, humanitarianism, on the other realism, at more than their just valuation, in matters of art. It is that odd instinct of the intellect, the necessity of carrying things to their furthest point of development, to be more logical than either life or art, two very wayward and illogical things, in which conclusions do not always follow from premises.

Well, and nothing followed, after this turning-point, as it seemed, in a career. "Whatever actually occurs is spoiled for art," Oscar Wilde has said. One hoped, but he had known at least himself, from the beginning. Nothing followed. Wit remained, to the very end, the least personal form of speech, and thus the kindest refuge for one who had never loved facts in themselves. "I am dying beyond my means" was the last word of his which was repeated to me.

His intellect was dramatic, and the whole man was not so much a personality as an attitude. Without being a sage, he maintained the attitude of a sage; without being a poet, he maintained the attitude of a poet; without being an artist, he maintained the attitude of an artist. And it was precisely in his attitudes that he was most sincere. They represented his intentions; they stood for the better, unrealised part of himself. Thus his attitude, towards life and towards art, was untouched by his conduct; his perfectly just and essentially dignified assertion of the artist's place in the world of thought and the place of beauty in the material world being in nowise invalidated by his own failure to create pure beauty or to become a quite honest artist. A talent so vividly at work as to be almost genius was incessantly urging him into action, mental action. Just as the appropriate word always came to his lips, so the appropriate attitude always found him ready to step into it, as into his own shadow. His mind was eminently reasonable, and if you look closely into his wit, you will find that it has always a basis of logic, though it may indeed most probably be supported by its apex at the instant in which he presents it to you. Of the purely poetical quality he had almost nothing; his style, even in prose, becomes insincere, a bewildering echo of Pater or of some French writer, whenever he tries to write beautifully. Such imagination as he had was like the flickering of light along an electric wire, struck by friction out of something direct and hard, and, after all, only on the surface.

"But then it is only the Philistine," he has said, in his essay on Wainewright, "who seeks to estimate a personality by the vulgar test of production. This young dandy sought to be somebody rather than to do something. He recognised that Life itself is an art, and has its modes of style no less than the arts that seek to express it." "Art never expresses anything but itself," he has said, in another essay in the same book, so aptly called "Intentions"; and that "principle of his new æsthetics" does but complete his view of the function of life. Art and life are to be two things, absolutely apart, each a thing made to a pattern, not a natural, or, as he would take it to be, an accidental, growth. It is the old principle of art for art's sake, pushed to its furthest limits, where every truth sways over into falsehood. He tells us that "the highest art rejects the burden of the human spirit, and gains more from a new medium or a fresh material than she does from any enthusiasm for art, or from any lofty passion, or from any fresh awakening of the human consciousness." But he forgets that he is only discussing technique, and that faultless technique, though art cannot exist without it, is not art.

And so with regard to life. Realising as he did that it is possible to be very watchfully cognisant of the "quality of our moments as they pass," and to shape them after one's own ideal much more continuously and consciously than most people have ever thought of trying to do, he made for himself many souls, souls of intricate pattern and elaborate colour, webbed into infinite tiny cells, each the home of a strange perfume, perhaps a poison. Every soul had its own secret, and was secluded from the soul which had gone before it or was to come after it. And this showman of souls was not always aware that he was juggling with real things, for to him they were no more than the coloured glass balls which the juggler keeps in the air, catching them one after another. For the most part the souls were content to be playthings; now and again they took a malicious revenge, and became so real that even the juggler was aware of it. But when they became too real he had to go on throwing them into the air and catching them, even though the skill of the game had lost its interest for him. But as he never lost his self-possession, his audience, the world, did not see the difference.

Among these souls there was one after the fashion of Flaubert, another after the fashion of Pater, others that had known Baudelaire, and Huysmans, and De Quincey, and Swinburne. Each was taken up, used, and dropped, as in a kind of persistent illustration of "the truth of masks." "A truth in art is that whose contradictory is also true." Well, it was with no sense of contradiction that the critic of beautiful things found himself appealing frankly to the public in a series of the wittiest plays that have been seen on the modern stage. It was another attitude, that was all; something external, done for its own sake, "expressing nothing but itself," and expressing, as it happened by accident, precisely what he himself was best able to express.

It may be, perhaps, now that the man is dead, that those who admired him too much or too little will do him a little justice. He was himself systematically unjust, and was never anxious to be understood too precisely, or to be weighed in very level balances. But he will be remembered, if not as an artist in English literature, at all events in the traditions of our time, as the supreme artist in intellectual attitudes.

1901.

Gabriele d'Annunzio

GABRIELE D'ANNUNZIO

Gabriele d'Annunzio comes to remind us, very definitely, as only an Italian can, of the reality and the beauty of sensation, of the primary sensations; the sensations of pain and pleasure as these come to us from our actual physical conditions; the sensation of beauty as it comes to us from the sight of our eyes and the tasting of our several senses; the sensation of love, which, to the Italian, comes up from a root in Boccaccio, through the stem of Petrarch, to the very flower of Dante. And so he becomes the idealist of material things, while seeming to materialise spiritual things. He accepts, as no one else of our time does, the whole physical basis of life, the spirit which can be known only through the body, the body which is but clay in the shaping or destroying hands of the spirit. And, in spite of a certain affectation of ideas, not always quite happily selected from Nietzsche and others, he takes nature very simply, getting sheer away from civilisation in his bodily consciousness of things, which he apprehends as directly, with however much added subtlety, as a peasant of his own Abruzzi.

For d'Annunzio the beauty of all beautiful things is a curiously elaborated beauty, made out of physical pain or pleasure in its absorption of the visible world, at every moment, as a part of one's breath. He seems to feel, more passionately than others, the heat of sunlight, the juicy softness of a ripe fruit, the texture of women's hair, and also the distress of rain, of rough garments, of the cloud that interrupts the sunlight;

and his sense of the beauty and ugliness of these things comes, more directly than with others, from the exact force of their physical action upon him. It is here that he is so Latin, so specifically Italian; for the Italians, among all Latin races, are the least sophisticated in their acceptance of physical fact. They have no reticence in speaking of what they feel, and they have none of those unconscious reticences in feeling which races drawn further from nature by civilisation have thought it needful to invent in their relations with nature. This is one of the things which people mean when they say that d'Annunzio's writing is immoral. Well, nature is immoral. Birth is a grossly sexual thing, death is a brutally physical thing, the ending, certainly, of the animal, whatever may remain over, inside that white forehead in which the brain has stopped working.

This physically sincere, attentive, impressionable self, then, which d'Annunzio finds in his own nature, and which he lends to the scarcely differentiated heroes of his books, is but the basis of a more extended and a more conscious self. Beginning by that intent waiting upon sensation in the first place, he ends by expanding the creature of acute sensation into a kind of Renaissance personality, in which sensation becomes complex, cultivated, the flower of an elaborate life. The Italy of the Renaissance cultivated personalities as we cultivate orchids; and, there also, the rarest beauty came from a heightening of nature into something not quite nature, a perversity of beauty which might be poisonous, as well as merely curious. The one thing was, that it should be the absolute. Now, to the seeker after the absolute, there exist in the world but two possibilities, love and wisdom; and of these only one is within the reach of more than singularly few. The passion for abstract ideas is not likely to commend itself, at all events to the exclusion of that other passion, to a nature so satisfied with the very pain of pleasure. Nor is the study of the passion for abstract ideas a very fruitful or extensive subject for the novelist. It is thus in the study of love chiefly, in the analysis of that very mortal passion which beats at so many of the closed doors of the universe, that d'Annunzio has chosen to show us what he chooses to show us of life. He has shown us the working of the one universal, overwhelming, and transfiguring passion, with a vehement patience, and with a complete disregard of consequences, of the moral prejudice. To him, as to the men of the Renaissance, moral qualities are variable things, to be judged only by æsthetic rules. Is an action beautiful, has it that intensity which, in the stricter sense, is virtue? Other considerations may, if you please, come afterwards, but these are the essential. For to d'Annunzio life is but a segment of art, and æsthetic living the most important thing for the artist who is not merely an artist in words, or canvas, or marble, but an artist in life itself. These passionate and feeble and wilful people of his are at least trying to come near such an ideal. Not every one can become the artist of his own life, or can have either the courage or the consistency to go on his own way, to his own end. It is needless to moralise against such an intention. Few will attain it.

It is but in the natural process of a deduction from these principles that d'Annunzio chooses to concern himself, in his novels, with temperament, not with either character or society. His novels are states of mind, sometimes, as in "Le Vergini delle Rocce," not leading to any conclusion; and these states of mind interest him supremely, for their own sake, and not for the sake of any conclusion to which they may lead. We should not recognise one of his persons if we met him in the street; but his jealousy, or his corrupt love of art, or his self-pity, will seem to us part of ourselves, seen in a singular kind of mirror, if we have ever been sincere enough with ourselves to recognise an obscure likeness when we see it. The great exterior novels, we may well believe, have been written; the inter-action of man upon man has been at least sufficiently described; what remains, eternally interesting, eternally new, is man, the hidden, inner self which sits silent through all our conversation, and may sit blind to its own presence there, not daring to find itself interesting.

It is this intrinsic self, the only part of our mechanism which, if it speaks, cannot lie, that d'Annunzio tries to find words for; and he turns, naturally, to himself, as at all events what he knows best in the universe. Thus to say that his heroes are but images of himself, changed a little here and there, directed along certain roads, is but to say that he has succeeded in doing precisely what he has tried to do. What he seeks are not those superficial differences by which we distinguish man from man, as we distinguish our friends at a distance by their clothes, but the profound similarities by which all men are men. This aim, which has always been the aim of poetry, has in the past been the aim of poetry alone; and for this very reason it has always been difficult to take fiction quite seriously as an imaginative art. I cannot remember a book of fiction, except "Don Quixote," which I could in any sense put on a level, as imaginative writing, with a great poem. The novel, in the past, has appealed to an altogether lower audience; its fatal first aim of interesting people having always been against it. Poetry, as Rossetti has wisely said, must indeed be as "amusing" as prose; but it is not amusing first, and poetry afterwards. But fiction, dealing with circumstance, which is the accident of time, and character, which is the accident of temperament; with society, which is the convention of external intercourse; with life seen from its own level, and judged by its temporary laws, has been a sort of composite art, working at once for two masters. It has never freed itself from the bondage of mere "truth" (likeness, that is, to appearances), it is only now, faintly and hesitatingly, beginning to consider beauty as its highest aim. No art can be supreme art if it does not consider beauty as its highest aim. It may be asked, it may even be doubted, whether such an aim will ever be practically possible for the novel. But to answer in the negative is to take away the novel's one chance of becoming a great imaginative art.

To d'Annunzio there exist in the world only two things, sex and art. He desires beauty with the rage of a lover; and, to him, sex is the supreme beauty. The visible world "exists" for him as an entirely satisfying thing, which the soul, or the needs of the soul, could but trouble, to no purpose. Studious of the origins of emotion, he finds them wholly in the physical action of the senses, and seems to have discovered nothing in human nature which cannot be rendered to the eye by some image. A woman moves to meet her lover, and what he notices is "the cry, the gesture, the start, the sudden stop, the vibration of her muscles under her garments, the light in her face extinguished like a flame that becomes ashes, the intensity of her look that was like a gleam of battle, the breath which parted her lips like the heat that breaks open the life of earth"; and he recognises in her "the Dionysian creature, the living material capable of receiving the impress of the rhythm of art, of being fashioned according to the laws of poetry." "I would that I could live the whole of life, and not be only a brain," he confesses, in his desire to fuse life, sensual life, and art, the art of the senses. And it is in the intensity of this twofold desire, of these two flames that burn towards each other that they may burn the higher together, that he obtains a kind of idealism out of two elements, one of which might easily sink into merely ignoble animalism, and the other deviate into a merely trivial æstheticism. His adoration of beauty is a continual fever, and in the intoxication of physical desire he is conscious that passion, also, is a supreme art. This quality comes to him because he is not so much a novelist as a poet, a poet who writes better in prose than in verse, but who never thinks in prose. "Le Vergini delle Rocce" is a shadowy poem, in which beautiful ghosts wander, "as if seen in a great mirror"; they are tired with waiting for life, their souls wasted away by dreams, their bodies famished with desires too vague to find a name. In the "Trionfo della Morte" passion has concentrated itself within a narrow circle, where it turns upon itself, grown deadly, exhausting life as it seems to live with so swift a vehemence. In its monotony we find the monotony of everything that ebbs and flows, as the sea does, without progress. Passion, into which the mind comes only as a reproach, a remembrance, or a troubling anticipation, has never been chronicled with a minuter fidelity than in this sombre book. "Il Fuoco" is a kind of symphony in which many voices cry together out of many instruments, building the elaborate structure. Here, passion is no longer unconscious of everything but itself; it is aware of its term, and it is able to conceive of that term as something that need be neither death nor any other annihilation of the future. "This thing I can do which even love could not do," says the woman, preparing herself for the sacrifice which will restore her lover to himself and to his finer self, art. In "La Gioconda" there is again the conflict of love and art, and here art is in league with the passions, implacable, a destroyer. In "La Città Morta" the emotion is sustained throughout on the level of poetic emotion. There is nothing but emotion, and thus hardly what we can call a play; these beings whom we apprehend so vaguely in their relations with the world about them are electrical to each other, at a touch, a word, a thought; each is obsessed, as if by an actual witchcraft, a malign influence coming out of the tombs of the dead city; they are already phantoms, tortured with the desires of the living. And so, while they have passed away from the world which alone, perhaps, can be made actual to us on the stage, they have entered into that imaginative world, the world of poetry, in which the passions are known for their beauty, not for the deeds which they have made men commit.

And so, in his novels, there are no stories, only states of mind and pictures. On the one side it is a going back to the origins of the novel, in such "confessions" as "Adolphe," for example; the novelty lies in the combination of what in "Adolphe" is a consciousness vaguely placed in the world, a world absolutely invisible to us, with an atmosphere itself as much a "state of mind" as Amiel's, and a universe as solid and coloured as Gautier's. His few personages are as little seen in their relation with society, as closely absorbed in their own sensations, as the single personage of Benjamin Constant, the man in whom one sees also the woman, as in a mirror. But with d'Annunzio, as he tells us in the preface to the "Trionfo della Morte," "the play of action and reaction between the single sensibility and exterior things is established on a precise woof of direct observation." Man, "the model of the world," is seen living in his own universe, which he creates continually about him; a world as personal to himself, and, to d'Annunzio and his people, as intimately realised, as the thought of the brain, or any passion.

D'Annunzio is an idealist, but he is an idealist to whom the real world is needful to the eyes, and feelings actually experienced are needful to the memory, before he can begin to make his art. All his work, all, at least, of his finest work, is something remembered, by a transfiguring act of the mind; not something which has come to him as vision, out of the darkness. With so personal an apprehension of the world, it is the world, always, that he needs, his soul being no world to him. In a monk's cell, or with dim eyes, he would have created nothing; he would never have been able to imagine beauty without a pattern.

But, to d'Annunzio, in that "seemingly exclusive predominance in his interests, of beautiful physical things, a kind of tyranny of the senses over him" (that phrase of Pater seems to have been made beforehand for his definition) things seen are already things felt; the lust of the eye, in him, is a kind of intellectual energy. The soul of visible things seems to cry out to him, entreating a voice: he hears, and is the voice. At times, delicate human sympathies come to him, through his mere sympathy with soulless things: the sense of pity, which stirs in him over the fading of flowers, and so over the ageing of human beauty. He realises sorrow, because it is a soiling of the texture of life; death, because it is the end of the weaving. One fancies, sometimes, that his very feeling for art, for the arts of music, painting, literature even, is the feeling of one to whom these things are of the nature of ripe fruit, golden sunshine, a luxury of the senses, rather than a need of the soul.

And he is all this because, being himself a Latin, he has known how to carry on the Latin traditions, confining himself to these for the most part, and, whenever he ventures away from them, turning aside into directions obviously not his own. He has read Nietzsche and Tolstoi, and can fancy himself the *sopra-uomo* and a brother to peasants. Only at such moments does he become vague, as he loses some of that sharpness of the senses through which he apprehends the universe. Intellect means as little to him, really, as human feeling; he can never think abstract thoughts, any more than he can care nobly for men and women. That idea of the *sopra-uomo*, which fascinates him in Nietzsche, fascinates him because it is a deification of one's own individuality, in the narrowest sense; the creation of a new tyrant, in whom intellect is no more than a means of power, indeed, is properly no more than strength of will. The act of thought, with him, is a calling up of images, a process of symbolism. And so his feeling narrows itself down to what can be hurt or gratified in himself, or in some one imagined after the pattern of himself. It is for this reason, perhaps, that while his prose is so full of diffused poetry, his actual poetry remains a hard, positive thing, of which he may truly say

"le feste ho celebrato
De' suoni, de' colori e de le forme,"

but in which there is little underneath these sounds, colours, and forms, which exist for their own sake, and not for the sake of what they have to express. He is not a dreamer, and poetry is not to be spun out of any coarser web than dreams. So, in his verse, even more than in his prose, he is precise, clear in detail, hard in outline; often artificial, but artificial in the direction of fantastically defined form; always bound to the visible shapes of reality, even when he seems to choose and arrange them with the most lawless freedom. Take, for instance, a piece of pure fancy, like this sonnet, and see how curiously knitted to fact it remains:

> "Lazily pasture on the grassy walls
> The Asiatic horses of the King,
> Herod's swift horses; and at intervals
> Among the roses the faint fluttering
> Of their long, slumberous tails rises and falls;
> About the rocks the palms are slumbering,
> And now and then a quivering sea-voice calls,
> Among things sleeping like a waking thing.
>
> But if Jacín with a hoarse cry appear,
> The scattered herd rises and runs thereto,
> Looking on him with troubled fixedness.
>
> Even so I love to image for you, dear,
> My swift desires that rise and run to you
> Like horses pastured upon rose-bushes."

I have translated this sonnet to show how precise in his pictures d'Annunzio can be, especially when he is most apparently remote from reality, as in this image of the mind. Even more precise in its imagery, even fainter in its suggestion of any meaning beyond the feel of words like things, is another sonnet which I will translate from "Il Piacere":

> "I am as one who lays himself to rest
> Under the shadow of a laden tree;
> Above his head hangs the ripe fruit, and he
> Is weary of drawing bow or arbalest.
>
> He shakes not the fair bough that lowliest
> Droops, neither lifts he hand, nor turns to see;
> But lies, and gathers to him indolently
> The fruits that drop into his very breast.

> In that juiced sweetness, over-exquisite,
> He bites not deep; he fears the bitterness;
> Yet sets it to his lips that he may smell,
>
> Sucks it with pleasure, not with greediness,
> And he is neither grieved nor glad at it.
> This is the ending of the parable."

That could have been written only by one to whom the eating of a fruit meant just as much, at all events relatively, as the doing of a good or bad deed. Virtue and Vice are terms that never occur in his work, as the ideas implied by those words seem never to have occurred to his mind. Is a thing beautiful? he asks; is it the expression of an individuality? If not, then it is bad, that is, worthless; if so, then it is good, that is, effectual, answering its end. And thus to gather the full enjoyment which can be gathered from eating a fruit, is already to have succeeded, so far, in filling a moment with ecstasy, that is, in accomplishing one of the purposes of life. Does not the word morality sound a little out of place in dealing with so frank an acceptance of pleasure, for its own sake, at its simplest? Those lovers, in his books, to whom passion means everything, living more and more greedily on their own sensations, and drinking in ecstasy with so bitter a taste on the tongue, have but gone on from the first symbolical eating of the fruit, adding pang after pang to delight. No new element enters into them; they have discovered nothing new in their souls.

To the northern temperament, built up out of uncomfortable weather and a conscience uneasy about sin, this attitude of mind is almost unthinkable, or to be thought of only as a thing wholly brutal and degraded. Certainly it does not tend to the strenuous virtues, but it does not exclude much of a kind of virtue. There is no moral value in enduring needless discomfort, and one who is not sensitive to the little daily differences between the pleasant and unpleasant passing of the time, to air, fire, light, the ministry of flowers and jewels, and beautiful clothes to wear, and soft things to touch, and low voices, and the vivid relief of rest, can have but an imperfect sense of reality, and is lacking in one of the main faculties of life. No beautiful thing ever grew, or was ever woven together out of the many growths of the world, except for the sake of those amateurs in life who are able to accept all gifts, in all the gratitude of enjoyment. With us, as a race, but only since Puritanism has changed the race, moral earnestness has eaten up the delicate, passive virtues of mere exquisite receptiveness; so that we cannot rest long enough to take pleasure in what we have possessed violently. The Latin temperament, content with so much less, and so warmly happy in contentment, accepts the world, making the world its own, not by conquest but by enjoyment.

Yet (and here, perhaps, the northern attitude of mind may seem to take its revenge) these books of d'Annunzio, in which every earthly delight is so eagerly accepted, possessed so passionately, are all tragedies, often tragedies ending in gross material horror, and they are tragedies because no man has yet found out a remedy against the satiety of pleasure, except the remedies hidden away somewhere in the soul. Youth passes, desire fades, attainment squeezes the world into a narrow circuit; there is nothing left over, except dreams that turn into nightmares, or else a great weariness. Is it that something has been left out of the world, or that something has come disturbingly into it? D'Annunzio scarcely seems to ask the question, not caring much, apparently, to come to any conclusion.

"I must speak only of my soul under the veil of some seductive allegory," he says in "Il Fuoco"; and, on another page, wonders "why the poets of our day wax indignant at the vulgarity of their age and complain of having come into the world too early or too late. I believe that every man of intellect can, to-day as ever, create his own beautiful fable of life. We should both look into life's confused whirl in the same spirit of fancy that the disciples of Leonardo were taught to adopt in gazing at the spots on a wall, at the ashes of fire, at clouds, even mud and other similar objects, in order to find there 'admirable inventions' and 'infinite things.' The same spirit prompted Leonardo to add: 'In the sound of bells you will find every word and every name that you choose to imagine.'" "In him," he says, speaking of the poet, "there was ever an unlimited ardour of life"; and, defining the poet on his other side, "he was only the means by which beauty held out the divine gift of oblivion." Personal ardour, then, a flaming search after every beauty that exists in the world or in our sense of it: that, to him, must be the foundation of art, the basis of the artist's character. And he must render always his own vision of things, "creating his beautiful fable," first out of life itself, and then, under a transformation in which everything shall become brighter, but nothing be changed, in the forms of his art. Symbolism, therefore, must come of itself, in the mere endeavour to do over again in another medium what our creating minds are always doing with the world. If things are as we see them, and if there is nothing inert or passionless to us in the world, every elaborate beauty which art can add to nature will be, at the utmost, no more than a reflection of some beauty actually seen there. Thus the "veil of seductive allegory" will be rather a medium for light than a curtain darkening with shadow. The world of the novelist, what we call the real world, is a solid theft out of space; colour and music may float into it and wander through it, but it has not been made with colour and music, and it is not itself a part of the consciousness of its inhabitants. To d'Annunzio, this "materialist" beauty is the most real thing in the world, and our creation of beauty, in sight, touch, hearing, in our passions and our reverences, in the energy of our acceptance of happiness, and in the persistence of our search after personal satisfaction, the most important part of life. It is only at the end of a long day fully enjoyed, that an uneasy thought comes to him, and that he seems to say with Mallarmé:

> "La chair est triste, hélas! et j'ai lu tous les livres."

1898, 1900.

A NOTE ON GEORGE MEREDITH

George Meredith, though he has written novels, is essentially a poet, not a novelist. He is a poet who is not in the English tradition; a seeker after some strange, obscure, perhaps impossible, intellectual beauty, austere and fantastic. If he goes along ways that have never been travelled in, that is because he is seeking what no one before him has ever sought; and, more absolutely than most less-absorbed travellers, he carries the world behind his eyes, seeing, wherever he goes, only his own world, a creation less recognisable by people in general than the creation of most image-making brains. That is why he is so difficult to follow, and why you will be told that his writing is unnatural or artificial. Certainly it is artificial. "Let writers find time to write English more as a learned language," said Pater; but Meredith has always written English as if it were a learned language. Aiming, as he has done in verse, at something which is the poetry of pure idea, in prose, at something which is another kind of intellectual poetry, he has invented a whole vocabulary which has no resemblance with the spoken language, and whose merit is that it gives sharp, sudden expression to the aspects under which he sees things. So infused is vision in him with intellect, that he might be said to see things in words; the unusual, restless, nervous words being a part of that world which he has made for himself out of the tangle of the universe.

The problem of Meredith is the problem of why a poet has spent most of his life in writing novels, novels which are the most intellectual in the language, but not great novels; while the comparatively small amount of verse which he has written is even further from being great poetry. Probably for the reason which made Gautier, a born painter, put down the brushes and paint in words; a mere question of technique, as people say; or, as they should say, that fundamental question. To so deliberate an artificer as Meredith, technique must always have been valued at by no means less than its true worth. Having written a lovely poem in "Love in the Valley," and a fascinating, strangely exciting, not quite satisfying poem in "Modern Love," he must have realised that such achievements with him were too much of the nature of happy accidents to be very many times repeated. It was the period, and he was the friend, of Rossetti, of Morris, of Swinburne, each a born poet, and each, in his own way, an instinctively perfect craftsman. Conscious that he had something new to say, and knowing that he could never say it in verse as these poets had said what they had to say, he turned to prose, and began by inventing "The Shaving of Shagpat," which is like nothing that any one, least of all an Arabian story-teller, had ever said before. English literature has not a more vividly entertaining book, nor has the soul of a style been lost more spectacularly.

It is only by realising that Meredith began by a volume of poems, continued in the Arabian entertainment of "The Shaving of Shagpat" and the Teutonic fantasy of "Farina," and only then, at the age of thirty-one, published his first novel, "The Ordeal of Richard Feverel," that we can hope in any measure to understand the characteristics of so disconcerting a mind, so apparently inexplicable a career. Remember that he has the elliptical brain of the poet, not the slow, cautious, logical brain of the novelist; that he has his own vision of a world in which probable things do not always happen, and that words are to him as visual as mental images. Then consider the effect on such a brain, from the first impatient, intolerant, indefatigable, of a training in consciously artificial writing, on subjects which are a kind of sublime farce, without relation to any known or supposed realities in the universe. Writing prose, then, as if it were poetry, with an endeavour to pack every phrase with imaginative meaning, every sentence, you realise, will be an epigram. And as every sentence is to be an epigram, so every chapter is to be a crisis. And every book is to be at once a novel, realistic, a romance, a comedy of manners; it is to exist for its story, its characters, its philosophy, and every interest is to be equally prominent. And all the characters in it are to live at full speed, without a moment's repose; their very languors are to be fevers. And they will live (can you doubt?) in a fantastic world in which only the unexpected happens; their most trivial moments being turned, by the manner of their telling, into a fairy story.

All this may be equally refreshing or exhausting, but it is not the modesty of nature; and as certainly as it is not the duty of the poet, so certainly is it the duty of the novelist, to respect the modesty of nature. Every novel of Meredith is a series of situations, rendered for the most part in conversation, as if it were a play. Each situation is grouped, and shown to us as if the light of footlights were cast upon it; between each situation is darkness, and the drop-curtain. And his characters have the same inconsequent vividness. They are never types, but always individuals, in whom a capricious intellectual life burns with a bright but wavering flame. They are like people whom we meet in drawing-rooms, to-day in London, next month in

Rome, and the month after in Paris. They fascinate us by their brilliance, their energy, their experience, their conversation; they have in their faces the distinction of birth, of thought, of culture; they are always a little ambiguous to us, and by so much the more attractive; they move us to a singular sympathy, with which is mingled not a little curiosity; we seem to become their friends; and it is only when we think of them in absence that we realise how little we really know them. Of their inner life we know nothing; their eloquent lips have always been closed on all the great issues of things. Of their characters we know only what they have told us; and they have told us for the most part anecdotes, showing their bearing under trying circumstances, which have proved them triumphantly to be English gentlemen and ladies, without, it would seem, always settling those obscurer judgments in which the soul is its own accuser and judge. We remember certain extraordinarily vivid looks, words, attitudes, which they have had in our company; and we remember them by these, rather than remember that these had once been a momentary part of them.

Not such wandering friends, coming and going about us as if we had made them, are Lear, Don Quixote, Alceste, Manon Lescaut, Grandet, Madame Bovary, Anna Karenina. These seem to flow into the great rhythms of nature, as if their life was of the same immortal substance as the life of the plants and stars. These are organic, a part of the universe; the others are enchanting exceptions, breaking the rhythm, though they may, with a new music.

And the books in which they live are at once too narrow and too wide for them. Their histories are allowed to develop as they will, or as the situations in them become interesting to their creator. Yet, like almost every English novelist, Meredith is the bond-slave of "plot." Plot must be an intricate web, and this web must never be broken; and the stage must be crowded with figures, each with his own life to be accounted for, and not one of them will Meredith neglect, however long his hero or heroine may be kept waiting on the way. But, to be quite frank, what English novelist, from Fielding onwards, has ever been able to resist the temptation of loitering, especially if it is over a humorous scene? Humour is the curse of the English novelist. Certainly he possesses it; he has always possessed it; but his humour is not the wise laughter of Rabelais, in whom laughter is a symbol; and it is always a digression. Dickens, in particular, from the very brilliance of what is distressing in him, has left his fatal mark on the English novel. And it is often Dickens, bespangled with all the gems of Arabia, that I find in Meredith's comic scenes; never, certainly, when he is writing good comedy. Then, as we might infer from that "Essay on Comedy," which is his most brilliant piece of sustained writing, he is intellect itself, a Congreve who is also a poet.

"The Tragic Comedians," which is the title of one of Meredith's novels, might well be applied to the whole series, so picturesquely, under the light of so sharp a paradox, does he conceive of human existence. But he is too impatient, too forgetful of the limits of prose and the novel, to work out a philosophy in that indirect, circumambient way in which alone it can minister to fiction. Life may indeed be a tragic comedy at every moment, but it is not visibly and audibly at every moment a tragic comedy. In spite of the fact that action, in Meredith's novels, seems often to linger on the way, his novels are always in action. To him and his people,

> "to do nought
> Is in itself almost an act";

every conversation is a hurry of mental action; the impressiveness with which nothing happens, when nothing is happening, is itself a strain on the energy. And the almost German romance which tempers in him the French wit, adding a new whirl of colours to the kaleidoscope, helps to withdraw this world of his creating further and further from the daylight in which men labour without energy, and are content without happiness, and dream only vague dreams, and achieve only probable ends. He conceives his characters as pure intelligences, and then sets them to play at hide-and-seek with life, as if England were a treasure island in the Pacific.

Again, it is the question of technique which comes to enlighten us. We have seen, I think, that with Meredith the question of how to write must have arisen before the question of what to write, certainly before the choice of the novel. A style conceived in verse, and brought up on Arabian extravaganzas and German fantasies, could scarcely be expected to adapt itself to the narration of the little, colourless facts of modern English society. With such a style, above all things literary, life recorded becomes, not a new life, but literature about life; and it is of the essence of the novel that life should be reborn in it, in the express image of its first shape. Where poetry, which must keep very close to the earth, is condemned, even, to avoid the soiling of the dust of the streets, the novel must not, at its peril, wander far from those streets. Before the novelist, human life is on its trial; he must see it with cold, learned eyes; he must hear it with undisturbed attention; he must be neither kind nor cruel, but merely just, in his judgment. Now Meredith's is not a style which can render facts, much less seem to allow facts to render themselves. Like Carlyle, but even more than Carlyle, Meredith is in the true, wide sense, as no other English writer of the present time can be said to be, a Decadent. The word Decadent has been narrowed, in France and in England, to a mere label upon a particular school of very recent writers. What Decadence, in literature, really means is that learned corruption of language by which style ceases to be organic, and becomes, in the pursuit of some new expressiveness or beauty, deliberately abnormal. Meredith's style is as self-conscious as Mallarmé's. But, unlike many self-conscious styles, it is alive in every fibre. Not since the Elizabethans have we had so flame-like a life possessing the wanton body of a style. And with this fantastic, poetic, learned, passionate, intellectual style, a style which might have lent itself so well to the making of Elizabethan drama, Meredith has set himself to the task of writing novels of contemporary life, in which the English society of to-day is to be shown to us in the habit and manners of our time.

Is it, then, to be wondered at that every novel of Meredith breaks every rule which could possibly be laid down for the writing of a novel? I think it follows; but the strange thing which does not follow is that the work thus produced should have that irresistible fascination which for many of us it certainly has. I find Meredith breaking every canon of what are to me the laws of the novel; and yet I read him in preference to any other novelist. I say to myself: This pleasure, which I undoubtedly get from these novels, must surely be an irrational kind of pleasure; for it is against my judgment on those principles on which my mind is made up. Here am I, who cannot read without the approval of an unconscious, if not of a definitely conscious, criticism; I find myself reading these novels with the tacit approval of this very difficult literary conscience of mine: certainly it approves me in admiring them; and yet, when I set myself to think coldly over what I have been reading, I am forced to disapprove. How can these two views exist side by side in the same mind? How is it that that side of me which approves does not condemn that side of me which disapproves, nor that which disapproves condemn that which approves? There are some secrets which will never be told: the secret of why beauty is beauty, of why love is love, of why poetry is poetry. This woman, this book, this writer, attracts me: you they do not attract. Yet I may admit every imperfection which you can point out to me, and at the end of your logic meet you with perhaps but a woman's reason. I shall never believe that such an instinct can be false: inexplicable it may be.

The fascination of Meredith is not, I think, quite inexplicable. It is the unrecognised, incalculable attraction of those qualities which go to make great poetry, coming to us in the disguise of prose and the novel, affecting us in spite of ourselves, as if a strange and beautiful woman suddenly took her seat among the judges in a court of law, where they were deciding some dusty case. Try to recall to yourself what has most impressed you in Meredith's novels, and you will think first, after a vague consciousness of their unusual atmosphere, of some lyric scene, such as the scene in "Richard Feverel," where Richard and Lucy meet in the wood; and that, you will see, is properly not prose at all, but a poem about first love. Then you will think of some passionate love-scene, one of Emilia's in "Sandra Belloni"; or the Venetian episode in "Beauchamp's Career"; or the fiery race of events, where dawn and darkness meet, in "Rhoda Fleming"; and all of them, you will see, have more of the qualities of poetry than of prose. The poet, struggling against the bondage of prose, flings himself upon every opportunity of evading his bondage. Even if he fails, he has made us thrillingly conscious of his presence. It is thus by the very quality which has been his distraction that Meredith holds us, by the intensity of his vision of a world which is not our world, by the living imagination of a language which is not our language, by the energy of genius which has done so much to achieve the impossible.

1897.

A NOTE ON ZOLA'S METHOD

THE art of Zola is based on certain theories, on a view of humanity which he has adopted as his formula. As a deduction from his formula, he takes many things in human nature for granted, he is content to observe at second-hand; and it is only when he comes to the filling-up of his outlines, the *mise-en-scène*, that his observation becomes personal, minute, and persistent. He has thus succeeded in being at once unreal where reality is most essential, and tediously real where a point-by-point reality is sometimes unimportant. The contradiction is an ingenious one, which it may be interesting to examine in a little detail, and from several points of view.

And, first of all, take "L'Assommoir," no doubt the most characteristic of Zola's novels, and probably the best; and, leaving out for the present the broader question of his general conception of humanity, let us look at Zola's manner of dealing with his material, noting by the way certain differences between his manner and that of Goncourt, of Flaubert, with both of whom he has so often been compared, and with whom he wishes to challenge comparison. Contrast "L'Assommoir" with "Germinie Lacerteux," which, it must be remembered, was written thirteen years earlier. Goncourt, as he incessantly reminds us, was the first novelist in France to deliberately study the life of the people, after precise documents; and "Germinie Lacerteux" has this distinction, among others, that it was a new thing. And it is done with admirable skill;

as a piece of writing, as a work of art, it is far superior to Zola. But, certainly, Zola's work has a mass and bulk, a *fougue*, a *portée*, which Goncourt's lacks; and it has a savour of plebeian flesh which all the delicate art of Goncourt could not evoke. Zola sickens you with it; but there it is. As in all his books, but more than in most, there is something greasy, a smear of eating and drinking; the pages, to use his own phrase, "grasses des lichades du lundi." In "Germinie Lacerteux" you never forget that Goncourt is an aristocrat; in "L'Assommoir" you never forget that Zola is a bourgeois. Whatever Goncourt touches becomes, by the mere magic of his touch, charming, a picture; Zola is totally destitute of charm. But how, in "L'Assommoir," he drives home to you the horrid realities of these narrow, uncomfortable lives! Zola has made up his mind that he will say everything, without omitting a single item, whatever he has to say; thus, in "L'Assommoir," there is a great feast which lasts for fifty pages, beginning with the picking of the goose, the day before, and going on to the picking of the goose's bones, by a stray marauding cat, the night after. And, in a sense, he does say everything; and there, certainly, is his novelty, his invention. He observes with immense persistence, but his observation, after all, is only that of the man in the street; it is simply carried into detail, deliberately. And, while Goncourt wanders away sometimes into arabesques, indulges in flourishes, so finely artistic is his sense of words and of the things they represent, so perfectly can he match a sensation or an impression by its figure in speech, Zola, on the contrary, never finds just the right word, and it is his persistent fumbling for it which produces these miles of description; four pages describing how two people went upstairs, from the ground floor to the sixth storey, and then two pages afterwards to describe how they came downstairs again. Sometimes, by his prodigious diligence and minuteness, he succeeds in giving you the impression; often, indeed; but at the cost of what *ennui* to writer and reader alike! And so much of it all is purely unnecessary, has no interest in itself and no connection with the story: the precise details of Lorilleux's chain-making, bristling with technical terms: it was *la colonne* that he made, and only that particular kind of chain; Goujet's forge, and the machinery in the shed next door; and just how you cut out zinc with a large pair of scissors. When Goncourt gives you a long description of anything, even if you do not feel that it helps on the story very much, it is such a beautiful thing in itself, his mere way of writing it is so enchanting, that you find yourself wishing it longer, at its longest. But with Zola, there is no literary interest in the writing, apart from its clear and coherent expression of a given thing; and these interminable descriptions have no extraneous, or, if you will, implicit interest, to save them from the charge of irrelevancy; they sink by their own weight. Just as Zola's vision is the vision of the average man, so his vocabulary, with all its technicology, remains mediocre, incapable of expressing subtleties, incapable of a really artistic effect. To find out in a slang dictionary that a filthy idea can be expressed by an ingeniously filthy phrase in *argot*, and to use that phrase, is not a great feat, or, on purely artistic grounds, altogether desirable. To go to a chainmaker and learn the trade name of the various kinds of chain which he manufactures, and of the instruments with which he manufactures them, is not an elaborate process, or one which can be said to pay you for the little trouble which it no doubt takes. And it is not well to be too certain after all that Zola is always perfectly accurate in his use of all this manifold knowledge. The slang, for example; he went to books for it, in books he found it, and no one will ever find some of it but in books. However, my main contention is that Zola's general use of words is, to be quite frank, somewhat ineffectual. He tries to do what Flaubert did, without Flaubert's tools, and without the craftsman's hand at the back of the tools. His fingers are too thick; they leave a blurred line. If you want merely weight, a certain kind of force, you get it; but no more.

Where a large part of Zola's merit lies, in his persistent attention to detail, one finds also one of his chief defects. He cannot leave well alone; he cannot omit; he will not take the most obvious fact for granted. "Il marcha le premier, elle le suivit"; well, of course she followed him, if he walked first: why mention the fact? That beginning of a sentence is absolutely typical; it is impossible for him to refer, for the twentieth time, to some unimportant character, without giving name and profession, not one or the other, but both, invariably both. He tells us particularly that a room is composed of four walls, that a table stands on its four legs. And he does not appear to see the difference between doing that and doing as Flaubert does, namely, selecting precisely the detail out of all others which renders or consorts with the scene in hand, and giving that detail with an ingenious exactness. Here, for instance, in "Madame Bovary," is a characteristic detail in the manner of Flaubert: "Huit jours après, comme elle étendait du linge dans sa cour, elle fut prise d'un crachement de sang, et le lendemain, tandis que Charles avait le dos tourné pour fermer le rideau de la fenêtre, elle dit: 'Ah! mon Dieu!' poussa un soupir et s'évanouit. Elle était morte." Now that detail, brought in without the slightest emphasis, of the husband turning his back at the very instant that his wife dies, is a detail of immense psychological value; it indicates to us, at the very opening of the book, just the character of the man about whom we are to read so much. Zola would have taken at least two pages to say that, and, after all, he would not have said it. He would have told you the position of the chest of drawers in the room, what wood the chest of drawers was made of, and if it had a little varnish knocked off at the corner of the lower cornice, just where it would naturally be in the way of people's feet as they entered the door. He would have told you how Charles leant against the other corner of the chest of drawers, and that the edge of the upper cornice left a slight dent in his black frock-coat, which remained visible half an hour afterwards. But that one little detail, which Flaubert selects from among a thousand, that, no, he would never have given us that!

And the language in which all this is written, apart from the consideration of language as a medium, is really not literature at all, in any strict sense. I am not, for the moment, complaining of the colloquialism and the slang. Zola has told us that he has, in "L'Assommoir," used the language of the people in order to render the people with a closer truth. Whether he has done that or not is not the question. The question is, that he does not give one the sense of reading good literature, whether he speaks in Delvau's *langue verte*, or according to the Academy's latest edition of classical French. His sentences have no rhythm; they give no pleasure to the ear; they carry no sensation to the eye. You hear a sentence of Flaubert, and you see a sentence of Goncourt, like living things, with forms and voices. But a page of

Zola lies dull and silent before you; it draws you by no charm, it has no meaning until you have read the page that goes before and the page that comes after. It is like cabinet-makers' work, solid, well fitted together, and essentially made to be used.

Yes, there is no doubt that Zola writes very badly, worse than any other French writer of eminence. It is true that Balzac, certainly one of the greatest, does, in a sense, write badly; but his way of writing badly is very different from Zola's, and leaves you with the sense of quite a different result. Balzac is too impatient with words; he cannot stay to get them all into proper order, to pick and choose among them. Night, the coffee, the wet towel, and the end of six hours' labour are often too much for him; and his manner of writing his novels on the proof-sheets, altering and expanding as fresh ideas came to him on each re-reading, was not a way of doing things which can possibly result in perfect writing. But Balzac sins from excess, from a feverish haste, the very extravagance of power; and, at all events, he "sins strongly." Zola sins meanly, he is penuriously careful, he does the best he possibly can; and he is not aware that his best does not answer all requirements. So long as writing is clear and not ungrammatical, it seems to him sufficient. He has not realised that without charm there can be no fine literature, as there can be no perfect flower without fragrance.

And it is here that I would complain, not as a matter of morals, but as a matter of art, of Zola's obsession by what is grossly, uninterestingly filthy. There is a certain simile in "L'Assommoir," used in the most innocent connection, in connection with a bonnet, which seems to me the most abjectly dirty phrase which I have ever read. It is one thing to use dirty words to describe dirty things; that may be necessary, and thus unexceptionable. It is another thing again, and this, too, may well be defended on artistic grounds, to be ingeniously and wittily indecent. But I do not think a real man of letters could possibly have used such an expression as the one I am alluding to, or could so meanly succumb to certain kinds of prurience which we find in Zola's work. Such a scene as the one in which Gervaise comes home with Lantier, and finds her husband lying drunk asleep in his own vomit, might certainly be explained and even excused, though few more disagreeable things were ever written, on the ground of the psychological importance which it undoubtedly has, and the overwhelming way in which it drives home the point which it is the writer's business to make. But the worrying way in which *le derrière* and *le ventre* are constantly kept in view, without the slightest necessity, is quite another thing. I should not like to say how often the phrase "sa nudité de jolie fille" occurs in Zola. Zola's nudities always remind me of those which you can see in the Foire au pain d'épice at Vincennes, by paying a penny and looking through a peep-hole. In the laundry scenes, for instance in "L'Assommoir," he is always reminding you that the laundresses have turned up their sleeves, or undone a button or two of their bodices. His eyes seem eternally fixed on the inch or two of bare flesh that can be seen; and he nudges your elbow at every moment, to make sure that you are looking too. Nothing may be more charming than a frankly sensuous description of things which appeal to the senses; but can one imagine anything less charming, less like art, than this prying eye glued to the peep-hole in the Gingerbread Fair?

Yet, whatever view may be taken of Zola's work in literature, there is no doubt that the life of Zola is a model lesson, and might profitably be told in one of Dr Smiles's edifying biographies. It may even be brought as a reproach against the writer of these novels, in which there are so many offences against the respectable virtues, that he is too good a bourgeois, too much the incarnation of the respectable virtues, to be a man of genius. If the finest art comes of the intensest living, then Zola has never had even a chance of doing the greatest kind of work. It is his merit and his misfortune to have lived entirely in and for his books, with a heroic devotion to his ideal of literary duty which would merit every praise if we had to consider simply the moral side of the question. So many pages of copy a day, so many hours of study given to mysticism, or Les Halles; Zola has always had his day's work marked out before him, and he has never swerved from it. A recent life of Zola tells us something about his way of getting up a subject. "Immense preparation had been necessary for the 'Faute de l'Abbé Mouret.' Mountains of note-books were heaped up on his table, and for months Zola was plunged in the study of religious works. All the mystical part of the book, and notably the passages having reference to the cultus of Mary, was taken from the works of the Spanish Jesuits. The 'Imitation of Jesus Christ' was largely drawn upon, many passages being copied almost word for word into the novel—much as in 'Clarissa Harlowe,' that other great realist, Richardson, copied whole passages from the Psalms. The description of life in a grand seminary was given him by a priest who had been dismissed from ecclesiastical service. The little church of Sainte Marie des Batignolles was regularly visited."

How commendable all that is, but, surely, how futile! Can one conceive of a more hopeless, a more ridiculous task, than that of setting to work on a novel of ecclesiastical life as if one were cramming for an examination in religious knowledge? Zola apparently imagines that he can master mysticism in a fortnight, as he masters the police regulations of Les Halles. It must be admitted that he does wonders with his second-hand information, alike in regard to mysticism and Les Halles. But he succeeds only to a certain point, and that point lies on the nearer side of what is really meant by success. Is not Zola himself, at his moments, aware of this? A letter written in 1881, and printed in Mr Sherard's life of Zola, from which I have just quoted, seems to me very significant.

"I continue to work in a good state of mental equilibrium. My novel ('Pot-Bouille') is certainly only a task requiring precision and clearness. No *bravoura*, not the least lyrical treat. It does not give me any warm satisfaction, but it amuses me like a piece of mechanism with a thousand wheels, of which it is my duty to regulate the movements with the most minute care. I ask myself the question: Is it good policy, when one feels that one has passion in one, to check it, or even to bridle it? If one of my books is destined to become immortal, it will, I am sure, be the most passionate one."

"Est-elle en marbre ou non, la Vénus de Milo?" said the Parnassians, priding themselves on their muse with her "peplum bien sculpté." Zola will describe to you the exact shape and the exact smell of the rags of his naturalistic muse; but has she, under the tatters, really a human heart? In the whole of Zola's works, amid all his exact and impressive descriptions of misery, all his endless annals of the poor, I know only one episode which brings tears to the eyes, the episode of the child-martyr Lalie in "L'Assommoir." "A piece of mechanism with a thousand wheels," that is indeed the image of this immense and wonderful study of human life, evolved out of the brain of a solitary student who knows life only by the report of his documents, his friends, and, above all, his formula.

Zola has defined art, very aptly, as nature seen through a temperament. The art of Zola is nature seen through a formula. This professed realist is a man of theories who studies life with a conviction that he will find there such and such things which he has read about in scientific books. He observes, indeed, with astonishing minuteness, but he observes in support of preconceived ideas. And so powerful is his imagination that he has created a whole world which has no existence anywhere but in his own brain, and he has placed there imaginary beings, so much more logical than life, in the midst of surroundings which are themselves so real as to lend almost a semblance of reality to the embodied formulas who inhabit them.

It is the boast of Zola that he has taken up art at the point where Flaubert left it, and that he has developed that art in its logical sequence. But the art of Flaubert, itself a development from Balzac, had carried realism, if not in "Madame Bovary," at all events in "L'Education Sentimentale," as far as realism can well go without ceasing to be art. In the grey and somewhat sordid history of Frédéric Moreau there is not a touch of romanticism, not so much as a concession to style, a momentary escapc of the imprisoned lyrical tendency. Everything is observed, everything is taken straight from life: realism, sincere, direct, implacable, reigns from end to end of the book. But with what consummate art all this mass of observation is disintegrated, arranged, composed! with what infinite delicacy it is manipulated in the service of an unerring sense of construction! And Flaubert has no theory, has no prejudices, has only a certain impatience with human imbecility. Zola, too, gathers his documents, heaps up his mass of observation, and then, in this unhappy "development" of the principles of art which produced "L'Education Sentimentale," flings everything pell-mell into one overflowing *pot-au-feu*. The probabilities of nature and the delicacies of art are alike drowned beneath a flood of turbid observation, and in the end one does not even feel convinced that Zola really knows his subject. I remember once hearing M. Huysmans, with his look and tone of subtle, ironical malice, describe how Zola, when he was writing "La Terre," took a drive into the country in a victoria, to see the peasants. The English papers once reported an interview in which the author of "Nana," indiscreetly questioned as to the amount of personal observation he had put into the book, replied that he had lunched with an actress of the Variétés. The reply was generally taken for a joke, but the lunch was a reality, and it was assuredly a rare experience in the life of solitary diligence to which we owe so many impersonal studies in life. Nor did Zola, as he sat silent by the side of Mlle. X., seem to be making much use of the opportunity. The language of the miners in "Germinal," how mnch of local colour is there in that? The interminable additions and divisions, the extracts from a financial gazette, in "L'Argent," how much of the real temper and idiosyncrasy of the financier do they give us? In his description of places, in his *mise-en-scène*, Zola puts down what he sees with his own eyes, and, though it is often done at utterly disproportionate length, it is at all events done with exactitude. But in the far more important observation of men and women, he is content with second-hand knowledge, the knowledge of a man who sees the world through a formula. Zola sees in humanity *la bête humaine*. He sees the beast in all its transformations, but he sees only the beast. He has never looked at life impartially, he has never seen it as it is. His realism is a distorted idealism, and the man who considers himself the first to paint humanity as it really is will be remembered in the future as the most idealistic writer of his time.

1893.

THE RUSSIAN SOUL: GORKI AND TOLSTOI

I

MAXIM GORKI was born at Nijni-Novgorod in 1868 or 1869; he is not sure of the year of his birth. His parents were poor people, and they died when he was a boy, leaving him penniless. He apprenticed himself to a shoemaker, but, tiring of the trade, ran away, and worked with an engraver, then with a painter of icons, then with a cook, then with a gardener, then again with a cook, on board a steamboat. This cook was a reader of novels, and Gorki began to read Gogol and Dumas. He was taken, he tells us, with a "ferocious desire" to learn, and he left the steamboat and made his way to Kazan, thinking that a poor fellow could be taught for nothing. He found that it was not the custom, and he got work at a baker's, living on twelve roubles a month. When he could endure the bakery no longer he began to wander about, reading, learning all that he could, living with vagabonds, sometimes drinking, sometimes working, a sawyer, a coal-heaver, a gatekeeper, a street seller of apples or of kvass. He made the acquaintance of a lawyer, who helped him and lent him books; but he was soon wandering again, and it was in an obscure provincial paper that he published his first story, "Makar Tchoudra," a gipsy narrative in which he had not yet learnt to use his strange material simply. In 1893 he met Korolenko, the novelist, who interested himself in him, and helped him to publish one of his stories, "Tchelkache." Its success was immediate, and since then Gorki has written many short stories, besides a novel, "Fomá Gordeïev," and several plays. "Les Vagabonds," a volume of short stories translated by Ivan Strannik, first introduced Gorki to France; other volumes of translations followed, first in French, then in English; the novel, "Fomá Gordeïev," has been translated into English, as well as many of the short stories. The novel is not so good as the best of the short stories, but it is a strange, chaotic, attractive book, which we may read either for its story, or because we want to find out something more about the mysterious Russian soul.

"I was born," he tells us in one of his stories, "outside society, and for that reason I cannot take in a strong dose of its culture without soon feeling forced to get outside it again, to wipe away the infinite complications, the sickly refinements, of that kind of existence. I like either to go about in the meanest streets of towns, because, though everything there is dirty, it is all simple and sincere, or else to wander about on the highroads and across the fields, because that is always interesting; it refreshes one morally, and needs no more than a pair of good legs to carry one." It is this feeling, the feeling which first made him a wanderer, that has made him a writer, and his stories are made directly out of the life which he has lived. In many of them he appears under his own name, telling the story as if it were something which had actually happened to him. Thus the scene of "Konovalov" is the baker's shop at Kazan, the underground kitchen with its yeasty atmosphere, in which everything looked dim, and the window high up, through which could be seen "a little scrap of blue sky with two stars: one was large, and shone like an emerald; the other, quite near, was hardly visible." His method is simple. In a few bold strokes he brings before us a corner of the country, a sea-beach, a quay, a shop, a street; then a man and a woman, two men, some simple incident, and the men and women go out as quietly as they had come in. But meanwhile a strange temperament has expressed itself in a few words, some disconcerting action, a significant silence; and what we have felt is just what is deepest, most unconscious, in that nature, to which speech is so difficult, though so painful, and action a kind of despairing start away from the logic of things. Along with this simple and profound human quality there is a power of rendering very subtle sensation, as in this sentence: "All about us reigned that aching quiet, from which one seems to be awaiting something, and which, if it lasted, would drive a man mad with its absolute peace, its utter absence of sound, the living shadow of motion." In "Mon Compagnon" there is a long description of a boat in a storm, as minute as Defoe, and with an imaginative quality of minuteness. When in summer, the two vagabonds light a fire in the field, because a fire would look beautiful; when in the midst of a thunderstorm on the steppe, one of the vagabonds begins to sing with all his might, and the other attacks him in a kind of savagery of terror; in the Meunier-like pictures of labour, as in the building of the embankment at Theodocia, there is something large, lyrical, as if the obscure forces of the earth half awakened and began to speak. In all this Gorki does but continue, in his own way, what other Russian novelists have done before him; he enters into the tradition, the youngest and most fruitful tradition in Europe. Other races, too long civilised, have accustomed themselves to the soul, to mystery, to whatever is most surprising in life and death. Russia, with centuries of savagery behind it, still feels the earth about its roots, or the thirst in it of the primitive animal. It has lost none of its instincts, and it has just discovered the soul. And it is ceaselessly perturbed by that strange inner companion; it listens to a voice which is not the voice of the blood; it listens to both voices, saying contrary things; and it is astonished, melancholy, questioning. Other novelists tell us of society; tell us, that is, what we are when we are not ourselves. The Russian novelists show us the soul when it is alone with itself, unconscious or morbidly conscious, gay, uneasy, confident, suspicious, agonised with duty, a tyrannous slave or a devout and humble master.

Every Russian is born a philosopher; he reasons as a child might reason, an ignorant, unhappy child, wondering why things are as they are. These vagabonds of Gorki are conscious that something is wrong, with the world or with them, and they cannot understand what. "I live, and I am bored," says Konovalov. "Why? I don't know at all. How shall I say it? There's a spark wanting in my soul. Something is wanting in me, that's all. Do you see? Well, then, I seek, and I am bored, and it all comes to——I dont know what." They pity themselves, with a kind of impersonal pity, not accusing any one. "We are by ourselves, we should be reckoned with by ourselves; because we are good for nothing in life, and we take up somebody else's place, and we get in other people's way. Whose fault is it? It is our fault against life. We haven't the joy of living, nor any feeling for ourselves. Our mothers gave birth to us in a bad hour, that's all!" There is only one good thing, liberty, the freedom at least to suffer in one's own way: "to walk to and fro on the earth this way and that; you walk, and you see new things, and then you don't think." "When one thinks, one gets disgusted with living," says Serejka; and all these people, to whom life is never quite mechanical, because they are living outside the laws, and have the leisure to lie down and watch the sea moving, or the black earth secretly alive, are all afraid of thinking. They cannot help thinking, but it frightens them. "You," says Vassili to Malva, "you don't know anything of these things; but sometimes I can't help thinking about life, and I am afraid. Especially at night, when I can't sleep." They know so little, and all the problems of the universe come to them without the intervention of books, or beliefs, or any knowledge. They see themselves, as Vassili does, when he lies awake at night, "so small, so small, and it seems as if the earth moved under me, and there were nobody on the earth but me." They move from place to place, like consumptive people, who think, if they could but be somewhere else, they would be quite well. But it is always somewhere else. All the roads of the world lead to six feet of earth, and all the way there has been a losing of the way.

To Gorki the vagabond is the most interesting failure in the world, where everything must be a failure. He has affirmed his independence, he has been resolutely himself, he has had the energy to stand up against the inevitable, realising at least his own courage, perhaps his own strength. Unlike most others, he knows that he has only himself to rely on in the world, and that it is only that self which matters.

II

The Russian novel is the novel of uncivilised people who give us their impressions of civilisation, or who show us how one can do without civilisation. They try to find out the meaning of life, each for himself, as if no one had ever thought about the matter before. They are troubled about the soul, which they are unable to realise, with Balzac, as "nervous fluid"; with Thackeray, as the schoolboy's response to his master. Like Fomá Gordeïev "they bear within them something heavy and uncomfortable, something which they cannot comprehend." Russian novels are the only novels in which we see people acting on their impulses, unable to resist their impulses or to account for them. They are never in doubt as to what they feel: it is as simple as when one says, I am cold, I am hungry. They say, I love this woman, I hate this man, I must go to Sevastopol though I shall probably be killed if I go there, I am convinced that this or that is my duty. Sometimes they reason out their feelings, but the reasoning never makes any difference to their feelings. The English novelist shows us an idea coming into a man's head; when he has got the idea he sometimes proceeds to feel as the idea suggests to him. The French novelist shows us a sensation, tempered or directed by will, coming into a man's consciousness; even his instincts wait on the instinctive criticism of the intelligence; so that passion, for instance, cools into sensuality while it waits. But to the Russian there is nothing in the world except the feeling which invades him like an atmosphere, or grows up within him like a plant putting out its leaves, or crushes him under it like a great weight falling from above. He wonders at this strange thing which takes possession of him so easily, so unexpectedly, so irresistibly. He may fight against it, but it will be as Jacob fights against the angel, in Nettleship's remarkable design: he is held in the mere hollow of a hand, while he conceives himself to be wrestling with the whole of that unseen force.

Tolstoi is so abnormally normal that he can express every feeling without having to allow for any personal deviation. He feels everything, and he feels to the roots of the emotion, and he can put one thing into words as simply as another thing. He does not say, this is good feeling and that bad, this is perverse, that natural; he says, this is the feeling. Gorki, like Dostoieffski, often feels awry, is not content with things as they are, or must choose to his purpose only crooked and ugly things. He takes sides frankly with the vagabonds, deifies them a little, turns them at times into Uebermenschen; he has none of the impartiality of mere justice, "pardoning," in the expressive phrase, only those whom he "understands." If we are disposed to over-estimate what is remarkable in the younger man, we have only to turn to a volume of Tolstoi, written at the age of twenty-seven, "Sevastopol," and we shall see at once all the difference between the most brilliant fever and the unalterable energy of health.

I have been turning over the pages of "Lavengro" these last few days, and it has struck me that there is something in that wonderful book more like the early writings of Tolstoi than anything we have in English. Borrow too writes as if civilisation did not exist, or as if it were still quite possible to exist outside civilisation, and he obtains, in his indirect way, an extraordinary effect of directness. Really the most artificial of writers, he is always true to that "peculiar mind and system of nerves" of which he was so well aware, and which drove him into all sorts of cunning ways of telling the truth, and making it at once bewildering and convincing. Take, in "Lavengro," the chapter describing his paroxysm of fear in the dingle, and contrast those pages with the pages in "Sevastopol" describing Praskhoúhin's sensations before and after the bomb strikes him. I know nothing of the kind, in any language, equal to those pages of Borrow; they go deep down into some "obscure night of the soul"; what Tolstoi gives us is not even an exceptional thing, it is so simple as to seem almost self-evident, but it is the elementary feeling, the normal human feeling. Yes, Tolstoi is abnormally normal, and every development of his art, his thought, and his conduct comes from his unquestioning obedience to impulse, in which he carries the instinct of his race to its ultimate limits.

Tolstoi's position of calm and dogged and well-thought-out revolt could only have been adopted or maintained in Russia, and in Russia it is conspicuous only because Tolstoi is a man of genius. It is the acting-out of an impulse, a childlike following of feeling to its logical consequences. The same sincerity to a conviction, to a conviction which has become an irresistible feeling, is seen in every Nihilist who strikes at the Tsar. It is the sincerity of the savage, who throws off the whole of civilisation with ease, as he would throw off a great-coat. The Russian has been civilised for so short a while that he has not yet got accustomed to it. Civilisation has no roots in him. Laws have been made for chaining him down, as if he were a dangerous wild beast, and the laws were made by those who knew his nature and had determined to thwart it. If he cannot have his way, he is always ready to be a martyr. And

Tolstoi, who has the peasant in him and the martyr, has done just as countless fanatics have done before him; and, being a man of genius and a great novelist, has done it successfully, appealing to all Europe. He strikes at civilisation, society, patriotism, with an infinitely greater force than the Nihilist; but he strikes in the same direction and from the same impulse. His convictions carry him against these barriers; he acts out his convictions: so does the Nihilist. He is for peace and the other for destruction; but that is only the accident by which the same current brings one straw to land and hurries the other straw over the weir. And wherever we look in Russian novels we shall see the same practical logic setting men and women outside the laws, for good or evil, deliberately or unconsciously. Fomá Gordeïev, when he thrashes the man in the club, "brimming with the ardent sensation of malice, quivering all over with the happiness of revenge, dragging him over the floor; bellowing dully, viciously, in fierce joy," is hardly aware why he is doing what he does; the feeling takes him, and he does it. "During those minutes he experienced a vast sensation—the sensation of liberation from a wearisome burden, which had already long oppressed his breast with sadness and impotency." He feels the need of asserting his own nature, of expressing himself; with his fists, as it happens: it is as if, being an artist, he had written his sonnet or painted the sky into his picture. Well, and to the Nihilist, that disinterested artist in life, the killing of somebody is merely the finishing of a train of thought, an emphatic, conclusive way of demonstrating a problem.

1901.

TOLSTOI ON ART

I

THE theory which makes feeling the test of art, and an ennobling influence upon the emotions the aim of art, has never received so signal a discomfiture as in the book by Tolstoi, called "What is Art?" in which that theory is put forward as the only possible one, and carried, in the most logical way, to its final conclusions. Tolstoi, as it seems to me, is more essentially a man of genius than any writer now living. He has carried the methods of the novel further into the soul of man than any novelist who ever lived; and he has at the same time rendered the common details of life with a more absolute illusion of reality than any one else. Since he has given up writing novels, he has written a study of the Christian religion which seems to me, from the strictly Christian point of view, to leave nothing more to be said; and he has followed out his own conclusions in life with the same logic as that with which he has carried them out in writing. He is unique in our time in having made every practical sacrifice to his own ideal. Everything he writes, therefore, we are bound to receive with that respect which is due alike to every man of genius and to every man of unflinching sincerity. It is impossible that he should write anything which is without a value of its own, not necessarily the value which he himself attaches to it. It may scarcely seem, indeed, that Tolstoi has much more of the necessary equipment for writing a book on art than, let us say, Bunyan would have had. Yet if Bunyan had sat down to write a book on art, in which he had given us his real opinion of Milton in the present and Shakespeare in the past, such a book, if it had told us nothing worth knowing about Shakespeare and Milton, would still have been well worth reading, for the sake of Bunyan himself and of the better understanding of that Puritan conscience which Bunyan embodied. In the same way this book of Tolstoi's, trying as it is to read, and little as it tells us about the questions it sets out to enlighten, has an undeniable value as the utterance of Tolstoi, and as the legitimate *reductio ad absurdum* of theories which have had so many more cautious and less honest defenders.

Tolstoi is not an abstract thinker, a philosopher by temperament, though he has come finally to have a consistent philosophy of life, not, as with Nietzsche, a mere bundle of intuitions. His mind is logical, and it is also that of a man of action: it goes straight to conclusions, and acts upon them, promptly and humbly. He desires, first of all, to become clear himself, to "save his own soul"; then he will act upon others by the instinctive exercise of his goodness, of what he is, not by some external reform. All his reforms would begin with the head and with the heart; he would "convince" the world of what to him is righteousness, taking it for granted that men will naturally do what they see ought to be done. Thus he has no belief in Socialism or in Anarchism, in any mechanical readjustment of things which is not the almost unconscious result of a personal feeling or conviction. To Tolstoi the one question is: What is the purpose of my life? and his answer, explains the interpreter, is this: "The purpose of my life is to understand, and, as far as possible, to do, the will of that Power which has sent me here, and which actuates my reason and conscience." Preferring, as he tells us, to seek goodness "by the head" rather than "by the heart," to begin with the understanding, he has none of the artist's disinterested interest in "problems," as Ibsen, for instance, has. When Ibsen concerns himself with questions of conduct, with the "meaning of life," he has no interest in their solution, only in their development, caring only to track the evil, not to cure it. They are his material, from which he holds himself as far aloof as the algebraist from his *x*. Now Tolstoi is what he is just because he has been through all this, and has found himself compelled to leave it behind. He is a personality, and the artist in him has never been more than a part of his personality. Tolstoi first lived, then wrote, now he draws the moral from both careers, working upon life itself rather than upon a painting after life. His final attitude is the postscript adding a conclusion to his novels. As a novelist he had kept closer to actual life, to the dust of existence, than any other novelist; so that "Anna Karenina" is perhaps more painful to read than any other novel. It gives us body and soul, and it also gives us the clothes of life, society. There are none of the disguises of the novelist with a style, or of the novelist with a purpose. It is so real that it seems to be speaking to us out of our own hearts and out of our own experience. It is so real because it is the work of one to whom life is more significant than it is to any other novelist. Thus the final step, the step which every novelist, if he goes far enough, may be impelled, by the mere logic of things, to take, is easier, more inevitable, for him than for any other. The novelist, more than any other artist, is concerned directly with life. He has to watch the passions at work in the world, the shipwreck of ideals, the action of society upon man, of man upon society. When he is tired of considering these things with the unimpassioned eyes of the artist, he begins to concern himself about them very painfully: he becomes a moralist. Perhaps he has been one: he becomes a reformer.

Tolstoi's theory of art, then, is this: "There is one indubitable indication distinguishing real art from its counterfeit, namely, the infectiousness of art. If a man, without exercising effort and without altering his standpoint, on reading, hearing, or seeing another man's work, experiences a mental condition which unites him with that man, and with other people who also partake of that work of art, then the object evoking that condition is a work of art. . . . And not only is infection a sure sign of art, but the degree of infectiousness is also the sole measure of excellence in art." Art, thus distinguished, is to be divided into two classes; first, religious art, and secondly, universal art. "The first, religious art—transmitting both positive feelings of love to God and one's neighbour, and negative feelings of indignation and horror at the violation of love—manifests itself chiefly in the form of words, and to some extent also in painting and sculpture: the second kind (universal art), transmitting feelings accessible to all, manifests itself in words, in painting, in sculpture, in dances, in architecture, and, most of all, in music."

Now here is a theory which, in the cautious hands of most critics, would produce but one result. We should be told that, judged by such a standard, modern writers were all wrong and older writers all right; that Verlaine, Huysmans, Manet, Liszt, Rodin, had departed from the "obvious," or the "well-recognised," or the "inevitable," or the "classical" lines of religious and universal art, while Shakespeare, Goethe, Raphael, Bach, Michelangelo, remained, perfect in their several ways, to show us by their perfection the laws which our uncouth and extravagant generation had broken. But this is not at all what the theory really means, and Tolstoi shows us what it really means. Tolstoi shows us that on this theory we have to get rid of the "rude, savage, and, for us, often meaningless works of the ancient Greeks: Sophocles, Euripides, Æschylus, and especially Aristophanes; of modern writers, Dante, Tasso, Milton, Shakespeare"; in painting, Michelangelo's "absurd Last Judgment," and "every representation of miracles, including Raphael's 'Transfiguration'"; in music, everything but "Bach's famous violin *aria*, Chopin's nocturne in E flat major, and perhaps a dozen bits (not whole pieces, but parts) selected from the works of Haydn, Mozart, Schubert, Beethoven, and Chopin." On the other hand, we are to accept "as examples of the highest art, flowing from love of God and man (both of the higher, positive, and of the lower, negative kind)," in literature: "The Robbers," by Schiller, Victor Hugo's "Les Pauvres Gens" and "Les Misérables," the novels and stories of Dickens, "The Tale of Two Cities," "The Christmas Carol," "The Chimes," and others; "Uncle Tom's Cabin," Dostoieffski's works, especially his "Memoirs from the House of Death," and "Adam Bede," by George Eliot; in painting, a picture by Walter Langley, in the Royal Academy of 1897, "a picture by the French artist Morlon," pictures by Millet, "and, particularly, his drawing, 'The Man with the Hoe,' also pictures in this style by Jules Breton, L'Hermitte, Drefregger, and others"; all of which Tolstoi has seen only in reproductions.

Here, then, is what the theory really leads to; and it cannot be said that Tolstoi is less emphatic in his condemnation of contemporary art than of that art which we are accustomed to call classical. Wagner is "only a limited, self-opinionated German of bad taste and bad style"; Baudelaire and Verlaine were "two versifiers, who were far from skilful in form and most contemptible and commonplace in subject matter"; some of Kipling's short stories are "absolutely unintelligible both in form and in substance"; his own works are all bad art, except two short stories, "God sees the Truth," and "The Prisoner of the Caucasus"; and in one of his lists of "spurious counterfeits of art," we are scornfully told that "people of our time and of our society are delighted with Baudelaires, Verlaines, Moréases, Ibsens, and Maeterlincks in poetry; with Monets, Manets, Puvis de Chavannes, Burne-Joneses, Stucks and Böcklins in painting; with Wagners, Liszts, Richard Strausses, in music; and they are no longer capable of comprehending either the highest or the simplest art." A good deal of this is what we have so often heard, from such very different lips. But never before has any one been keen-sighted enough, and honest enough, to see and admit how logically one-half of this condemnation depends on the other. Our critics have condemned Wagner for the qualities by which they have come to praise Beethoven; Verlaine for the innovations which they applaud in Hugo; Rodin for the imagination which they adore in Michelangelo. It is only Tolstoi who sees that all these artists are obeying, in their various measures, in their various ways, the same laws; that to condemn one is to condemn all the others as well: and he condemns all.

II

Tolstoi's theory of art, which we have found to lead to what is practically the entire condemnation of art, with a few arbitrary exceptions, is based on a generous social doctrine of equality, a conviction of the "brotherhood of man," and a quite unjustifiable assumption that art is no more than "an organ of progress." To Tolstoi it seems astonishing that any one at the present day should be found to maintain the conception of beauty held by the Greeks; that "the very best that can be done by the art of nations after nineteen hundred years of Christian teaching is to choose as the ideal of their life the ideal that was held by a small, semi-savage, slave-holding people who lived two thousand years ago, who imitated the nude human body extremely well, and erected buildings pleasant to look at." Yet he himself selects as examples of "good, supreme art" the "Iliad," the "Odyssey," the stories of Isaac, Jacob, and Joseph, the Hebrew prophets, the Psalms, the Gospel parables, the story of Sakya Muni, and the hymns of the Vedas; and I do not think he would contend that his list of modern works of art (Dickens, Dostoieffski, George Eliot, "Uncle Tom's Cabin," and the rest) shows any artistic or spiritual advance upon those masterpieces of the very earliest ages. If, then, the only modern works which he admits to be written on sound principles cannot for a moment be compared with the ancient works to which he gives the same theoretic sanction, what room is left for astonishment that an ideal of art, divined two thousand years ago, should still remain essentially the highest ideal of art?

Closely linked with this confusion of art with progress is another application of Socialistic theories to questions of art, not less demonstrably false. "A good and lofty work of art," he tells us, "may be incomprehensible, but not to simple, unperverted labourers (all that is highest is understood by them)." And he declares that the "Iliad" and "Odyssey," the Bible narratives, including the Prophetic Books, and the other masterpieces of ancient art of which I have given his list, are "quite comprehensible now to us, educated or uneducated, as they were comprehensible to the men of those times, long ago, who were even less educated than our labourers." But such a statement is absolutely unjustifiable: it has no foundation in fact. The "Iliad," to an English labourer, would be completely unintelligible. Imagine him sitting down to the simplest translation which exists in English, the prose translation of Lang, Butcher, and Leaf; imagine him reading: "Upon the flaming chariot set she her foot, and grasped her heavy spear, great and stout, wherewith she vanquisheth the ranks of men, even of heroes with whom she of the awful sire is wroth!" To the English labourer the Bible comes with an authority which no other book possesses for him; he certainly reads it, but does he read with an intelligent pleasure, does he really understand, large portions of the Prophetic Books? It is as certain that he does not as it is certain that he does read with pleasure, and understand, the Gospel parables and the stories of Isaac, Jacob, and Joseph. But does this fact of his understanding one, and not understanding the other, set the parables higher as art than the Prophetic Books, or the stories of Isaac, Jacob, and Joseph higher than the "Iliad"? On Tolstoi's own theory it would do so, but would Tolstoi himself follow his theory to that extremity?

To such precipices are we led at every moment by the theory which makes feeling the test of art. Tolstoi tells us that he once saw a performance of "Hamlet" by Rossi, and that he "experienced all the time that peculiar suffering which is caused by false imitations of works of art." He read a description of a theatrical performanee by savages, and from the mere description he "felt that this was a true work of art." Is this quite fair to the instincts, is it not a little deliberate, a choice decided upon beforehand rather than a simple record of personal feeling? Even if it is a preference as instinctive as it is believed to be, of what value is the mere preference of one man, even a man of genius; and of what value in the defining of a work of art is it for any number of people to tell me that it has caused them a genuine emotion? Come with me to the Adelphi; there, in no matter what melodrama, you shall see a sorrowful or heroic incident, acted, as it seems to you, so livingly before you, that it shall make you hot or cold with suspense, or bring tears to your eyes. Yet neither you nor I shall differ in our judgment of the melodrama as a work of art; and Tolstoi, if he were to see it, would certainly condemn it, from his own point of view, as strongly as you or I. Yet it has answered, in your case or mine, to his own test of a work of art; and certainly, to the quite simple-minded or uneducated people there present, it has been accepted without any critical after-thought as entirely satisfying.

No, neither the uneducated judgment nor the instincts of the uneducated can ever come to have more than the very slightest value in the determination of what is true or false in art. A genuine democracy of social condition may or may not be practically possible; but the democracy of intellect, happily, is impossible. There, at all events, we must always find an aristocracy; there, at all events, the stultifying dead-weight of equality must for ever be spared to us. In material matters, even, in matters most within his reach, has the labourer ever been able to understand a machine, which he will come in time to prize for its service, until it has been laboriously explained to him, and, for the most part, forced upon him for his good? How, then, is he to understand a poem, which must always continue to seem to him a useless thing, useless at all events to him? Tolstoi, throughout the whole of this book on art, has tried to reduce himself intellectually, as, in practice, he has reduced himself socially, to the level of the peasant. And, with that extraordinary power of assimilation which the Russians possess, he has very nearly succeeded. It is a part of the Russian character to be able to live a fictitious life, to be more western than the Westerns, more sympathetic, out of indolence and the dramatic faculty, than one's intimate friends. And Tolstoi, who is in every way so typically a Russian, has in addition the genius of the novelist. So he is now putting himself in the place of the peasant, speaking through the peasant's mouth, in all these doctrines and theories, just as he used to put himself in the place of the peasant, and speak through the peasant's mouth, in his stories. The fatal difference is that, in the stories, he knew that he was speaking dramatically, while, in the doctrines and theories, he imagines that he is speaking in his own person.

1898.

A CENSOR OF CRITICS

In a polemical book called "Ephemera Critica; or, Plain Truths about Current Literature," Mr Churton Collins, the Timon of critics, "spoke out," with emphasis, on many questions. I am concerned with only one of them, and with him only as with a voice crying, very loudly, in the wilderness. Where I am concerned with Mr Collins is in his examination of current criticism, and in his protest against the manufacture of cheap reputations. He points scornfully to the spectacle of the ignorant applauding the ignorant, both comfortable in the ditch together. Only, he is a little apt to see bad intentions where there are really no intentions of any kind whatever. Mr Collins, as it seems to me, expends a good deal of needless anger over what he calls "the prevalence, or rather the predominance, of mere prejudice, the prejudice of cliques in favour of cliques, the prejudice of cliques against cliques." I do not believe much in cliques, so far as that word is used to represent a somewhat unfair or malicious banding together of persons professing the same loves or hates. The wicked clique is as empty a convention as the wicked baronet. Few baronets in real life, whatever their intentions, have the intellectual vigour and consistency attributed to them in fiction; they remain, as a rule, comparatively harmless. And cliques, if cliques exist, so far from pushing incompetence and frustrating competence for personal motives, or doing mischief for mischief's sake, are usually of the most pitiable honesty, and applaud what they really think to be good, condemn what they really think to be bad. I have not the slightest doubt that the supporters of what is, I believe, called the Kailyard School of fiction, have supported that school in all sincerity of admiration; that those persons who compare Mr Stephen Phillips with Milton, or, as Mr Churton Collins himself does, with Leopardi, do so in all simplicity; that there are dramatic critics who really consider Mr Pinero a dramatist of great intellectual capacity, superior on many points to Ibsen; musical critics who really imagine themselves to be moved by the music of Dr Parry or Sir Alexander Mackenzie; art critics who find it quite impossible to find merit in the sculpture of Rodin. I am more charitable than Mr Collins; where he sees perfidy and depravity, "the work of deliberate fraud," I can see only ignorance and bad taste, a helpless ignorance, a hopeless bad taste. Now taste can neither be acquired nor eradicated; it is an essence, not a property; once in existence, it can be trained to finer and subtler perceptions; but it must be born, like genius, and no one is responsible for its possession, any more than he is responsible for the colour of his eyes or hair. Ignorance is indeed a more remediable matter; but even here let us not be unjust. Few men are ignorant by preference, but rather by misfortune; and against misfortune, who is fully armed? Probably many of the hasty gentlemen who review books in the newspapers have a sincere envy of Mr Collins' knowledge of many literatures; but circumstances have not left them the leisure to attain that knowledge. Some of them, lacking knowledge, possess a certain measure of taste; there are others who, lacking taste, possess a certain measure of knowledge. And I maintain that, as a rule, these gentlemen do their best. They should be treated more gently; and, in particular, it should be explained to them that enthusiasm is a good thing, but that unintermittent enthusiasm tends to mental exhaustion.

Or, what if after all the newspaper critics are right, and Mr Collins and a few other people wrong? What if English literature has never known so brilliant an epoch as the present; what if the poets and novelists whom we meet or pass in the Strand or at the Authors' Club are really the greatest we have ever had? I will relate an experience which happened to me lately, just as it happened: was I perhaps nearer the truth then, in my ingenuous wonder, my trustful acceptance of a surprising piece of good news, than I am now, when reflection has brought back the old doubts again?

I do not often read novels, finding that the very interesting art of the novelist requires a closer attention in following its processes, with a more abundant leisure, than I care to give or happen to possess. When I do, however, read a novel it is generally a French one; and I confess that, up to the other day, I was under the impression that in following a natural preference I was also on the footsteps of wisdom. But, the other day, happening to take up a novel translated from the Norwegian, I found at the end of the volume thirty-two closely printed pages of advertisements, giving the opinions of the press on thirty-two English novels. The volume was dated a few years back, and the novels had been published, apparently, within a year or two of that date. I read these opinions of the press with a keen interest, which I found presently growing into something like astonishment, and when I had come to the end of them I began to wonder how I could possibly have overlooked so many works of so high a genius. The newspapers whose opinions I had been reading were the best-known newspapers in England; they seemed, so far as I could judge, to represent every kind of opinion throughout the country. Well, according to these newspapers, every one of these thirty-two books was, in its way, something of a masterpiece. "Mr Hall Caine," I read, "reaches heights which are attained only by the greatest masters of fiction. . . . I think of the great French writer Stendhal, at the same moment as the great English writer." It is Mr T. P. O'Connor who thinks of Stendhal at the same moment as of Mr Hall Caine; but the *Scotsman* is very bold, and goes further, finding another novel of the same writer "distinctly ahead of all the fictional literature of our time, and fit to rank with the most powerful fictional writing of the past century"; while the *Christian World* realises how great is the "fascination of being present, as it were, at the birth of a classic"; of "The Manxman" that is. Of another book by another writer, the *Daily Chronicle* assures me "It has not a dull page from first to last. Any one with normal health and taste can read a book like this with real pleasure"; while the *Westminster Gazette* and the *Speaker*, referring to, I should suppose, two singularly different books, declare, with singular unanimity of language, of one "that there is cleverness enough in it to furnish forth a dozen novels"; of the other, that the writer has "put enough observation, humour, and thought into this book to furnish forth half-a-dozen ordinary novels"; only half-a-dozen, it is true, this time. Then the *Globe* tells me, of yet another story, that "this is a remarkable story—a story that fascinates, tingling with life, steeped in sympathy with all that is best and saddest"; I turn the page, I see the name of yet another story, and here it is the *Standard* assuring me that this too is "a remarkable story; it abounds with dramatic situations, the interest never for a moment flags, and the characters are well drawn and consistent." Robert Louis Stevenson is on the next page, and of him I read neither more nor less than of all the others. But on the next page I find Mr Zangwill, and the *Queen* "has not the least doubt that 'The Master' will always be reckoned one of our classics." Before a book of Mr Henry James the *Manchester Guardian* can only gasp: "To attempt to criticise a creation so exquisite, so instinct with the finest and purest human feeling, so penetrated with the fastidious distinction of a sensitive spirit, would indeed be superfluous, if not impertinent." The *Manchester Courier* is more explicit, and discovers that Mrs Lynn Linton "writes with all the bitterness of Dean Swift"; and the *Pall Mall Gazette* discovers that Mr C. F. Keary "is less witty than Mr Meredith, but more responsible"; and the *Times* and the *World*, in almost the same words, mention that a novel of Mr W. E. Tirebuck is "the most remarkable contribution made by fiction to the history of the working classes since 'Mary Barton'" ("since Mrs Gaskell wrote her 'Mary Barton' we have seen no more interesting novel on the condition of the working classes"), "and it has a wider range and import of deeper gravity." After this it cannot surprise us that one book "must be pronounced," by the *Daily Chronicle*, "an almost unqualified triumph"; and that the *World* finds without difficulty "a work to which the much-used adjective 'beautiful' may be applied with full intention and strict justice."

It is doubtless my loss that, not being a novel reader, I have not read more than two out of the thirty-two novels of which, I suddenly realise, such wonderfully attractive things have been said. One of these books I certainly admired, the other I did not. A few of the others I have taken up; and, it now appears, laid down too hastily; for it did not occur to me to continue reading them. In the future, I fear, I shall have but little time for my French novels; for I confess that, interesting as I found some of them in their degree, I should not have been disposed to apply anything like the same unqualified praise to any one of them which all these critics apply to every one of the thirty-two English works. I therefore feel it my duty (I am sure it will be my privilege) to turn my attention at once to contemporary English novels; and, these critics impress upon me, I shall have no difficulty of choice: all are good, almost all are supremely good. Nothing, for a long time, has interested me so much as this sudden renaissance of the novel in England; or, should I say, in all modesty, my sudden discovery of it? During the whole of the nineteenth century, prior to this year of grace, there have been perhaps a dozen novelists whom the world in general has agreed to consider more or less novelists of the first rank. Here, in one publisher's list, are twice that number of writers, about each of whom our responsible critics have spoken in terms which would only barely escape flattery if applied to all but the greatest of the others. I repeat: all this has interested me profoundly, for, assuming that one publisher is not alone in publishing for men and women of genius, how incalculable must be the number of great novelists now writing in England, their very names, perhaps, unknown to others as ill-informed in these matters as myself!

Now who is right, these gentlemen with their enthusiasm, or Mr Collins with his little suggestion about "hyperbole heaped on hyperbole, rhodomontade on rhodomontade," his statement: "It is not that a good book will not be praised, but that bad books are praised still more"; his conclusion: "Measured and discriminating eulogy, which means precisely what it expresses, and which is always the note of sound and just criticism, is to the uninitiated poor recommendation compared with that which has no limitation but extremes"? If these gentlemen are wrong, if they have no clearer sense of what they are saying than the foreigner who begins his crescendo of eulogy with "splendid," "superb," "magnificent," and ends it with "nice," then may not Mr Collins be within measurable distance of the truth in saying of much contemporary criticism: "Without standards, without touchstones, without principles, without knowledge, it appears to be regarded as the one calling for which no equipment and no training are needed"? "As a rule the men who write bad books are the men who criticise bad books," he reminds us; and again: "The writer of a single good book is soon forgotten by his contemporaries; but the writer of a series of bad books is sure of reputation and emolument." Is or is not all this true? Is there any remedy for it? Is there any likelihood that the remedy will be found and applied?

Mr Collins tells us, as if he were telling us something startling, that "the sole encouragement now left to authors to produce good books is the satisfaction of their own conscience, and the approbation of a few discerning judges." But has not that, with a very few exceptions, always been the case? Good art, except sometimes the very greatest, so great that it possesses every quality, even commercial value, has never been a money-making commodity. A choice lies before the artist, if that can be called choice where the true artist will never know what it is to hesitate at the parting of the ways. There has never been a time or a country where the populace has wanted beauty, has wanted, that is, any form of art. Mr Collins himself points out that, at the great epochs, in the Athens of Pericles, the Rome of Augustus, the Florence of the Medici, art was made for the few good judges, not for the judgment of the crowd; and it was the good fortune of the artists that there was a Pericles, an Augustus, a Pope of the Medici, who happened to care greatly for art. Even in our own days there was a king who cared greatly for art, who made it possible for Wagner to conquer the world during his own lifetime, and on his own terms; who made possible the greatest achievement in art of our times. People said he was mad: that is the difference; they deposed him and allowed him to drown himself. No doubt he ruled Bavaria with a certain eccentricity; he built many expensive palaces, and was unconventional in his methods, and sometimes disturbed the sleep of his people by driving noisily past their windows at night; but he did no great wrong to his nation or to the world, caused no bloodshed, had none of the typical vices and bourgeois ambitions which bring about great calamities meanly; and he was a prince to art. There has been no other since Louis XIV., and thus the populace has never had art thrust upon it. Why, then, should it be expected to encourage or support artists? There was a time when it was the custom for the impoverished man of letters to appeal to the charity of some wealthy and instructed nobleman. The custom has changed, and yet, still, is not a painter of originality often obliged to depend for long periods on the intelligent generosity of a single buyer? The public has never known good art from bad; it has never, of its own accord, encouraged good art; it is unreasonable to expect that it ever will. The present time is not exceptional in its disregard for good art; there it is but repeating history. Where it is exceptional is in its creation of a new order of merit, in its assumption that, as Mr Collins says, "the criteria of the multitude need be the only criteria of what is addressed to the multitude," in its enfranchisement of ignorance grown restless with new ambitions.

The world is becoming more and more democratic, and with democracy art has nothing to do. What is written for the crowd goes to the crowd; it lives its bustling day there, and is forgotten, like to-day's newspaper to-morrow. The catalogue of novels which I chanced to take up was some few years old; if I turned to the catalogue which has replaced it, I am sure that I should see the same eulogies, but on other, newer books. For the first time in the history of the world, as Mr Collins points out, the crowd has found for itself a loud, multitudinous voice. It has thrown off its chains, the chains of good taste; it has won liberty, the liberty to misbehave. It is sick of enduring the sight of masterpieces; it is weary of waiting for some new excellence to be discovered for its admiration. It is powerful now, it must have its own bread and games, and the slave's revenge on its masters. Books multiply, praise is tossed about; but the artist stands aside, not even *hors concours*, because there are no longer any judges, or their voice is drowned by the gabble of the jurymen, as they disagree among themselves, and refer the verdict to the bystanders.

1901.

WHAT IS POETRY?

A SCHOLARLY critic, Mr W. J. Courthope, wrote a book called "Life in Poetry: Law in Taste," in which he tried to prove that "the secret of life in poetry lies in the power to give individual form to universal ideas of nature adapted for expression in any of the recognised classes of metrical composition." By the words life in poetry, he told us, "I mean the qualities in poetry, whatsoever they are, whencesoever they are derived, which have the power of producing enduring pleasure; and I have endeavoured to ascertain their nature by examining the works of poets who have been acknowledged, *semper, ubique, ab omnibus*, to be the living poets of the world." Mr Courthope, who has edited Pope, naturally brings Pope into the question, and gives away much of his argument by doing so. He finds in Pope both his "life" and his "universal," and he apologises for the "limited idea of Nature, of the Universal," which he does, in a way, acknowledge, by saying, first, that "this restriction of knowledge to self-knowledge is only the completion of a tendency of thought which reveals itself in 'Paradise Lost'"; and, secondly, that Pope's idea of Nature must be compared only with that of "the false wits of the seventeenth century, Phineas and Giles Fletcher, Donne, Crashaw, Quarles, and Cowley." But the question really is, whether Pope is, in the true sense, a poet at all; whether the prose force and finish of his character of Atticus, quoted elsewhere in the book, are, simply as poetry, the equivalent of the lines of Crashaw "On a Prayer-book sent to Mrs R.," quoted as self-evidently ridiculous. I would assert that the two last lines of this quotation,

> "Dropping with a balmy shower
> A delicious dew of spices,"

represent a level of poetry to which Pope never attained, in spite of his consummate ability. Pope is the most finished artist in prose who ever wrote in verse. It is impossible to read him without continuous admiration for his cleverness, or to forget, while reading him, that poetry cannot be clever. While Crashaw, with two instinctively singing lines, lets us overhear that he is a poet, Pope brilliantly convinces us of everything that he chooses, except of that one fact. The only moments when he trespasses into beauty are the moments when he mocks its affectations; so that

> "Die of a rose in aromatic pain"

remains his homage, unintentional under its irony, to that "principle of beauty in all things" which he had never seen.

In discussing the nature and function of metre, Mr Courthope quotes from Marlowe:

> "Was this the face that launched a thousand ships,
> And burned the topless towers of Ilium?"

and tells us: "It is certain that he could only have ventured on the sublime audacity of saying that a face launched ships and burned towers by escaping from the limits of ordinary language, and conveying his metaphor through the harmonious and ecstatic movements of rhythm and metre." Now, on the contrary, any writer of elevated prose, Milton or Ruskin, could have said in prose precisely what Marlowe said, and made fine prose of it; the imagination, the idea, a fine kind of form, would have been there; only one thing would have been lacking, the very finest kind of form, the form of verse. It would have been poetical substance, not poetry; the rhythm transforms it into poetry, and nothing but the rhythm.

Poetry is first of all an art, and, in art, there must be a complete marriage or interpenetration of substance and form. The writer like Walt Whitman, who seems to contain so much material for poetry, which he can never shape into anything tangibly perfect, is not less disqualified from the name of poet than a writer like Pope, who has the most exquisite control over an unpoetical kind of form which exactly fits an unpoetical kind of substance. Crashaw, who had poetical substance of a particular kind, with only an intermittent power over it, remains a genuine but imperfect poet, whom we must sift with discrimination. Milton, who has almost every quality of form, and many of the finest qualities of substance, becomes the great poet whom he is universally admitted to be, because he is almost always successful in the fusion of substance and form.

It is only after this intimate union has been consummated that we can begin to consider relative qualities of merit. The writer of one perfect song in one of the Elizabethan song-books is a poet, but, if he has written no more, or no more of such merit, he will remain a small, a limited poet. Pollok's "Course of Time" may be as long as "Paradise Lost," but Pollok does not enter into the competition. In distinguishing between poet and poet, in the somewhat fruitless task of assigning places, Mr Courthope's rules, among others, come fairly into use. They are useless in distinguishing what is poetry from what is not poetry, and they would be useless in the presence of any new writer claiming to be a poet.

It is less difficult to be just to Virgil and Milton than to be just to Verlaine or to Mr Yeats. Nor will the mere testing of Mr Yeats or of Verlaine by Milton or by Virgil avail to keep the critic to the truth. Every new force has its own novel form of beauty, and if our latest poet is not essentially different from his predecessors, no amount of affinity to them will save him. It is profoundly important, as Mr Courthope asserts, to examine and to keep in mind "the works of poets who have been acknowledged, *semper*, *ubique*, *ab omnibus*, to be the living poets of the world"; but it is not less important to be on the watch for every stirring of new life, whether or not our reading has prepared us for it, in the form in which we find it.

1901.

CAMPOAMOR

RAMÓN DE CAMPOAMOR Y CAMPOOSORIO, who died at Madrid on the 12th of February 1901, was born at Navia, in the province of Asturias, on the 24th of September 1817. His career covers almost the whole century: he was the contemporary of Quintana, Espronceda, Zorrilla, yet absolutely untouched by the influences which made of Quintana a lesser Cowper, of Espronceda a lesser Byron, and of Zorrilla a lesser Longfellow. Coming into a literature in which poetry is generally taken to be but another name for rhetoric, he followed, long before Verlaine, Verlaine's advice to "take rhetoric and wring its neck." The poetry of words, of sounds, of abstractions, that poetry which is looked upon in Spain as the most really poetical kind of poetry, left him untouched; he could but apply to it the Arab proverb: "I hear the tic-tac of the mill, but I see no flour." In his "Poética" he declares, boldly: "If we except the *Romancero* and the *cantares*, Spain has almost no really national lyric poetry." "There are very well-built verses, that are lads of sound body, but without a soul. Such are those of Herrera and of almost all his imitators, the grandiloquent poets." In the simple masculine verse of Jorge Manrique (whose great poem, the "Coplas por la muerte de su Padre," is known to most English readers in its admirable translation by Longfellow) he saw an incomparable model, whose grave and passionate simplicity might well have been the basis of a national style. "Poetry," he declares, in what seemed to his critics an amusing paradox, "is the rhythmical representation of a thought through the medium of an image, expressed in a language which cannot be put in prose more naturally or with fewer words. . . . There is in poetry no immortal expression that can be said in prose with more simplicity or with more precision." Prose, indeed, seemed to him not really an art at all, and when Valera, a genuine artist in prose, defended his own ground by asserting that "metaphysics is the one useless science, and poetry the one useless art," Campoamor replied in verse, defining prose as "la jerga animal del ser humano" ("the jabber of the human animal"). "What are philosophical systems," he asks, "but poems without images?" and, protesting against the theory of "art for art," and suggesting "art for ideas," or "transcendental" art, as a better definition of what was at least his own conception, he sums up with his customary neatness: "Metaphysics is the science of ideas, religion is the science of ideas converted into sentiments, and art the science of ideas converted into images. Metaphysics is the true, religion the good, and æsthetics the beautiful." By calling art "transcendental" he means, not that it should be in itself either philosophical or didactic, much less abstract, for "art is the enemy of abstractions, . . . and whatever becomes impersonal evaporates," but that it should contain in itself, as its foundation, a "universal human truth," without which "it is no more than the letters of tattling women." "All lyric poetry should be a little drama." "In the drama of the Creation everything was written by God in sympathetic ink. We have but to apply the reagent, and hold it to the light. The best artist is the best translator of the works of God." "It has been my constant endeavour," he tells us, "to approach art through ideas, and to express them in ordinary language, thus revolutionising the substance and form of poetry, the substance with the *Doloras* and the form with the *Pequeños Poemas*." Beginning at first with fables, he abandoned the form of the fable, because it seemed to him that the fable could only take root in countries in which the doctrine of the transmigration of souls was still believed. "The *Dolora*, a drama taken direct from life, without the metaphors and symbols of indirect poetry, seemed to me a form more European, more natural, and more human than that of the oriental fable." But the *Dolora* was to retain thus much of the fable, that by means of its drama it was to "solve some universal problem," the solution growing out of the actual structure of the story. Thus, in poetry, subject is all-important, subject including "the argument and the action." "In every pebble of the brook there is part of an Escurial: the difficulty and the merit are in building it." "Novelty of subject, regularity of plan, the method with which that plan is carried out": these, together with the fundamental idea, which is to be of universal application, "transcendental," as he calls it, are the requisites of a work of art; it is on these grounds that a work of art is to be judged. "Every work of art should be able to reply affirmatively to these four questions:

The subject: can it be narrated?
The plan: can it be painted?
The design: has it a purpose?
The style: is it the man?"

Campoamor was no classical scholar, and it is but hesitatingly that he suggests, on the authority of "a French critic, who had it from Aristotle," that the theory of the Greeks in poetry was in many points similar to his. If we turn to Matthew Arnold's preface to his Poems, we shall find all that is fundamental in Campoamor's argument stated finally, and in the form of an appeal to classical models. "The radical difference between their poetical theory" (the Greeks', that is) "and ours consists, it appears to me, in this: that with them the poetical character of the action in itself, and the conduct of it, were the first consideration; with us attention is fixed mainly on the value of the separate thoughts and images which occur in the treatment of an action." And, further on in that admirable preface, Matthew Arnold assures "the individual writer" that he "may certainly learn of the ancients, better than anywhere else, three things which it is vitally important for him to know: the all-importance of the choice of a subject, the necessity of accurate construction, and the subordinate character of expression." Is not this precisely the aim of Campoamor? and is it not as a natural corollary to this severe theory of poetical construction that he tells us: "Style is not a question of figures of speech, but of electric fluid"; "rhythm alone should separate the language of verse from that of prose"; yet that language should have always an inner beauty, "the mysterious magic of music, so that it should say, not what the writer intends, but what the reader desires"? And so we come, not unnaturally, to his ideal in writing: "To write poems whose ideas and whose words had been, or seemed to have been, thought or written by every one."

Upon these theories, it might well seem to us, a writer is left at all events free, and with a very reasonable kind of liberty, to make the most of himself. Only, after all, the question remains: What was Campoamor's conception of subject and development; how far was his precision a poetical precision; did he, in harmonising the language of prose and of verse, raise the one or lower the other?

The twelve volumes of Campoamor's collected poems contain "El Drama Universal," a sort of epic in eight "days" and forty-seven scenes, written in heroic quatrains, and worthy, a Spanish critic assures us, of "an Ariosto of the soul"; "Colon," a narrative poem in sixteen cantos, written in *ottava rima;* "El Licenciado Torralba," a legendary poem in eight cantos, written in iambic verse of varying length; three series of "Pequeños Poemas," each containing from ten to twelve narrative poems written in a similar form of verse; two series of "Doloras," short lyrical poems, of which I have already quoted his own definition; a volume of "Humoradas," containing some hundreds of epigrams; and two volumes of early work, brought together under the name of "Poesias y Fábulas." Besides these, he wrote some plays, the admirable volume called "Poética: Polémicas Literárias," and a contribution to metaphysics called "Lo Absoluto." Of his long poems, only one is what Rossetti called "amusing," only "El Licenciado Torralba" has that vital energy which keeps a poem alive. With this exception we need consider only the three collections in which a single thing, a consistent "criticism of life," is attempted under different but closely allied forms: the "Humoradas," which are epigrams; the "Doloras," which he defines as "dramatised 'Humoradas'"; and the "Pequeños Poemas," which he defines as "amplified 'Doloras.'"

Applied by a great poetical intellect, Campoamor's theories might have resulted in the most masterly of modern poems; but his intellect was ingenious rather than imaginative; his vivid human curiosity was concerned with life more after the manner of the novelist than of the poet; his dramas are often anecdotes; his insight is not so much wisdom as worldly wisdom. He "saw life steadily," but he saw it in little patches, commenting on facts with a smiling scepticism which has in it something of the positive spirit of the eighteenth century. Believing, as he tells us, that "what is most natural in the world is the supernatural," he was apt to see the spiritual side of things, as the Spanish painters have mostly seen it, in a palpable detachment from the soil, garlanded in clouds. Concerned all his life with the moods and casuistries of love, he writes of women, not of woman, and ends, after all, in a reservation of judgment. Poetry, to him, was a kind of psychology, and that is why every lyric shaped itself naturally into what he called a drama. His whole interest was in life and the problems of life, in people and their doings, and in the reasons for what they do. Others, he tells us, may admire poetry which is descriptive, the delineation of external things, or rhetorical, a sonorous meditation over abstract things; all that he himself cares for are "those reverberations that light up the windings of the human heart and the horizons that lie on the other side of material life." Only, some imaginative energy being lacking, all this comes, for the most part, to be a kind of novelette in verse, in the "Pequeños Poemas," a versified allegory, in the "Doloras," or an epigram, in the "Humoradas."

Can verse in which there is no ecstasy be poetry? There is no ecstasy in the verse of Campoamor; at the most a talking about ecstasy, as in some of the "Pequeños Poemas," in which stories of passion are told with exquisite neatness, precision, sympathetic warmth; but the passion never cries out, never finds its own voice. Once only in his work do I find something like that cry, and it is in "El Licenciado Torralba," the story of a kind of Faust, who, desiring love without unrest, makes for himself an artificial woman ("la mujer mas mujer de las mujeres") *Muliercula*, to whom he gives

"el ánimo del bello paganismo,
que, siendo ménos que alma, es mas que vida."

Torralba is arrested by the Inquisition as a necromancer, and Muliercula is burnt at the stake. I have translated the description of her death:

"Midmost, as if the flame of the burning were
A bed of love to her,
Muliercula, with calm, unfrightened face,
Not without beauty stood,
And her meek attitude
Had something of the tiger's natural grace.
She suffers, yet, no less,
Dying for him she loves, broods there,
Within the burning air,
Quiet as a bird within a wilderness.
The wild beast's innocency all awake
Enraps her, and as she burns,
The intermittent flaming of the stake
To the poor fond foolish thing now turns
Into a rapture, dying for his sake;
And then, because the instinct in her sees
This only to be had,
Nothingness and its peace,
For her last, surest end, utterly glad,
With absolute heart and whole,
That body without a soul,
As if the bright flame brings
Roses to be its bed,
Dies, and so enters, dead,
Into the august majesty of things!"

There, in that fantastic conception of "la belleza natural perfecta" of woman, as the thinker, above all others, has desired to find her, I seem to discover the one passionate exception to Campoamor's never quite real men and women, the novelist's lay-figures of passion, about whom we are told so many interesting anecdotes. A witty story-teller, a sympathetic cynic, a transcendental positivist, he found the ways of the world the most amusing spectacle in nature, and for the most part his poems are little reflections of life seen as he saw it, with sharp, tolerant, worldly eyes. At his best, certainly most characteristic, when he is briefest, as in the "Humoradas," he has returned, in these polished fragments, to the lapidary style of Latin poetry, reminding us at times of another Spaniard, Martial. Idea, clearness, symmetry, point, give to this kind of verse something of the hardness and glitter of a weapon, even when the intention is not satirical. With Campoamor the blade is tossed into the air and caught again, harmlessly, with all the address of an accomplished juggler. He plays with satire as he plays with sentiment, and, when he is most serious, will disguise the feeling with some ironical afterthought. Here are some of the "Humoradas," in Spanish and English. I have translated them, as will be seen, quite literally, and I have tried to choose them from as many moods as I could.

"*Al mover tu abanico con gracejo*
Quitas el polvo al corazon mas viejo."

"You wave your fan with such a graceful art,
You brush the dust off from the oldest heart."

"*Las niñas de las madres que amé tanto*
Me besan ya como se besan á un santo."

"The children of the mothers I loved, ah see,
They kiss me as though they kissed a saint in me!"

"*Jamas mujer alguna*
Ha salido del todo de la cuna."

"No woman yet, since they were made all,
Has ever got quite outside of the cradle."

"*Prohibes tu amor con tus desdenes.*
Sin frutos prohibidos no hay Edenes."

"Let your consent with your disdain be hidden:
No Paradise whose fruit is not forbidden."

"*No le gusta el placer sin violéncia,*
Y por eso y á cree la desgraciada
Que ni es pasion, ni es nada,
El amor que no turba la conciéncia."

"She tastes not pleasure without strife,
And therefore, hapless one, she feels
That love's not good enough for life
Which hales not conscience by the heels."

"*Si es fácil una hermosa,*
Voy y la dejo;
Si es difícil la cosa,
Tambien me alejo,
Niñas, cuidad
De amar siempre con fácil
Dificultad."

"If too easy she should be,
I, beholding, quit her;
If the thing's too hard for me,
Trying proves too bitter.
Girls, now see,
Best it is to love with easy
Difficulty."

"*Niegas que fuiste mi mejor amiga?*
Bien, bien; lo callaré: nobleza obliga."

"That you were my best friend, do you deny?
Well, well; noblesse oblige; then so will I."

"*Te he visto no sé donde, ni sé cuando.*
Ah! si; ya lo recuerdo, fué soñando."

"Have I not seen you? Yes, but where and when?
Ah, I remember: I was dreaming then."

"*Te es infiel! y la quieres? No me extraña;*
Yo adoro á la esperanza, aunqué me engaña."

"She's faithless, and you love her? As you will:
Hope I adore, and hope is faithless still."

"*Vas cambiando de amor todos los años,*
Mas no cambias jamas de desengaños."

"You change your love each year; yet Love's commandment
Is, that you never change your disenchantment."

"*Por él la simetria es la belleza,*
Aunqué corte á las cosas la cabeza."

"Beauty for him was symmetry, albeit
He sometimes cut the heads off things, to see it."

I will add three short pieces from the "Doloras."

"Shamed though I be, and weep for shame, 'tis true,
I loved not good what evil I love in you."

"They part; years pass; they do not see
Each other: after six or seven:
'Good Heaven! and is it really he?'
'And is it really she? good Heaven!'"

The Soul for Sale.

"One day to Satan, Julio, flushed with wine:
'Wilt buy my soul?' 'Of little worth is it.'
'I do but ask one kiss, and it is thine.'
'Old sinner, hast thou parted with thy wit?'
'Wilt buy it?' 'No.' 'But wherefore?' 'It is mine.'"

In such work as this there is much of what the Spaniards call "salt": it stings healthily, it is sane, temperate, above all, ingenious; and the question as to whether or not it is poetry resolves itself into a question as to whether or not the verse of Martial, indeed Latin epigrammatic verse in general, is poetry. To the modern mind, brought up on romantic models, only Catullus is quite certainly or quite obviously a poet in his epigrams; and his appeal to us is as personal as the appeal of Villon. He does not generalise, he does not smile while he stabs; the passion of love or hate burns in him like a flame, setting the verse on fire. Martial writes for men of the world; he writes in order to comment on things; his form has the finish of a thing made to fulfil a purpose. Campoamor also writes out of a fruitful experience, not transfiguring life where he reflects it. If what he writes is not poetry, in our modern conception of the word, it has at least the beauty of adjustment to an end, of perfect fitness; and it reflects a temperament, not a great poetical temperament, but one to which human affairs were infinitely interesting, and their expression in art the one business of life.

1901.

Robert Bridges

ROBERT BRIDGES

Mr Bridges appears to me, in his "Shorter Poems," to be alone in our time as a writer of purely lyric poetry, poetry which aims at being an "embodied joy," a calm rapture. Others have concerned themselves with passions more vehement, with thoughts more profound, with a wilder music, a more variable colour; others have been romantic, realistic, classical, and tumultuous; have brought a remote magic into verse, and have made verse out of sorrowful things close at hand. But while all these men have been singing themselves, and what they have counted most individual in themselves, this man has put into his verse only what remains over when all the others have finished. It is a kind of essence; it is what is imperishable in perfume; it is what is nearest in words to silence. Of the writer of "Will love again awake," or "I love all beauteous things," you know no more than you know of the writer of "Kind are her answers," or of "O Love, they wrong thee much," in the Elizabethan song-books. You know only that joy has come harmoniously into a soul, which, for the moment at least, has been purged of everything less absolute than the sheer responsiveness of song. And so, better than the subtlest dramatist, the lyric poet, in his fine, self-sacrificing simplicity, can speak for all the world, scarcely even knowing that he is speaking for himself at all. And in this poetry, it should be noted, nothing is allowed for its own sake, not even the most seductive virtue, as pathos, the ecstasy of love or of religion; but everything for the sake of poetry. Here is an artist so scrupulous that beauty itself must come only in sober apparel, joy only walking temperately, sorrow without the private disfiguring of tears. Made, as it is, out of what might be the commonplace, if it were not the most select thing in the world; written, as it is, with a deliberateness which might be cold if it were not at that quiet heat in which rapture is no longer astonished at itself; realising, as it does, Coleridge's requirement that "poetry in its higher and purer sense" should demand "continuous admiration, not regular recurrence of conscious surprise"; this poetry, more than almost any in English, is art for art's sake; and it shows, better certainly than any other, how that formula saves from excess, rather than induces to it. So evenly are form and substance set over against one another that it might be said, with as much or as little justice, that everything exists for form, or that nothing is sacrificed to it.

Listen, for instance, to a song which gives us Mr Bridges at his best:

"I have loved flowers that fade,
Within whose magic tents
Rich hues have marriage made
With sweet unmemoried scents.
A honeymoon delight,—
A joy of love at sight,
That ages in an hour:—
My song be like a flower!

I have loved airs, that die
Before their charm is writ
Along a liquid sky
Trembling to welcome it.
Notes, that with pulse of fire
Proclaim the spirit's desire,
Then die, and are nowhere:—
My song be like an air!

Die, song, die like a breath,
And wither as a bloom:
Fear not a flowery death,
Dread not an airy tomb!
Fly with delight, fly hence!
'Twas thine love's tender sense
To feast; now on thy bier
Beauty shall shed a tear."

Technique in the writing of a song which shall be simply a song, and in the purity and subtlety of style, can go no further; every word seems to be chosen for its beauty, and yet, if we look into it, is chosen equally for its precision; every word sings, and yet says what it means, as clearly as if it had no musical notes to attend to. And here, as elsewhere in Mr Bridges' work, every epithet has at once originality and distinction, a gentlemanly air of ease at finding itself where it is, though in a society wholly new to it. "Magic tents," for the enveloping petals of a flower; the word "unmemoried," used of scents, to which it is common to attribute the memories they awaken or recall in human minds; "faint attire of frightened fire," used of the palm willow in spring; the vision of "uncanopied sleep flying from field and tree" at dawn; the "astonisht" Saracen, whom the Crusader, before

"His hands by death were charm'd
To leave his sword at rest,"

crossed the sea to send into hell; the "soft unchristen'd smile" of Eros: all these unusual and inevitable epithets, each an act of the imagination, sharp, unerring, but never surprising, seem to unite in themselves just those contrary qualities which should combine to make perfect style in verse. Mr Meredith, caring mostly for originality, invents for every noun an adjective which has never run in harness with it, and which champs and rears intractably at its side. Mr Swinburne, preferring what goes smoothly to what comes startlingly from a distance, chooses his epithets for their sound and for their traditional significance, their immediate appeal, sensuous or intellectual. Mr Bridges obtains his delicate, evasively simple effects by coaxing beautiful, alien words to come together willingly, and take service with him, as if they had been born under his care.

Unlike most poets, Mr Bridges is a cultivated musician, and has, indeed, twice written the "book of words" for music: once for Sir Villiers Stanford's oratorio, "Eden," and once, in the form of a Purcell Ode, for the setting of Sir Hubert Parry. Neither experiment is altogether fortunate, but the study of music has taught Mr Bridges what the daily practice of it taught the song-writers of the age of Elizabeth: a delicate, and in time instinctive, sense of the musical value of words and syllables, the precise singing quality of rhythms, with all kinds of dainty tricks, which, if they come at all, can come only by some rare accident to the song-writer who is not a musician. To Mr Bridges it is part of his science, of his equipment as an artist. I doubt if many of his effects, irresponsible as they often come to seem, have come to him in his sleep; it is almost a point of honour with him, the artist's scrupulous honour, to know beforehand what he is going to do, and to do it precisely as he decides upon doing it.

Mr Bridges' style in verse has been said to lack originality, and it is true that his finest lyrics might have found their place among the lyrics in an Elizabethan song-book. And yet they are not archaic, a going back to the external qualities of style, but a thinking back, as of one who really, in thought, lives in another age, to which his temper of mind is more akin. They are very personal, but personal in a way so abstract, so little dependent on the accidents of what we call personality, that it seems the most natural thing in the world for him to turn to a style which comes to him with a great, anonymous tradition. He has never had that somewhat prosaic desire to paint himself "with all the warts," and he is quite indifferent to the self-consciousness which goes by the name of originality. Just as, in his plays, he borrows frankly from any one who deals in his own merchandise, so in his lyrics he tries to write only what might have been written in any time or in any country. In the note to "Achilles in Scyros" we read: "One passage in my play (I. 518 and foll.) is an imitation of Calderon; but this is after Muley's well-known speech in the *Principe Constante*, which is quoted in most books on Calderon." He seems almost impersonal in his work, indifferent whose it is, his own or another's, as if only its excellence interested him. And this work, when it is most narrowly personal, does not so much render moods of a temperament as aspects of a character. Nobility of character, a moral largeness, which becomes one with an intellectual breadth, a certain gravity, simplicity, sincerity: these count for so much in his work, which indeed they seem to make. Here is a poem, strangely named "The Affliction of Richard," which gives us, with spare dignity, all this side of Mr Bridges' work:

"Love not too much. But how,
When thou hast made me such,
And dost thy gifts bestow,
How can I love too much?
Though I must fear to lose,
And drown my joy in care,
With all its thorns I choose
The path of love and prayer.

Though thou, I know not why,
Didst kill my childish trust,
That breach with toil did I
Repair, because I must:
And spite of frighting schemes,
With which the fiends of Hell
Blaspheme thee in my dreams,
So far I have hoped well.

But what the heavenly key,
What marvel in me wrought
Shall quite exculpate thee,
I have no shadow of thought.
What am I that complain?
The love, from which began
My question sad and vain,
Justifies thee to man."

There are no heats of passion, no outcries, but an equable sensitiveness to fine emotions; a kind of brooding, almost continual ecstasy, the quietest ecstasy known to me in poetry. He demands, and seems to attain,

"Simple enjoyment calm in its excess,
With not a grief to cloud, and not a ray
Of passion overhot my peace to oppress;
With no ambition to reproach delay,
Nor rapture to disturb my happiness."

But, among all these suave negatives, he finds or makes for himself an astringent quality of austere self-control. It is with a kind of religious fervour, as of one expressing an old, settled belief, that he says, in perhaps his best-known lyric:

"I love all beauteous things,
I seek and adore them;
God hath no better praise,
And man in his hasty days
Is honoured for them.

I too will something make
And joy in the making;
Altho' to-morrow it seem
Like the empty words of a dream
Remembered on waking."

Made, as it is, on so firm a basis of a character, his art is concerned with results rather than (as with most lyric poets) with processes. How many of his poems seem to lead from meditation straight to action; to be expressing something more definite, more formed and settled, than a feeling divorced from consequences! When, as so often, he finds words for an almost inarticulate delight, it is, for the most part, no accidental but rather an organic delight to which he gives utterance: the response of nature to his nature, of his nature to nature.

Mr Bridges' art is made for simple thoughts, and direct, though delicate, emotions; these it renders with a kind of luminous transparency; when the thought or emotion becomes complex the form becomes complicated, and all the subtlety of its simplicity goes out of it, as a new kind of subtlety endeavours to come in. Mr Bridges' poetic heat is intermittent, and thus his felicity; for all charm in verse, however "frail and careful," is born of some energy at white heat. At rare times, even in the short poems, and not only in so long a poem as, for instance, "Prometheus the Firegiver," one feels that the wave of thought or emotion does not flow broadly and strongly to the end, but breaks on the way. And so the plays, with all their meditative and lyrical beauty, their quaint, delicate dialogue, a grave playing with love and life, a serious trifling, bookish and made for an artist's pleasure, remain, for the most part, interesting experiments, not achievements. Singularly insubstantial things, spun out of gossamer, a web of dainty thoughts and song-like meditations about passion, with a somewhat uncertain humour spinning it, they seem to have been made for the sake of making them, as a poet might write Latin verses.

By the way one finds all manner of delightful things, unsubstantial things, things which seem unessential, but which, all the same, have an enchantment and a wisdom of their own. There is always delight in reading any verse which Mr Bridges writes, however he writes it; it will have something at least of the unseizable form of poetry; that is to say, of the true spirit of poetry. He thinks in verse; he writes verse learnedly and instinctively. Ordinary things when he says them take on a gravity which is not the gravity of even the best prose; they have air about them, and they sing out of the air. The words in these plays are for the most part very simple, the things said are very simple; but beauty is rarely absent from them. Often enough it is a beauty of mere adjustment; the ordinary appropriate thing is said fittingly. Only occasionally does any exceptional beauty come into the work, from which, indeed, it seems to be deliberately excluded. Part of the charming, disconcerting manner of the plays consists in precisely this ordinary unemphatic manner of writing, this poetry which would be so very near prose if it were not something wholly different. Mr Bridges will not indulge himself or you; there are no baits for attention, no splendours or violences, not much passion, not much emotion, not a very vivid or active life. You are to resign yourself to a somewhat lulling spell; you must dream to the end, otherwise the entertainment is closed to you.

The fact is that Mr Bridges can only reach his highest point of intensity in the lyric, not in the play.

These twilight characters who take distracting events gently, and can moralise on them as bookish people would at the moment of their happening (sometimes condensing the essence of the situation into a few lovely undramatic lines), have in them but little of the life-blood which went to the making of the best of the "Shorter Poems." The genius of Mr Bridges is reticent, exquisitely unemphatic. Drama is all emphasis, of a kind; emphasis which it is, indeed, the dramatist's art to suspend, not to exclude. Mr Bridges has no emphasis in his dramas; he writes them as he writes his lyrics, treating the stage much as he has treated metre. He has turned metre into his own ways; he has drawn out of it his own music, which comes to us through the plays like violin music written out for a full orchestra.

In the two parts of "Nero," not intended for the stage, as most of the other plays are, we find, perhaps, the nearest approach to what is essentially drama, in characters and subject-matter. In "The Return of Ulysses," where the framework and part of the substance are ready made in Homer, and in "Achilles in Scyros," which is full of happy poetry, not twisted into some childish shape for the mere ingenuity of the twisting, we find a more continuous quality of charm than in the other plays, with merits less purely technical. But even in these it is beauty of detail, rather than structural beauty, which appeals to us; and, in these as in the other plays, we remember single lines and passages rather than either characters or situations.

"Prometheus" returns to me in these lines:

> "I see the cones
> And needles of the fir, which by the wind
> In melancholy places ceaselessly
> Sighing are strewn upon the tufted floor;"

"Achilles" in such lines as

> "that old god
> Whose wisdom buried in the deep hath made
> The unfathomed water solemn,"

or

> "questioning the high decrees
> By which the sweetly tyrannous stars allot
> Their lives and deaths to men;"

and "The Humours of the Court" characterises itself in the wholly undramatic picture-making of this beautiful speech:

> "All this hour
> I have seemed in Paradise: and the fair prospect
> Hath quieted my spirit: I think I sail
> Into the windless haven of my life
> To-day with happy omens: as the stir
> And sleep-forbidding rattle of the journey
> Was like my life till now. Here all is peace:
> The still fresh air of this October morning,
> With its resigning odours; the rich hues
> Wherein the gay leaves revel to their fall;
> The deep blue sky; the misty distances,
> And splashing fountains; and I thought I heard
> A magic service of meandering music
> Threading the glades and stealing on the lawns."

"Eros and Psyche," a narrative after Apuleius, has the coldness of work done, however sympathetically, as task-work, and is but half alive. Like the plays, it is an experiment, one of the learned, laborious diversions of the scholar who is part of this poet.

In the sixty-nine sonnets, called "The Growth of Love," we find another kind of experiment. Here Mr Bridges plays solemn variations on the theme which is, he tells us,

> "My contemplation and perpetual thought."

Every sonnet has a calm, temperate skill of its own; some of the sonnets come to us with precisely the accent of the lyrics; some might be belated Elizabethan sonnets; others translations from early Italian poetry; others, as here, have almost the note of Milton:

"The dark and serious angel, who so long
Vex'd his immortal strength in charge of me,
Hath smiled for joy and fled in liberty
To take his pastime with the peerless throng.
Oft had I done his noble keeping wrong,
Wounding his heart to wonder what might be
God's purpose in a soul of such degree;
And there he had left me but for mandate strong.

But seeing thee with me now, his task at close
He knoweth, and wherefore he was bid to stay,
And work confusion of so many foes:
The thanks that he doth look for, here I pay,
Yet fear some heavenly envy, as he goes
Unto what great reward I can not say."

But with all this fine skill, this serious and interesting substance, even these sonnets are work which is not Mr Bridges' real work. They are written around a subject, they do not give inevitable words to that love to which they are consecrated. As we read each sonnet we say: How fine this is! and when we have read them all we say: How fine they all are! The poet who, in his lyrics, seems to speak for all the world, telling every one some intimate secret which has never whispered itself before, speaks now for himself, and finds himself unconsciously generalising. He seems to repeat only what others have said before him; admirable things, to which he adds the belief of experience, but with no quickening of the pulses.

The exact filling of a given form has always been one of the main preoccupations of this artist, as it should be of every artist. And it is not necessary to read Mr

Bridges' treatise on the prosody of Milton to realise how completely he has apprehended everything that is to his purpose in the science of verse. Limiting himself, indeed, far less than Coventry Patmore, Mr Bridges has somewhat the same resoluteness in subordinating technique to style. His verse has a unity of effect, so carefully prolonged that only by reading attentively do you discover the elaboration of this severe, simple, unemphatic verse, in which a most learned and complex variety of cadence is used to support, with adornment, indeed, but with no weak or distracting adornment, the single structure. Where many artists have the air of offering you their choicest things with a certain (what shall I say?) emphasis, as if calling your attention to what you might possibly overlook, Mr Bridges, when he is most lavish, uses the most disguise, and would gladly pass off upon you his gold coin as if it were a counter. It is all the modesty of his pride: be assured that he knows the worth of his gold far better than you do.

In one of his sonnets Mr Bridges has told us very clearly what it is that he aims at, and what he refrains from, in his work. Let us take him at his word:

"I live on hope and that I think do all
Who come into this world, and since I see
Myself in swim with such good company,
I take my comfort whatsoe'er befall.
I abide and abide, as if more stout and tall
My spirit would grow by waiting like a tree;
And, clear of others' toil, it pleaseth me
In dreams their quick ambition to forestall.

And if thro' careless eagerness I slide
To some accomplishment, I give my voice
Still to desire, and in desire abide.
I have no stake abroad; if I rejoice
In what is done or doing, I confide
Neither to friend nor foe my secret choice."

"The art that most I loved, but little used," he says, speaking of poetry, and contrasts himself with those of his friends who have sought positive attainments,

> "While I love beauty, and was born to rhyme."

He wraps a haughty indifference round him like a mantle, not without some of that sensitiveness which resents praise no less than censure, because it demands acceptance, unquestioning homage, rather than even so much equality as the man who praises must claim towards the man whose worth he has weighed before praising. Mr Bridges takes some pains to impress upon us that he is something more than a poet, and that, even in so far as he is a poet, he is not wholly at our service. In another sonnet he tells us what select kind of immortality he chooses to desire for himself:

> "O my uncared-for songs, what are ye worth,
> That in my secret book with so much care
> I write you, this one here and that one there,
> Marking the time and order of your birth?
> How, with a fancy so unkind to mirth,
> A sense so hard, a style so worn and bare,
> Look ye for any welcome anywhere
> From any shelf or heart-home on the earth?
>
> Should others ask you this, say then I yearn'd
> To write you such as once, when I was young,
> Finding I should have loved and thereto turn'd.
> 'Twere something yet to live again among
> The gentle youth beloved, and where I learn'd
> My art, be there remembered for my song."

Even this reward, he seems to say to us, he can do without, reserving to himself his "joy in the making."

To Mr Bridges, undoubtedly, there is something of an actual "joy" in making poetry, in the mere writing of verse. No one in our time has written verse more consciously and more learnedly, with a more thorough realisation of all those effects which are commonly supposed to come to poets by some divine accident. Moreover, he has thought out the question of English prosody in a way of his own, correcting, as it seems to me, certain errors of theorists, and correcting them upon a principle which has consciously or unconsciously been present to the best writers of English verse in all ages. I will quote from his book on Milton's prosody what seems to be the essential part of his theory:

"Immediately English verse is written free from a numeration of syllables, it falls back on the number of stresses as its determining law: that is its governing power, and constitutes its form; and this is a perfectly different system from that which counts the syllables. It seems also the most natural to our language; and I think that the confusion which exists with regard to it is due to the fact that stress cannot be excluded from consideration even in verse that depends primarily on the number of syllables. The two systems are mixed in our tradition, and they must be separated before a prosody of stress can arise. But if once the notion be got rid of that you must have so many syllables in a line to make a verse, or must account for the supernumerary ones in some such manner as the Greeks or Latins would have done, then the stress will declare its supremacy, which, as may be seen in Shakespeare and Milton, it is burning to do. Now the primary law of pure stressed verse is, that there shall never be a conventional or imaginary stress: that is, *the verse cannot make the stress, because it is the stress that makes the verse*. . . . If the number of stresses in each line be fixed, and such a fixation would be the metre, and if the stresses be determined only by the language and its sense, and if the syllables which they have to carry do not overburden them, then every line may have a different rhythm; though so much variety is not of necessity. . . . I will only add that when English poets will write verse governed honestly by natural speech-stress, they will discover the laws for themselves, and will find open to them an infinite field of rhythm as yet untouched. There is nothing which may not be done in it, and it is perhaps not the least of its advantages that it is most difficult to do well."

All Mr Bridges' work in verse is an illustration of this theory, and it is because this theory is, as he says, "too simple to be understood," that he has been accused of writing verse which is difficult to scan. Read verse for the sense (that is what he really says to us), and if the verse is correctly written the natural speech-emphasis will show you the rhythm. Take, for instance, the last of the "Shorter Poems." The last stanza reads:

> "Fight, to be found fighting: nor far away
> Deem, nor strange thy doom.
> Like this sorrow 'twill come,
> And the day will be to-day."

The first line of the poem reads:

> "Weep not to-day: why should this sadness be?"

a line which appears quite normal, from the conventional standpoint of syllables and according to a conventional accent. Yet what a surprising and altogether admirable variety is introduced into this metre by the first line which I have quoted from the last stanza! Read it according to the rules by which, we are commonly taught, English verse is governed, and it is incorrect, scarcely a verse at all. Read for the sense, say it as you would say it if it were prose, and you were speaking it without thinking about accents or syllables, and its correct ease, its legitimate beauty, its unforced expressiveness, reveal themselves to you at once. At times Mr Bridges does not trust his own words enough, and puts needless accents on them, as in the poem which begins with the wavering and delicate line:

> "The storm is over, the land hushes to rest,"

where he prints the last line but one in this barbarous way:

> "Sée! sléep hath fallen: the trees are asleep."

That line needs but to be read, like all the others, for its sense, with the natural pauses of the voice, and it cannot be read wrongly. It is only in one point that Mr Bridges seems to me inconsistent with his own theory, in which natural speech is so rightly accepted as the test and standard of verse. He admits, as in the lines I have quoted, inversions which would be impossible in natural speech:

> "nor far away
> Deem, nor strange thy doom."

Now an inversion for the sake of rhyme or rhythm is as bad as a conventional accent, is indeed an inexcusable blemish in a poem written frankly in the language of to-day, and presenting itself to us with so familiar a simplicity. It is a "poetic licence," and for poetic licences poetry, at all events modern poetry, has no room.

If the quality of Mr Bridges' poetry, apart from its many qualities as an art, were to be summed up in a word, there is but one word, I think, which we could use, and that word is wisdom; and for the quality of his wisdom there is again but one word, the word temperance. This poet, collectedly living apart, to whom the common rewards of life are not so much as a temptation, has meditated deeply on the conduct of life, in the freest, most universal sense; and he has attained a philosophy of austere, not unsmiling content, in which something of the cheerfulness of the Stoic unites with the more melancholy resignation of the Christian; and, limiting himself so resolutely to this sober outlook upon life, though with a sense of the whole wisdom of the ages:

> "Then oft I turn the page
> In which our country's name,

Spoiling the Greek of fame,
Shall sound in every age:
Or some Terentian play
Renew, whose excellent
Adjusted folds betray
How once Menander went:"

limiting himself, as in his verse, to a moderation which is an infinite series of rejections, he becomes the wisest of living poets, as he is artistically the most faultless. He has left by the way all the fine and coloured and fantastic and splendid things which others have done their utmost to attain, and he has put into his poetry the peace and not the energies of life, the wisdom and not the fever of love, the silences rather than the voices of nature. His whole work is a telling of secrets, and they are told so subtly that you too must listen to overhear them, as he has been listening, all his life, to the almost inaudible voices of those "flames of the soul" which are the desire and the promise of eternal beauty.

1901.

AUSTIN DOBSON

The qualities of Mr Austin Dobson's work are known, for, by an accident which sometimes comes to surprise even the most disinterested of workers, his work is popular. Many have even paid him the compliment, from their own point of view, of ranking him, as a poet, with those amiable, intelligent, often scholarly persons, such as Mr Locker-Lampson, who have made facile verses about books and wines on the afternoons when they were at leisure. He has written, it is true, a good deal of *vers de societé*, some of which he frankly acknowledges on the head-lines; and to distinguish between light verse, which is poetry, and *vers de societé*, which is what it calls itself, will certainly not be easy for the casual reader, especially as Mr Dobson is continually bridging the distance with flying *pontons.* It is reassuring to think that he is probably best known by his least valuable work, by what is sentimental in it, or merely amusing. But, in a certain sense, he is genuinely popular for many genuine qualities of his art, only these qualities mean something much more, something often different, to the careful student of his poetry. Who, then, does not know

> "The song where not one of the graces
> Tight-laces";

the verse which trips on daintier feet than any verse of our time; well-bred verse which dresses in quite the most severe French taste, wears no rouge except with fancy dress, and can sing with as fresh a voice as if it

Austin Dobson

were not singing in a drawing-room? His eighteenth-century muse passes easily from England to France, and it is not fanciful to note the partly French origin of this after all so English writer coming into evidence in a score of little ways, ways as minute as the preference for single and double rhymes intermingled, after the manner of French masculine and feminine rhyming. The scholarship turned courtly (as of some abbé who writes madrigals for the Marquise), the ease of fastidious wit, the fancy brought back from her far voyages, and at home, by preference, in a garden, all these, these unique qualities, it is impossible not to see in the poems of Mr Dobson. He paints, of course, *genre* pictures, brings the whole apparatus of the connoisseur daintily into verse, writes in imitation of Pope, of Prior, and with a worthy flattery in the action; renders Horace in triolets, and Holbein in a *chant royal.* His wit and significance in the use of proper names, allusions, the French language; his wit and delicacy in rhyme, the rare discretion of his epithets, are all evident, and not likely to be overlooked. And when he chooses to be entirely serious, as in perhaps his finest poem, "The Sick Man and the Birds," how natural it seems to him, after all his evasions, to speak, as it is most natural to the poet to speak, directly!

Most of his poetry is an evasion; and it becomes, in its very frivolity, poetry, because it is an evasion. In its indirect, smiling, deliberate way of dealing with life, choosing those hours of carnival, when for our allotted time we put on masks, and coloured dresses, and dance a measure or two with strangers, it is an escape, an escape from life felt to be about to become overpowering. Do we not, among ourselves, avoid the expression of a deeply-felt emotion, in order that we may not intensify the emotion itself by giving it words?

This light poetry, seeming to be occupied so largely with the things that matter least to us in the world, is human in a most closely human way; and by its very evasion it confesses the power and oppression of those deep emotions which it is like us in trying to escape.

The quality which I find, even in those which seem least likely to occasion it of these transparent "Proverbs in Porcelain," these lilting old French forms, these trotting ballads of the time of the Georges, is the quality of pathos. It is that pathos of things fugitive, flowers, beauty, the bloom on any fruit, sunshine in winter. It is what touches us, what we feel, without our quite realising the paradox of its appeal to us, not only in the frail, rose-leaf art of Watteau (where it is no doubt part of the intention), but in the certainly unintended suggestion of those eighteenth-century fans painted with gallant devices, those seventeenth-century gavottes written for courtly measures; and is there not perhaps something of the same reason for the melancholy so strangely islanded in the heart of whirling gaiety of the German dance-rhythms of to-day? In the Capitoline Museum at Rome, in a room filled with busts of the emperors, there is one bust, that of Julia, the daughter of Titus, which has for me precisely the charm and pathos of those fragile things to which this kind of art gives something of the consecration of time. The little fashionable head, so small, eager, curled so elaborately for its life of one fashionable day, and seeming to be so little at home in the unexpected, perpetuating coldness of marble: what has such as this to do with the dignity of death?

> "But where is the Pompadour, too?"

asks Mr Dobson:

> "*This* was the Pompadour's *Fan!*"

And it is because he has apprehended so deeply the carnival hours of life, with all that they have of the very unconsciousness of flight; because he has shown us youth, fashion, careless joy, in their unconcern of to-morrow, when youth will be one step further into the shadow it casts before it, and fashion will retire before other plumes, and careless joy sadden at a mere change of the wind; it is because he has these "artless, ageless things to say," with so vivid, and so reluctant, a sense of what can be said lightly, daintily, with sufficient sincerity, during that bright hour's "indefinite reprieve," that he is a poet, where most writers of light verse (to whom the moment is seen but from the moment's point of view) are but rhymers for drawing-rooms. Writing as he does of the matters, and apparently in the tone, which are sufficient for the day to most worldly-wise people, his point of view is never that of the worldly-wise gentleman of the clubs, who is often to be found admiring him for what he thinks is a similarity of tastes. It is always the point of view of the poet, and of a poet to whom no sensation comes without its delicate after-thought of wisdom.

I do not say that the whole of his work is of this value which I find typical of it. And, in particular, I do not say that this implicit quality of pathos is not sometimes, to its peril, explicit. Such popular pieces as "The Child-Musician," in which the pathos is said instead of seen, drop at once into a different order of work. A direct appeal to the sentiment of tears, a demand on one's sympathy: any of our Adelphi artificers can move us with that, and leave us ashamed of our emotion afterwards. A newspaper paragraph will do as much; the sight, in the street, of a woman sobbing in a doorway. That pathos, ethereal and yet enduring as the little life of roses living on in the immortality of the vinaigrette, which I find in whatever is good of Mr Dobson's work, is entirely a pathos of second thoughts; something which is not in the picture, but without which the picture would not be what it is, a picture of some *fête galante*, seeming to exist for itself, in so fragile a moment's happiness, that it appeals to our pity as irony does, touching the artistic sense in us of the paradox of life.

In Mr Dobson's work, as I have said, we get, frankly, *vers de société* as well as poetry; and it might be interesting to discriminate between whatever, in his work, belongs to the one or the other order. It is unsafe to neglect so much as a single piece in his collection, for you are never safe from a surprise, and you will find touches of genuine poetry in the most unexpected places. But for the most part he is at his best when he is furthest away from our time; and for an obvious enough reason. It is only past fashions that can appeal to us as being in themselves poetical. When they are of our time they are, in themselves, but so much decoration; they have even a touch of comedy in their nearness to us. That is why Mr Dobson's poems of the present day, in which he deals with manners as manners, are with difficulty accepted as poetry; and why the verse-writers of "tea-cup times," who in those times wrote of their tea-cups, scarcely seem to us poets. While the fan was still between the ringed fingers of the Pompadour, it was but a pretty piece of decoration; it is only now that the

> "Chicken-skin, delicate, white,
> Painted by Carlo Vanloo,"

becomes stuff for poetry, becoming a symbol of those silken ways by which the fates of nations went, when the fan was of equal weight with the sceptre. But Mr

Dobson, who has the true artist's love of difficulties to conquer, has done that most difficult of things, making poetry out of the ribbons of to-day, and for the wearer of those ribbons. Well, let the "English girl, divine, demure," for whom he has told us he sings, take the pretty compliment, as the probably not more comprehensive Marquise of Molière took the compliments of her "last poet": who should quarrel with the flattering tongue of a dedication? Mr Dobson knows well enough that he has not written his poems for young ladies, nor for to-day's homage. He has done his day's work for the work's sake, and he has finished perfectly a small, beautiful thing: a miniature, a bust, a coin.

> "All passes. Art alone
> Enduring stays to us;
> The Bust outlasts the throne—
> The Coin, Tiberius."

1897.

MR W. B. YEATS

I

Mr Yeats is the only one among the younger English poets who has the whole poetical temperament, and nothing but the poetical temperament. He lives on one plane, and you will find in the whole of his work, with its varying degrees of artistic achievement, no unworthy or trivial mood, no occasional concession to the fatigue of high thinking. It is this continuously poetical quality of mind that seems to me to distinguish Mr Yeats from the many men of talent, and to place him among the few men of genius. A man may indeed be a poet because he has written a single perfect lyric. He will not be a poet of high order, he will not be a poet in the full sense, unless his work, however unequal it may be in actual literary skill, presents this undeviating aspect, as of one to whom the act of writing is no more than the occasional flowering of a mood into speech. And that, certainly, is the impression which remains with one after a careful reading of the revised edition of Mr Yeats' collected poems and of his later volume of lyrics, "The Wind among the Reeds." The big book, now reissued with a cover by a young artist of subtle and delicate talent, Miss Althea Gyles, contains work of many kinds; and, among mainly lyrical poems, there are two plays, "The Countess Cathleen" and "The Land of Heart's Desire." "The Countess Cathleen" is certainly the largest and finest piece of work which Mr Yeats has yet done. Its visionary ecstasy is firmly embodied in persons whose action is

William Butler Yeats

indeed largely a spiritual action, but action which has the lyrical movement of great drama. Here is poetry which is not only heard, but seen; forming a picture, not less than moving to music. And here it is the poetry which makes the drama, or I might say equally the drama which makes the poetry; for the finest writing is always part of the dramatic action, not a hindrance to it, as it is in almost all the poetical plays of this century. In the long narrative poem contained in the same volume, "The Wanderings of Oisin," an early work, much rewritten, a far less mature skill has squandered lyrical poetry with a romantic prodigality. Among the lyrics in other parts of the book there are a few which Mr Yeats has never excelled in a felicity which seems almost a matter of mere luck; there is not a lyric which has not some personal quality of beauty; but we must turn to the later volume to find the full extent of his capacity as a lyric poet.

In the later volume, "The Wind among the Reeds," in which symbolism extends to the cover, where reeds are woven into a net to catch the wandering sounds, Mr Yeats becomes completely master of himself and of his own resources. Technically the verse is far in advance of anything he has ever done, and if a certain youthful freshness, as of one to whom the woods were still the only talkers upon earth, has gone inevitably, its place has been taken by a deeper, more passionate, and wiser sense of the "everlasting voices" which he has come to apprehend, no longer quite joyously, in the crying of birds, the tongues of flame, and the silence of the heart. It is only gradually that Mr Yeats has learnt to become quite human. Life is the last thing he has learnt, and it is life, an extraordinarily intense inner life, that I find in this book of lyrics, which may seem also to be one long "hymn to intellectual beauty."

The poems which make up a volume apparently disconnected are subdivided dramatically among certain symbolical persons, familiar to the readers of "The Secret Rose," Aedh, Hanrahan, Robartes, each of whom, as indeed Mr Yeats is at the trouble to explain in his notes, is but the pseudonym of a particular outlook of the consciousness, in its passionate, or dreaming, or intellectual moments. It is by means of these dramatic symbols, refining still further upon the large mythological symbolism which he has built up into almost a system, that Mr Yeats weaves about the simplicity of moods that elaborate web of atmosphere in which the illusion of love, and the cruelty of pain, and the gross ecstasy of hope, became changed into beauty. Here is a poet who has realised, as no one else, just now, seems to realise, that the only excuse for writing a poem is the making of a beautiful thing. But he has come finally to realise that, among all kinds of beauty, the beauty which rises out of human passion is the one most proper to the lyric; and in this volume, so full of a remote beauty of atmosphere, of a strange beauty of figure and allusion, there is a "lyrical cry" which has never before, in his pages, made itself heard with so penetrating a monotony.

There are love-poems in this book which almost give a voice to that silence in which the lover forgets even the terrible egoism of love. Love, in its state of desire, can be expressed in verse very directly; but that "love which moves the sun and the other stars," love to which the imagination has given infinity, can but be suggested, as it is suggested in these poems, by some image, in which for a moment it is reflected, as a flame is reflected in trembling water. "Aedh hears the cry of the sedge," for instance; and this is how the sedge speaks to him:

"I wander by the edge
Of this desolate lake
Where wind cries in the sedge:
Until the axle break
That keeps the stars in their round
And hands hurl in the deep
The banners of East and West
And the girdle of light is unbound,
Your head will not lie on the breast
Of your beloved in sleep."

By such little, unheard voices the great secret is whispered, the secret, too, which the whole world is busy with.

"O sweet everlasting Voices be still;
Go to the guards of the heavenly fold
And bid them wander obeying your will
Flame under flame, till Time be no more;
Have you not heard that our hearts are old,
That you call in birds, in wind on the hill,
In shaken boughs, in tide on the shore?
O sweet everlasting Voices be still."

To a poet who is also a mystic there is a great simplicity in things, beauty being really one of the foundations of the world, woman a symbol of beauty, and the visible moment, in which to love or to write love songs is an identical act, really as long and short as eternity. Never, in these love songs, concrete as they become through the precision of their imagery, does an earthly circumstance divorce ecstasy from the impersonality of vision. This poet cannot see love under the form of time, cannot see beauty except as the absolute beauty, cannot distinguish between the mortal person and the eternal idea. Every rapture hurries him beyond the edge of the world and beyond the end of time.

The conception of lyric poetry which Mr Yeats has perfected in this volume, in which every poem is so nearly achieved to the full extent of its intention, may be clearly defined; for Mr Yeats is not a poet who writes by caprice. A lyric, then, is an embodied ecstasy, and an ecstasy so profoundly personal that it loses the accidental qualities of personality, and becomes a part of the universal consciousness. Itself, in its first, merely personal stage, a symbol, it can be expressed only by symbol; and Mr Yeats has chosen his symbolism out of Irish mythology, which gives him the advantage of an elaborate poetic background, new to modern poetry. I am not sure that he does not assume in his readers too ready an acquaintance with Irish tradition, and I am not sure that his notes, whose delightfully unscientific vagueness renders them by no means out of place in a book of poems, will do quite all that is needed in familiarising people's minds with that tradition. But after all, though Mr Yeats will probably regret it, almost everything in his book can be perfectly understood by any poetically sensitive reader who has never heard of a single Irish legend, and who does not even glance at his notes. For he has made for himself a poetical style which is much more simple, as it is much more concise, than any prose style; and, in the final perfecting of his form, he has made for himself a rhythm which is more natural, more precise in its slow and wandering cadence, than any prose rhythm. It is a common mistake to suppose that poetry should be ornate and prose simple. It is prose that may often allow itself the relief of ornament; poetry, if it is to be of the finest quality, is bound to be simple, a mere breathing, in which individual words almost disappear into music. Probably, to many people, accustomed to the artificiality which they mistake for poetical style, and to the sing-song which they mistake for poetical rhythm, Mr Yeats' style, at its best, will seem a little bare, and his rhythm, at its best, a little uncertain. They will be astonished, perhaps not altogether pleased, at finding a poet who uses no inversions, who says in one line, as straightforward as prose, what most poets would dilute into a stanza, and who, in his music, replaces the aria by the recitative. How few, it annoys me to think, as I read over this simple and learned poetry, will realise the extraordinary art which has worked these tiny poems, which seem as free as waves, into a form at once so monumental and so alive! Here, at last, is poetry which has found for itself a new form, a form really modern, in its rejection of every artifice, its return to the natural chant out of which verse was evolved; and it expresses, with a passionate quietude, the elemental desires of humanity, the desire of love, the desire of wisdom, the desire of beauty.

II

I have said that Mr Yeats is the only one among the younger English poets who has the whole poetical temperament, and nothing but the poetical temperament. He is also the only one who combines a continuously poetical substance with continuous excellence of poetical technique. Celtic, if you will, in the quality of his imagination, he has trained that imagination to obey him, as the Celtic imagination rarely obeys those who are for the most part possessed by it. Seeming to many to be the most spontaneous of writers, he is really the most painstaking, the most laboriously conscientious. He makes his visible pictures out of what has come to him invisibly, in dreams, in the energetic abandonment of meditation; but he rarely falls into the error of most mystical poets, who render their visions literally into that other language of ordinary life, instead of translating them freely, idiom for idiom. His verse, lyric and dramatic, has an ecstasy which is never allowed to pass into extravagance, into rhetoric, or into vagueness. Though he has doubtless lost some of the freshness, the fairy quality, of his early work, that freshness and that fairy quality have been replaced by an elaborately simple art, which becomes more and more accomplished, and, in the best sense, precise. The grace of youth is bound to fade out of poetry as it fades out of faces; and all we can hope is that, as in life, the first grey hairs may bring with them some of the grey wisdom of experience, so, in art, time may strengthen what is strong and bring conscious mastery instead of the unconsciousness of early vigour. Mr Yeats could not again become so simple, so joyous, so untouched by human things, as to write another such poem as "The Lake-Isle of Innisfree"; but he can write now with a deeper and more passionate sense of beauty, more gravely, with a more remote and yet essentially more human wisdom. And his verse, though he has come to play more learned variations upon its rhythms, has become more elaborately simple, more condensed, nearer in form to what is most like poetry in being most like prose. It is the mistake of most writers in verse to form for themselves a purely artificial kind of rhythm, in which it is impossible to speak straight. Open "Herod," for instance, at random, and read:

> "Herod shall famous be o'er all the world,
> But he shall kill that thing which most he loves."

Now there, in a purely prosaic statement, are two inversions, which turn what might have been at all events the equivalent of good prose into what is only the parody of poetry. Take one of the most beautiful and imaginative passages out of "The Shadowy Waters," and read:

> "The love of all under the light of the sun
> Is but brief longing, and deceiving hope,
> And bodily tenderness; but love is made
> Imperishable fire under the boughs
> Of chrysoberyl and beryl and chrysolite
> And chrysoprase and ruby and sardonyx."

Is there a word or a cadence in these lines which could not have been used equally well in prose, or in conversation; and yet, can it be denied that those lines are exquisite verse, moving finely to their own music? To get as far from prose, or from conversation, as possible: that is the aim of most writers of verse. But really, the finest verse is that verse which, in outward form and vocal quality, is nearest to dignified prose or serious conversation. Turn to some passage in Shakespeare in which poetical subtlety seems to refine upon speech to its last possibility of expression; the words of Troilus, for instance, as he waits for Cressida in the orchard:

> "I am giddy; expectation whirls me round.
> The imaginary relish is so sweet
> That it enchants my sense: what will it be
> When that the watery palate tastes indeed
> Love's thrice repured nectar? Death, I fear me,
> Swooning destruction, or some joy too fine,
> Too subtle potent, tuned too sharp in sweetness,
> For the capacity of my ruder powers:
> I fear it much; and I do fear besides,
> That I shall lose distinction in my joys;
> As doth a battle, when they charge on heaps
> The enemy flying."

In all Shakespeare there is not a passage fuller of

the substance of poetry or finer in the technique of verse; yet might not every word have been said in prose, word for word, cadence for cadence, with the mere emphasis of ordinary conversation? And Mr Yeats has never failed to realise, not only that verse must be as simple and straightforward as prose, but that every line must be packed with poetical substance, must be able to stand alone, as a fine line of verse, all the more because it challenges at once the standards of prose and of poetry. If it has so simple a thing to say as this:

> "No, no, be silent,
> For I am certain somebody is dead":

it must say it with the same weight, the same gravity, as if it had to say:—

> "Her eyelids tremble and the white foam fades;
> The stars would hurl their crowns among the foam
> Were they but lifted up."

It was the error of Browning, it is the error of many who have learnt of him everything but his genius, to realise only that verse must be like speech, without realising that it must be like dignified speech. Browning has written the most natural, the most vocal, verse of any modern poet; but he has, only too often, chosen the speech of the clubs and of the streets, rather than the speech of those who, even in conversation, use words reverently.

Whether or not Mr Yeats is, or may become, a great dramatist, one thing is certain: he, and he alone among English poets since Shelley, has the dramatic sense and the speech of the dramatist. His plays may seem to lack something of the warmth of life; but they are splendidly centred upon ideas of life, and they speak, at their best, an heroic language which is the intimate language of the soul. When Seanchan, in "The King's Threshold," dying of hunger, says to the Chamberlain:

"You must needs keep your patience yet awhile,
For I have some few mouthfuls of sweet air
To swallow before I am grown to be as civil
As any other dust;"

when he says to the cripples:

"What bad poet did your mothers listen to
That you were born so crooked?"

we hear the note of great dramatic speech, in which poetry is content to seem simpler than prose. We hear the same speech, not more imaginative, but more elaborate, in "On Baile's Strand," when Cuchullain speaks to his sword, and calls it

"This mutterer, this old whistler, this sand-piper,
This edge that's grayer than the tide, this mouse
That's gnawing at the timbers of the world;"

and, more elaborately yet, but speech always, when he says:

"I think that all deep passion is but a kiss
In the mid battle, and a difficult peace
'Twixt oil and water, candles and dark night,
Hill-side and hollow, the hot-footed sun
And the cold sliding slippery-footed moon,
A brief forgiveness between opposites
That have been hatreds for three times the age
Of this long 'stablished ground."

We feel the instinct or sure science of the dramatist, his essential property, more than words, in the great discovery of Cuchullain that the man he has killed is his own son. Cuchullain is sitting on a bench beside a blind man and a fool, and the blind man cries out to the fool: "Somebody is trembling. Why are you trembling, fool? the bench is shaking, why are you trembling? Is Cuchullain going to hurt us? It was not I who told you, Cuchullain." And the blind man says: "It is Cuchullain who is trembling. He is shaking the bench with his knees." As a stage effect, and an effect which is greater drama than any words could be, greater than the fine words which follow, it would be hard to invent anything more direct, poignant, and inevitable.

We have often to complain, in reading poetical plays, that so far as there is poetry and so far as there is drama, the poetry at the best is but an ornament to the drama, no structural part of it. Here, on the other hand, both grow together, like bones and flesh. And, while it has usually to be said that the characters of poetical drama speak too much, here condensation is carried as far as it can be carried without becoming mere baldness. Each thing said is a thing which had to be said, and it is said as if the words flowered up out of a deep and obscure soil, where they had been germinating for a long time in the darkness. The silences of these plays are like the pauses in music; we have the consciousness, under all the beauty and clearness and precision of the words we hear, of something unsaid, something which the soul broods over in silence. The people who speak seem to think or dream long before speaking and after speaking; and though they have legendary names, and meet fantastically on a remoter sea than that which the Flying Dutchman sails over, or starve on the threshold of king's palaces that poetry may be honoured, or fight and die ignorantly and passionately among disasters which it is their fate to bring upon themselves, they are human as a disembodied passion is human, before it has made a home or a prison for itself among circumstances and within time. Their words are all sighs, they come out of

"that sleep
That comes with love,"

and out of

"the dreams the drowsy gods
Breathe on the burnished mirror of the world
And then smooth out with ivory hands and sigh."

They are full of weariness and of ecstasy, remembering human things, and mortality, and that dreams are certainly immortal, and that perhaps there may be a love which is also immortal. They speak to one another not out of the heart or out of the mind, but out of a deeper consciousness than either heart or mind, which is perhaps what we call the soul. There is wisdom in these plays as well as beauty; but indeed beauty is but half beauty when it is not the cloak of wisdom, and wisdom, if it is not beautiful, is but a dusty sign-post, pointing the way ungraciously.

1900, 1904.

MR STEPHEN PHILLIPS

THE principle of destruction is the principle of life. It is your business, if you are bringing a new force into the world, to begin by killing, or at least wounding, a tradition, even if the tradition once had all the virtues. There was never a dragon that Perseus or St George killed who had not been a centre of conservatism and a moral support. Perseus or St George, it has never thoroughly been understood, was only able to kill him because his day was over, and he was getting behind the times. Dragons in their old age grow weak, and their teeth drop out before the spear strikes through the roofs of their mouths. It is not always even so hard and heroic to put them to death as is generally supposed. But it is essential.

In poetry there is, indeed, the great unformulated tradition by which all poetry may be recognised, in virtue of which all poets are of the same race, as all well-bred persons are akin. But in exact opposition to this tradition, which cannot be dated, there is a literary tradition, new in every age, and at the most of only temporary value. The writers who found traditions are mostly good writers; but the greatest writers inspire poets without founding traditions. When Wordsworth destroyed the tradition of Pope he founded a new tradition of his own which has been fatal to every disciple. Keats and Shelley made no schools; we feel their influence to-day in every writer of fine English verse. Tennyson founded a tradition of his own, which has helped more indifferent and uninspired poets to pass themselves off as excellent and inspired poets than almost any other tradition in poetry. Tennyson's work seems to be the kind of work which one can do if one takes trouble enough. Sometimes it is; but, after all, has any one done it quite so well? is there not always some essential thing left out? Nothing was ever so easy to copy, and to copy well, well enough to take in the ignorant. Now the appeal of poetry must always be chiefly to the ignorant, for in no age have there been enough discriminating people to make what is called a public; that is, if we are speaking of the appeal of the work of any single generation to that generation. People to-day have Keats on their table instead of Robert Montgomery, and some of them are even beginning to have Mr Bridges instead of Robert Lord Lytton, because they have been told what to read by the people whose judgments really matter, and whose judgments only wait for a little of the corroboration of time. But the popular poet of a generation, or of a given moment of that generation, is never chosen because of his merit; if he happens to have merit, as in the case of Tennyson, or as in the case of Victor Hugo, that is a matter largely beside the question. The mob is not logical enough or thorough-going enough to choose always the worst. On the contrary, the mob frequently chooses a writer of merit, a writer who deserves tempered praise as well as not unmeasured reproof.

It is a common mistake to suppose that originality, perhaps a trifle meretricious, is likely to succeed where quiet merit passes unobserved. In verse, at all events, quiet merit (not perhaps so entirely admirable a thing in an art justly called "inspired") has every chance of success, where true originality will but disconcert the student of poetry who has come to love certain formulas, the formulas of his masters, which seem to him, as every form of truth must seem to "young ignorance and old custom," a form immortal in itself. That there is an eternal but certainly invisible beauty, it is the joy of the artist to believe. It is often well for him to believe also that the ray by which he apprehends infinite light is itself the essential light. But a limitation, which in the artist is often strength, shutting him in the more securely on his own path, in the critic is mere weakness of sight, an unpardonable blindness. In no two ages of the world has the eternal beauty manifested itself under the same form. A classic beauty of order to Sophocles, a Gothic beauty of exuberant and elaborate life to Shakespeare, perfume to Hafiz, a self-consuming flame to Catullus, it has revealed itself to every lover under a new disguise. We cannot study old masters too much, for they, by their surprising divergence from one another, teach us to express ourselves in a way as novel as their own. They ask for our homage in passing, then to be forgotten in a new life which has no leisure for looking back. They say to us: worship your idol, and then turn your back on your idol; we also burned the idols of our fathers, that we might warm ourselves at a fire, and put heat into our blood, and be ready for the next stage of the journey.

Now the merit by which Mr Stephen Phillips has attracted attention is not the merit by which a new force reveals itself. It is not a new revelation of beauty; it is the tribute to an already worshipped beauty by which a delicate and sensitive nature, too reverent to be a lover, proclaims the platonic limitations of his affection.

The problem of Mr Stephen Phillips lies in the answer to two questions: what constitutes original poetry? and what constitutes dramatic poetry? It is to the bar of these two questions that I propose to summon Mr Phillips.

First, let me state the case for the defence. Turning to the press-notices at the end of Mr Phillips' various volumes, I learn that, to the *Daily Chronicle*, "Christ in Hades," "has the Sophoclean simplicity so full of subtle suggestion, and the Lucretian solemnity so full of sudden loveliness; and the result is Virgilian." Mr Churton Collins, in the *Pall Mall Gazette*, is sure that "it may be safely said that no poet has made his *début* with a volume which is at once of such extraordinary merit and so rich in promise" as the "Poems." The *Times* finds in it "the indefinable quality which makes for permanence"; the *Globe*, "an almost Shakespearean tenderness and beauty." "Here is real poetic achievement—the veritable gold of song," cries the *Spectator*; and *Literature* asserts that "no man in our generation, and few in any generation, have written better than this." The famous names brought in for incidental comparison, on hardly less than terms of equality, are, not only, as we have seen, Shakespeare, Sophocles, Lucretius, and Virgil, but also Dante, Milton, Landor, and Rossetti. Of "Paolo and Francesca" we are told by Mr William Archer in the *Daily Chronicle* that here "Mr Phillips has achieved the impossible. Sardou could not have ordered the action more skilfully, Tennyson could not have clothed the passion in words of purer loveliness." In the *Morning Post*, Mr Owen Seaman tells us that "Mr Phillips has written a great dramatic poem which happens also to be a great poetic drama. We are justified in speaking of Mr Phillips' achievement as something without parallel in our age." Mr Churton Collins, in the *Saturday Review*, says that, "magnificent as was the promise of" the earlier poems, he "was not prepared for such an achievement as the present work." He finds that "it unquestionably places Mr Phillips in the first rank of modern dramatists and of modern poetry. It does more, it claims his kinship with the aristocrats of his art, with Sophocles and with Dante." Mr Sidney Colvin, in the *Nineteenth Century*, tells us that "to the rich poetical production of the nineteenth century it seems" to him "that Mr Phillips has added that which was hitherto lacking—notwithstanding so many attempts made by famous men—namely, a poetical play of the highest quality, strictly designed for, and expressly suited to, the stage." Mr William Archer, in the *World*, discovers in "Herod" "the elder Dumas speaking with the voice of Milton"; while the *Daily Graphic*, the *Globe*, and the *Athenæum*, as with one voice, announce in it "an intensity which entitles it to rank with the works of Webster and Chapman," and assert that "its grim imagination and fantasy may be compared with that of Webster," and that "it is not unworthy of the author of 'The Duchess of Malfi.'" To the *Morning Leader* it is "splendidly opulent in conception; perfect in construction; far beyond all contemporary English effort in the aptitude of its verse to the subject and to the stage." Of "Ulysses" I have no press notices at hand, but I see from an advertisement in the *Westminster Gazette*, entitled, "Is modern poetry read?" that one London bookseller is said to have ordered three times as many copies as he "would have taken of a new poem by Tennyson, four times as many as for one by Swinburne, six times as many as for one by Browning." Let this end the case for the defence.

Poetry is an act of creation which the poet shares with God, and with none of his creatures. Poetical feeling is a sensibility which the poet may share with the green-grocer walking arm-in-arm with his wife, in Hyde Park, at twilight on Sunday. To express poetical feeling in verse is not to make poetry. Poetical feeling can be rendered with varying success; it can be trained, improved, made the most of: poetry exists. But as there is nothing that has not been finely done that cannot be tamely copied, so in poetry we have continually before us copies or paraphrases which are often more successful in their appeal to the public than the originals which have inspired them. And, as all but the best judges in painting can be imposed upon by a finely executed copy of a masterpiece, so in poetry all but the best judges are often imposed upon by work done conscientiously and tastefully after good models. We can imagine the reader of Mr Phillips' "Poems" pausing before a line or a passage, and saying, That has almost the ring of Landor. Another reader will go a step further and say, It follows Landor so closely that it is as good as Landor. The third reader will content himself with saying, It is as good as Landor. And as he says it, you will not suspect what really lies at the root of the compliment; you will imagine to yourself something different from Landor, but as good as Landor in a different way.

Now Mr Phillips' poetry is of the kind that seems, when we hear it for the first time, to be vaguely familiar. We cannot remember where we have heard it; we cannot remember if we have heard it just as it is, or if it merely recalls something else. But we are at once disposed to say, It is poetry, because it reminds us of other poetry that we have read. There is a profound sense in which all poetry is alike; in which Villon may be recognised by his inner likeness, as well as by his outer unlikeness, to Homer, while Scott shall be discredited by his outer likeness, as well as by his inner unlikeness, to Homer. But the poetry that is at once recognised by its resemblance to other poetry must always be second-rate work, because it is work done at second-hand, work which has come into the world a foundling, and has had to adopt another man's house for its maintenance.

The most conspicuous influence on Mr Stephen Phillips in his "Poems" is Tennyson, and not the mature Tennyson, but the Tennyson of "Oenone," Tennyson at twenty-three. Take these lines, which represent the low average, hardly that, of "Oenone," and read them carefully, weighing all their cadences:

> "O mother, hear me yet before I die.
> Hath he not sworn his love a thousand times,
> In this green valley, under this green hill,
> Even on this hand, and sitting on this stone?
> Seal'd it with kisses, water'd it with tears?
> O happy tears, and how unlike to these!
> O happy Heaven, how canst thou see my face?
> O happy earth, how canst thou bear my weight?
> O death, death, death, thou ever-floating cloud,
> There are enough unhappy on this earth.
> Pass by the happy souls, that love to live:
> I pray thee pass before my light of life,
> And shadow all my soul, that I may die.
> Thou weighest heavy on the heart within,
> Weigh heavy on my eyelids: let me die."

Now read carefully these lines from "Marpessa," and weigh every cadence, comparing it with the cadences of Tennyson:

> "I should expect thee by the Western ray,
> Faded, not sure of thee, with desperate smiles,
> And pitiful devices of my dress
> Or fashion of my hair: thou wouldst grow kind;
> Most bitter to a woman that was loved.
> I must ensnare thee to my arms, and touch
> Thy pity, to but hold thee to my heart.
> But if I live with Idas, then we two
> On the low earth shall prosper hand in hand
> In odours of the open field, and live
> In peaceful noises of the farm, and watch

The pastoral fields burned by the setting sun.
And he shall give me passionate children, not
Some radiant god that shall despise me quite,
But clambering limbs and little hearts that err."

But for the awkward line ending with the word "quite," it would be possible to read out those two passages and to puzzle the hearer as to which was Tennyson and which Mr Phillips. It may be said that we are paying Mr Phillips a high compliment by saying that his verse might be mistaken for the verse of Tennyson. Is it, after all, a compliment? Would it be a true compliment if we were able to quote from Mr Phillips lines resembling these lines, which we take from one of the finer parts of "Oenone," lines which appear only in a later edition?

"Then to the bower they came,
Naked they came to that smooth-swarded bower,
And at their feet the crocus brake like fire,
Violet, amaracus, and asphodel,
Lotos and lilies: and a wind arose."

Or, to take Tennyson in a severer mood, read the concluding lines of "Ulysses":

"We are not now that strength which in old days
Moved earth and heaven; that which we are we are;
One equal temper of heroic hearts,
Made weak by time and fate, but strong in will
To strive, to seek, to find, and not to yield."

Even if, anywhere in Mr Phillips' work, we could find lines of that calibre exactly, so that they could be mistaken for those lines, would it be possible to commend Mr Phillips for any much greater achievement, because he had been able to do over again what Tennyson did well, than because he had been able to do over again what Tennyson did only moderately well? That is not the question. The question is, has this new poet killed the dragon of a literary tradition? has he brought the new life of a personal energy?

Poetry, I have said, is an act of creation; poetical feeling is a form of sensibility. Now in all Mr Phillips' verse we find poetical feeling; never the instant, inevitable, unmistakable thrill and onslaught of poetry. When Dante writes:

"Amor, che a nullo amato amar perdona";

when Shakespeare writes:

"O thou weed,
Who art so lovely fair and smell'st so sweet
That the sense aches at thee, would thou hadst ne'er been born!"

when Coleridge writes:

"She, she herself, and only she
Shone through her body visibly";

when Blake writes:

"When the stars threw down their spears,
And watered heaven with their tears,
Did He smile His work to see?
Did He who made the lamb make thee"?

we are convinced at once, we accept without question; there is nothing to argue about. A flower has come up out of the soil of the earth; it has all the age of the earth in its roots, and the novelty of the instant in its fragrant life. Turn to Mr Phillips, and to an admired passage:

"So bare her soul that Beauty like a lance
Pierced her, and odour full of arrows was."

One hesitates; one says, is that really good, or only apparently good? There is something in the idea, but has the idea found its "minutely appropriate words"? Change a word or two, turn it into prose, say it without inversion: "Her soul was so naked that Beauty pierced her like a spear, and odour was full of arrows to her." Is not that, in prose, finer than it was in verse? The verse, in Mr Phillips, reaches a high general level, but never the absolute. Now a high general level, without the absolute, means infinitely less than a general level, imperfect either in substance or in workmanship, with here and there the absolute. It is the difference between the "bounding line" of life and the more or less discernible outline of a shadow. In real poems, slight or brief though they may be, we have the single imaginative act; something has been done which has never been done before, and which will never be done again. Until that has been done it is of slight interest to consider how many other excellent qualities a work may contain. Mr Phillips has laid the paper, the sticks, and the coals neatly in the grate, where they remain, in undisturbed order, awaiting the flame that never wakens them into light or heat.

But we have as yet considered only one of the two questions I proposed to consider, the question: what constitutes original poetry? A second question remains: what constitutes dramatic poetry?

The essential thing in drama is that the drama should be based upon character, that the action should be made by the characters. Every speech which is not a new revelation of character is an intrusive speech, whatever irrelevant merit it may have as verse. In the poetic drama it is impossible to disentangle poetry from character, or character from poetry. If the two are not one, neither is satisfactorily present. Coleridge jots down, in one of his priceless notes: "Item, that dramatic poetry must be poetry hid in thought and passion—not thought or passion disguised in the dress of poetry." In the poetic drama every line of verse must come out of the heart of the man or woman who speaks it, and as straight from the heart as if it were in prose. Verse throws off none of the responsibilities of the playwright, but rather adds to them, though with its own compensations. Even a prose speech on the stage is not a precise verbal imitation of the words which people would probably use under given circumstances. It is permitted to the dramatist, by the very convention which makes drama, to express what his characters would like to express, in a more precise and a more profound way than that in which they would express themselves if they were real people. He must do so within the limits of plausibility; that is part of his art as a dramatist. But he must do so, or he will not convey to his audience what the imperfect stammerings of ordinary conversation convey to those who know already what to read into the words and how to interpret the pauses and the gestures.

In the poetic drama, which, by the mere fact of the language in which it is written, takes us still further from the external realities of ordinary conversation, speech may be, indeed, must be, still further lifted, its meaning still further deepened. All speech is an attempt, an admittedly imperfect attempt, to express the mind's conception of itself, of the universe, and of its relation to the universe. The best words that have yet been invented go only a little way into that mysterious inner world of which the outer world is but a shadow. Who can say that the first words which come to my lips when I am trying to tell some intimate secret of myself, a secret which I have only half understood, are nearer to the innermost meaning of that secret than the carefully chosen and, in some strange way, illuminated words by which, if I am a poet, I can hint at what no human tongue can wholly tell? When we talk with one another in any grave moment, we are like children who talk loudly in the dark to give themselves courage. We speak out of the midst of an enveloping darkness; we understand only a part of what we are saying, and only partly why we are saying it. The words are most often false to their real meaning; they are nothing. To imitate them precisely would be to come no nearer to your heart and to mine who have spoken them. The dramatist must bring speech nearer to that obscure thing of which speech is but a suggestion; the poetic dramatist, who speaks in a finer, more expressive, and therefore truer, language, may come much nearer to the truth, to the real meaning of words, than the dramatist who writes in prose can ever come.

Speech, then, in the poetic drama, is not the imitation of ordinary conversation, it is not the mere turning of ordinary conversation into verse; it is a beautiful and expressive saying aloud of what people have only thought, or meant, or felt, without being able to put those thoughts, or intentions, or emotions, into words. It comes nearer to humanity as it goes further from a merely literal turning into verse of people's failure to express themselves. It must carry always the illusion of words actually spoken; it must seem to us as if such or such a person of the drama might have said just those words if poetry had really been his native language, as it might be the language native to his soul; we must be tricked and led into believing some more subtle truth than that which our ears hear and our eyes see. But let us remember at what distance we are from the market-place.

Now in all Mr Phillips' plays the action is conceived first, the characters are fitted into it afterwards, and the verse is embroidered upon a stiff and empty canvas, with a merely decorative intention. Mr Phillips has attempted, to some extent, to copy the form of the Greek, rather than of the Elizabethan play, to follow Sophocles rather than Shakespeare. The attempt is interesting; it might have resulted in the creation of a new and wholly modern thing. The only dramatist since Sophocles in whom the essential qualities of Sophocles, as a dramatist, are to be seen, is Ibsen. Ibsen has invented for himself a form which seems to us absolutely new, and, above all things, modern. It is new, it is modern, but it is new and modern in a fine sense because it goes back to the moment when the drama was most faultlessly conceived and developed, and finds there, not a thing to copy, but a principle of life to which its own principle of life corresponds. Mr Phillips has tried to copy an outline, but the outline, drawn, as it is, with skill, remains empty, is neither filled nor finished, and, at the best, remains academic, not vital, the outline of Bouguereau, not of Ingres or of Degas, in whom a similar purity of drawing achieves such different ends.

Mr Phillips has written for the stage with a certain kind of success, and he has been praised, as we have seen, for having "written a great dramatic poem which happens also to be a great poetic drama." But this praise loses sight of the difference which exists between what is dramatic and what is theatrically effective. In "Paolo and Francesca," in "Herod," and in "Ulysses," there are many scenes which, taken in themselves, are theatrically effective; and it is through this quality, which is the quality most prized on the modern English stage, that these plays have found their way to Her Majesty's theatre and to St James's. But take any one of these scenes, consider it in relation to the play as a whole, think of it as a revelation of the character of each person who takes part in it, examine its probability as a natural human action, and you will find that the people do, not what they would be most likely to do, but what the author wishes them to do, and that they say, not what they would be most likely to say, but what the author thinks it would be convenient or impressive for them to say.

What Mr Phillips lacks is sincerity; and without sincerity there can be no art, though art has not yet begun when sincerity has finished laying the foundations. One is not sincere by wishing to be so, any more than one is wise or fortunate. Infinite skill goes to the making of sincerity. Mr Phillips, who has so much skill, devotes it all to producing effects by means of action, and to describing those effects by means of verse. Paolo and Francesca say gracious things to one another, gracious idyllic things, which one hears the poet prompting them to say; but they always say things, they do not speak straight out. Nothing that is said by Herod might not as well be said by Mariamne; nothing that is said by either Mariamne or Herod might not better be said by a third person. When Calypso and Ulysses talk for the last time on the island, we feel neither the goddess nor the hero; but the obvious thought, the expected emotion, is always exact to its minute. The people of a great dramatist seem to break away from their creator; having set them in motion, he is not responsible for the course they take; he is the automaton, not they. But Mr Phillips' people do but decorate his stage, on which they profess to live and move and have their being. They pass, and the scenery is changed, and they pass again, or others like them pass; and they have said graceful verse, with literary intentions, and they have committed violent actions, with theatrical intentions; and nothing that they have done has moved us, and nothing that they have said has moved us, and we can always discuss the acting and the staging.

The characters of a great drama are not limited for their existence to the three hours during which they move before our eyes on the other side of a luminous gulf. Their first words seem to echo back into a past in which they have already lived intensely; when they have left the stage at the end of the play they have all eternity before them in which to go on living. The first words of Cleopatra to Antony,

> "If it be love indeed, tell me how much,"

have told us already, before she begins to live her passionate, luxurious, and treacherous life before us, all that Shakespeare intends us to know of her secret. When she says proudly, at the moment of death,

> "I am fire and air; my other elements
> I give to baser life,"

she is but accepting her rank among the immortal forces. The mind cannot limit her to the frame of five acts; the five acts have existed in order to set her for ever outside them.

This, then, is the effect of great drama, we might say, of all genuine drama. With the end of "Ulysses" the masque is over; of "Herod," the melodrama; of "Paolo and Francesca," the idyl. What remains with us? First, the tumult and glitter of the spectacle;

next, the qualities of the acting; lastly, a few separate lines, not essential to the play as a whole, or to the revelation of any one of the characters, but interesting in themselves for their idea or for their expression. The canvas is stretched and threadbare, the pattern indistinct; here and there a colour asserts itself, coming self-consciously out of the pattern.

I have now examined Mr Phillips' work from the point of view of poetry, and from the point of view of drama; I have indicated why it seems to me that this work is neither original as poetry nor genuine as drama. I have indicated why the poetry has been praised by the critics; it remains to consider why the drama has been accepted by the public.

First of all, the public wants, or has been trained to want, spectacle at the theatre; and Mr Phillips provides them with spectacle, on which they can repose their eyes without troubling their minds by any further considerations. An enthusiastic admirer of "Ulysses," advising a friend to go and see the most beautiful play he had ever seen, and being answered, "But I have read the play, and do not care for it," exclaimed with conviction, "Oh, you won't hear the words!" Yet there are those who wish to hear the words, and to whom the words seem full of beauty. These are the people into whose hands modern education has put all the great books of the world, all the treasures of all the arts, and whom it has not taught to discriminate between what is good and what is second-rate. Ignorance has its felicities; the peasant who has read nothing but his Bible has at least not been trained in the wrong direction. But there is one thing more fatal than most other things in the world: the education which gives facts without reasons, opinions without thoughts, mental results without the long meditation through which they should have come into the mind. There is something which education, as we see it in our time, violently and ignorantly at work upon ignorance, can do; it can persuade the public that the middle class in literature is a fine form of intellectual democracy; it can change the patterns of our wall-papers into less aggressive patterns; it can exclude the antimacassar from the back of the chair on which we rest our head, and the mental image of the antimacassar from the head which rests on the back of the chair. But the change in the furniture, the vague consciousness that a certain piece of furniture is ugly or unseemly, has not turned an inartistic mind into an artistic mind; it has merely changed the model on the blackboard for a slightly better model. The taste for melodrama stark naked has faded a little in the public favour; we must have our melodrama clothed, and clothed elegantly. The verse which seemed good enough for poetical plays ten years ago is not good enough for us any longer; we were in the "third standard" then, we are in the "fourth standard" now.

In an essay on popular poetry Mr Yeats has pointed out, with unquestionable truth, that "what we call popular poetry never came from the people at all. Longfellow, and Campbell, and Mrs Hemans, and Macaulay in his Lays, and Scott in his longer poems, are the poets of the middle class, of people who have unlearned the unwritten tradition which binds the unlettered, so long as they are masters of themselves, to the beginning of time and to the foundation of the world, and who have not learned the written tradition which has been established upon the unwritten." "There is only one good kind of poetry," he reminds us; "for the poetry of the coteries, which presupposes the written tradition, does not differ in kind from the true poetry of the people, which presupposes the unwritten tradition." We live in a time when the middle class rules; when the middle class will have its say, even in art. The judgments of the crowd are accepted by the crowd; there are, alas, no longer tyrants. No man any longer admits that he is ignorant of anything; the gentleman who has made his money in South Africa talks art with the gentleman who has made his money on the Stock Exchange. Once he was content to buy; now he must criticise as well. The gambler from abroad takes the opinion of the gambler at home; between them they make opinion for their fellows. And they will have their popular poetry, their popular drama. They, and the shopkeeper, and the young man brought up at the board school, form a solid phalanx. They hold together, they thrust in the same direction. The theatres exist for them; they have made the theatres what they are. They will pay their money for nothing on which money has not been squandered. A poetical play must not be given unless it can be mounted at a cost of at least £2000; so much money cannot be risked unless there is a probability that the play will draw the crowd: is it not inevitable that the taste of the crowd should be consulted humbly, should be followed blindly? Commercialism rules the theatre, as it rules elsewhere than in the theatre. It is all a simple business matter, a question of demand and supply. A particular kind of article is in demand at the theatre: who will meet that demand? Mr Phillips comes forward with plays which seem to have been made expressly for the purpose. Their defects help them hardly more than their merits. They have just enough poetical feeling, just enough action, just enough spectacle; they give to the middle-class mind the illusion of an art "dealing greatly with great passions"; they give to that mind the illusion of being for once in touch with an art dealing greatly with great passions. They rouse no disquieting reflections ; they challenge no accepted beliefs. They seem to make the art of the drama easy, and to reduce poetry at last to the general level.

1902.

ERNEST DOWSON

I

The death of Ernest Dowson will mean very little to the world at large, but it will mean a great deal to the few people who care passionately for poetry. A little book of verses, the manuscript of another, a one-act play in verse, a few short stories, two novels written in collaboration, some translations from the French, done for money; that is all that was left by a man who was undoubtedly a man of genius, not a great poet, but a poet, one of the very few writers of our generation to whom that name can be applied in its most intimate sense. People will complain, probably, in his verses, of what will seem to them the factitious melancholy, the factitious idealism, and (peeping through at a few rare moments) the factitious suggestions of riot. They will see only a literary affectation, where in truth there is as genuine a note of personal sincerity as in the more explicit and arranged confessions of less admirable poets. Yes, in these few evasive, immaterial snatches of song, I find, implied for the most part, hidden away like a secret, all the fever and turmoil and the unattained dreams of a life which had itself so much of the swift, disastrous, and suicidal impetus of genius.

Ernest Christopher Dowson was born at The Grove, Belmont Hill, Lee, Kent, on August 2nd, 1867; he died at 26 Sandhurst Gardens, Catford, S.E., on Friday morning, February 23rd, 1900, and was buried in the Roman Catholic part of the Lewisham Cemetery on

February 27th. His great-uncle was Alfred Domett, Browning's "Waring," at one time Prime Minister of New Zealand, and author of "Ranolf and Amohia," and other poems. His father, who had himself a taste for literature, lived a good deal in France and on the Riviera, on account of the delicacy of his health, and Ernest had a somewhat irregular education, chiefly out of England, before he entered Queen's College, Oxford. He left in 1887 without taking a degree, and came to London, where he lived for several years, often revisiting France, which was always his favourite country. Latterly, until the last year of his life, he lived almost entirely in Paris, Brittany, and Normandy. Never robust, and always reckless with himself, his health had been steadily getting worse for some years, and when he came back to London he looked, as indeed he was, a dying man. Morbidly shy, with a sensitive independence which shrank from any sort of obligation, he would not communicate with his relatives, who would gladly have helped him, or with any of the really large number of attached friends whom he had in London; and, as his disease weakened him more and more, he hid himself away in his miserable lodgings, refused to see a doctor, let himself half starve, and was found one day in a Bodega with only a few shillings in his pocket, and so weak as to be hardly able to walk, by a friend, himself in some difficulties, who immediately took him back to the bricklayer's cottage in a muddy outskirt of Catford, where he was himself living, and there generously looked after him for the last six weeks of his life.

He did not realise that he was going to die, and was full of projects for the future, when the £600 which was to come to him from the sale of some property should have given him a fresh chance in the world;

began to read Dickens, whom he had never read before, with singular zest; and, on the last day of his life, sat up talking eagerly till five in the morning. At the very moment of his death he did not know that he was dying. He tried to cough, could not cough, and the heart quietly stopped.

II

I cannot remember my first meeting with Ernest Dowson. It may have been in 1891, at one of the meetings of the Rhymers' Club, in an upper room at the Cheshire Cheese, where long clay pipes lay in slim heaps on the wooden tables, between tankards of ale; and young poets, then very young, recited their own verses to one another with a desperate and ineffectual attempt to get into key with the Latin Quarter. Though few of us were, as a matter of fact, Anglo-Saxon, we could not help feeling that we were in London, and the atmosphere of London is not the atmosphere of movements or of societies. In Paris it is the most natural thing in the world to meet and discuss literature, ideas, one's own and one another's work; and it can be done without pretentiousness or constraint, because, to the Latin mind, art, ideas, one's work and the work of one's friends, are definite and important things, which it would never occur to any one to take anything but seriously. In England art has to be protected, not only against the world, but against oneself and one's fellow-artist, by a kind of affected modesty which is the Englishman's natural pose, half pride and half self-distrust. So this brave venture of the Rhymers' Club, though it lasted for two or three years, and produced two little books of verse which will some day be literary curiosities, was not quite a satisfactory kind of *cénacle.* Dowson, who enjoyed the real thing so much in Paris, did not, I think, go very often; but his contributions to the first book of the club were at once the most delicate and the most distinguished poems which it contained. Was it, after all, at one of these meetings that I first saw him, or was it, perhaps, at another haunt of some of us at that time, a semi-literary tavern near Leicester Square, chosen for its convenient position between two stage-doors? It was at the time when one or two of us sincerely worshipped the ballet; Dowson, alas, never. I could never get him to see that charm in harmonious and coloured movement, like bright shadows seen through the floating gauze of the music, which held me night after night at the two theatres which alone seemed to me to give an amusing colour to one's dreams. Neither the stage nor the stage-door had any attraction for him; but he came to the tavern because it was a tavern, and because he could meet his friends there. Even before that time I have a vague impression of having met him, I forget where, certainly at night; and of having been struck, even then, by a look and manner of pathetic charm, a sort of Keats-like face, the face of a demoralised Keats, and by something curious in the contrast of a manner exquisitely refined, with an appearance generally somewhat dilapidated. That impression was only accentuated later on, when I came to know him, and the manner of his life, much more intimately.

I think I may date my first impression of what one calls "the real man" (as if it were more real than the poet of the disembodied verses!) from an evening in which he first introduced me to those charming supper-houses, open all night through, the cabmen's shelters. I had been talking over another vagabond poet, Lord

Rochester, with a charming and sympathetic descendant of that poet, and somewhat late at night we had come upon Dowson and another man wandering aimlessly and excitedly about the streets. He invited us to supper, we did not quite realise where, and the cabman came in with us, as we were welcomed, cordially and without comment, at a little place near the Langham; and, I recollect, very hospitably entertained. The cooking differs, as I found in time, in these supper houses, but there the rasher was excellent and the cups admirably clean. Dowson was known there, and I used to think he was always at his best in a cabmen's shelter. Without a certain sordidness in his surroundings he was never quite comfortable, never quite himself; and at those places you are obliged to drink nothing stronger than coffee or tea. I liked to see him occasionally, for a change, drinking nothing stronger than coffee or tea. At Oxford, I believe, his favourite form of intoxication had been haschisch; afterwards he gave up this somewhat elaborate experiment in visionary sensations for readier means of oblivion; but he returned to it, I remember, for at least one afternoon, in a company of which I had been the gatherer and of which I was the host. I remember him sitting, a little anxiously, with his chin on his breast, awaiting the magic, half-shy in the midst of a bright company of young people whom he had only seen across the footlights. The experience was not a very successful one; it ended in what should have been its first symptom, immoderate laughter.

Always, perhaps, a little consciously, but at least always sincerely, in search of new sensations, my friend found what was for him the supreme sensation in a very passionate and tender adoration of the most escaping of all ideals, the ideal of youth. Cherished, as I imagine, first only in the abstract, this search after the immature, the ripening graces which time can only spoil in the ripening, found itself at the journey's end, as some of his friends thought, a little prematurely. I was never of their opinion. I only saw twice, and for a few moments only, the young girl to whom most of his verses were to be written, and whose presence in his life may be held to account for much of that astonishing contrast between the broad outlines of his life and work. The situation seemed to me of the most exquisite and appropriate impossibility. The daughter of a refugee, I believe of good family, reduced to keeping a humble restaurant in a foreign quarter of London, she listened to his verses, smiled charmingly, under her mother's eyes, on his two years' courtship, and at the end of two years married the waiter instead. Did she ever realise more than the obvious part of what was being offered to her, in this shy and eager devotion? Did it ever mean very much to her to have made and to have killed a poet? She had, at all events, the gift of evoking, and, in its way, of retaining, all that was most delicate, sensitive, shy, typically poetic, in a nature which I can only compare to a weedy garden, its grass trodden down by many feet, but with one small, carefully tended flower-bed, luminous with lilies. I used to think, sometimes, of Verlaine and his "girl-wife," the one really profound passion, certainly, of that passionate career; the charming, child-like creature, to whom he looked back, at the end of his life, with an unchanged tenderness and disappointment: "Vous n'avez rien compris à ma simplicité," as he lamented. In the case of Dowson, however, there was a sort of virginal devotion, as to a Madonna; and I think had things gone happily, to a conventionally happy ending, he would have felt (dare I say?) that his ideal had been spoilt.

But, for the good fortune of poets, things rarely do

go happily with them, or to conventionally happy endings. He used to dine every night at the little restaurant, and I can always see the picture, which I have so often seen through the window in passing: the narrow room with the rough tables, for the most part empty, except in the innermost corner, where Dowson would sit with that singularly sweet and singularly pathetic smile on his lips (a smile which seemed afraid of its right to be there, as if always dreading a rebuff), playing his invariable after-dinner game of cards. Friends would come in, during the hour before closing time; and the girl, her game of cards finished, would quietly disappear, leaving him with hardly more than the desire to kill another night as swiftly as possible.

Meanwhile she and the mother knew that the fragile young man who dined there so quietly every day was apt to be quite another sort of person after he had been three hours outside. It was only when his life seemed to have been irretrievably ruined that Dowson quite deliberately abandoned himself to that craving for drink, which was doubtless lying in wait for him in his blood, as consumption was also; it was only latterly, when he had no longer any interest in life, that he really wished to die. But I have never known him when he could resist either the desire or the consequences of drink. Sober, he was the most gentle, in manner the most gentlemanly, of men; unselfish to a fault, to the extent of weakness; a delightful companion, charm itself. Under the influence of drink, he became almost literally insane, certainly quite irresponsible. He fell into furious and unreasoning passions; a vocabulary unknown to him at other times sprang up like a whirlwind; he seemed always about to commit some act of absurd violence. Along with that forgetfulness came other memories. As long as he was conscious of himself, there was but one woman for him in the world, and for her he had an infinite tenderness and an infinite respect. When that face faded from him, he saw all the other faces, and he saw no more difference than between sheep and sheep. Indeed, that curious love of the sordid, so common an affectation of the modern decadent, and with him so genuine, grew upon him, and dragged him into more and more sorry corners of a life which was never exactly "gay" to him. His father, when he died, left him in possession of an old dock, where for a time he lived in a mouldering house, in that squalid part of the East End which he came to know so well, and to feel so strangely at home in. He drank the poisonous liquors of those pot-houses which swarm about the docks; he drifted about in whatever company came in his way; he let heedlessness develop into a curious disregard of personal tidiness. In Paris, Les Halles took the place of the docks. At Dieppe, where I saw so much of him one summer, he discovered strange, squalid haunts about the harbour, where he made friends with amazing innkeepers, and got into rows with the fishermen who came in to drink after midnight. At Brussels, where I was with him at the time of the Kermesse, he flung himself into all that riotous Flemish life, with a zest for what was most sordidly riotous in it. It was his own way of escape from life.

To Dowson, as to all those who have not been "content to ask unlikely gifts in vain," nature, life, destiny, whatever one chooses to call it, that power which is strength to the strong, presented itself as a barrier against which all one's strength only served to dash one to more hopeless ruin. He was not a dreamer; destiny passes by the dreamer, sparing him because he clamours for nothing. He was a child, clamouring for so many things, all impossible. With a body too weak for ordinary existence, he desired all the enchantments of all the senses. With a soul too shy to tell its own secret, except in exquisite evasions, he desired the boundless confidence of love. He sang one tune, over and over, and no one listened to him. He had only to form the most simple wish, and it was denied him. He gave way to ill-luck, not knowing that he was giving way to his own weakness, and he tried to escape from the consciousness of things as they were at the best, by voluntarily choosing to accept them at their worst. For with him it was always voluntary. He was never quite without money; he had a little money of his own, and he had for many years a weekly allowance from a publisher, in return for translations from the French, or, if he chose to do it, original work. He was unhappy, and he dared not think. To unhappy men, thought, if it can be set at work on abstract questions, is the only substitute for happiness; if it has not strength to overleap the barrier which shuts one in upon oneself, it is the one unwearying torture. Dowson had exquisite sensibility, he vibrated in harmony with every delicate emotion; but he had no outlook, he had not the escape of intellect. His only escape, then, was to plunge into the crowd, to fancy that he lost sight of himself as he disappeared from the sight of others. The more he soiled himself at that gross contact, the further would he seem to be from what beckoned to him in one vain illusion after another vain illusion, in the delicate places of the world. Seeing himself moving to the sound of lutes, in some courtly disguise, down an alley of Watteau's Versailles, while he touched finger-tips with a divine creature in rose-leaf silks, what was there left for him, as the dream obstinately refused to realise itself, but a blind flight into some Teniers kitchen, where boors are making merry, without thought of yesterday or to-morrow? There, perhaps, in that ferment of animal life, he could forget life as he dreamed it, with too faint hold upon his dreams to make dreams come true.

For, there is not a dream which may not come true, if we have the energy which makes, or chooses, our own fate. We can always, in this world, get what we want, if we will it intensely and persistently enough. Whether we shall get it sooner or later is the concern of fate; but we shall get it. It may come when we have no longer any use for it, when we have gone on willing it out of habit, or so as not to confess that we have failed. But it will come. So few people succeed greatly because so few people can conceive a great end, and work towards that end without deviating and without tiring. But we all know that the man who works for money day and night gets rich; and the man who works day and night for no matter what kind of material power, gets the power. It is the same with the deeper, more spiritual, as it seems vaguer issues, which make for happiness and every intangible success. It is only the dreams of those light sleepers who dream faintly that do not come true.

We get out of life, all of us, what we bring to it; that, and that only, is what it can teach us. There are men whom Dowson's experiences would have made great men, or great writers; for him they did very little. Love and regret, with here and there the suggestion of an uncomforting pleasure snatched by the way, are all that he has to sing of; and he could have sung of them at much less "expense of spirit," and, one fancies, without the "waste of shame" at all. Think what Villon got directly out of his own life, what Verlaine, what Musset, what Byron, got directly out of their own lives! It requires a strong man to "sin strongly" and profit by it. To Dowson the tragedy of his own life could only have resulted in an elegy. "I have flung roses, roses, riotously with the throng," he confesses, in his most beautiful poem; but it was as one who flings roses in a dream, as he passes with shut eyes through an unsubstantial throng. The depths into which he plunged were always waters of oblivion, and he returned forgetting them. He is always a very ghostly lover, wandering in a land of perpetual twilight, as he holds a whispered *colloque sentimental* with the ghost of an old love:

> "Dans le vieux parc solitaire et glacé,
> Deux spectres ont évoqué le passé."

It was, indeed, almost a literal unconsciousness, as of one who leads two lives, severed from one another as completely as sleep is from waking. Thus we get in his work very little of the personal appeal of those to whom riotous living, misery, a cross destiny, have been of so real a value. And it is important to draw this distinction, if only for the benefit of those young men who are convinced that the first step towards genius is disorder. Dowson is precisely one of the people who are pointed out as confirming this theory. And yet Dowson was precisely one of those who owed least to circumstances; and, in succumbing to them, he did no more than succumb to the destructive forces which, shut up within him, pulled down the house of life upon his own head.

A soul "unspotted from the world," in a body which one sees visibly soiling under one's eyes; that improbability is what all who knew him saw in Dowson, as his youthful physical grace gave way year by year, and the personal charm underlying it remained unchanged.

There never was a simpler or more attaching charm, because there never was a sweeter or more honest nature. It was not because he ever said anything particularly clever or particularly interesting, it was not because he gave you ideas, or impressed you by any strength or originality, that you liked to be with him; but because of a certain engaging quality, which seemed unconscious of itself, which was never anxious to be or to do anything, which simply existed, as perfume exists in a flower. Drink was like a heavy curtain, blotting out everything of a sudden; when the curtain lifted, nothing had changed. Living always that double life, he had his true and his false aspect, and the true life was the expression of that fresh, delicate, and uncontaminated nature which some of us knew in him, and which remains for us, untouched by the other, in every line that he wrote.

III

Dowson was the only poet I ever knew who cared more for his prose than for his verse; but he was wrong, and it is not by his prose that he will live, exquisite as that prose was at its best. He wrote two novels in collaboration with Mr Arthur Moore: "A Comedy of Masks," in 1893, and "Adrian Rome," in 1899, both done under the influence of Mr Henry James, both interesting because they were personal studies, and studies of known surroundings, rather than for their actual value as novels. A volume of "Stories and Studies in Sentiment," called "Dilemmas," in which the influence of Mr Wedmore was felt in addition to the influence of Mr James, appeared in 1895. Several other short stories, among his best work in prose, have not yet been reprinted from the *Savoy*. Some translations from the French, done as hack work, need not be mentioned here, though they were never without some traces of his peculiar quality of charm in language. The short stories were indeed rather "studies in sentiment" than stories; studies of singular delicacy, but with only a faint hold on life, so that perhaps the best of them was not unnaturally a study in the approaches of death: "The Dying of Francis Donne." For the most part they dealt with the same motives as the poems, hopeless and reverent love, the ethics of renunciation, the disappointment of those who are too weak or too unlucky to take what they desire. They have a sad and quiet beauty of their own, the beauty of second thoughts and subdued emotions, of choice and scholarly English, moving in the more fluid and reticent harmonies of prose almost as daintily as if it were moving to the measure of verse. Dowson's care over English prose was like that of a Frenchman writing his own language with the respect which Frenchmen pay to French. Even English things had to come to him through France, if he was to prize them very highly; and there is a passage in "Dilemmas" which I have always thought very characteristic of his own tastes, as it refers to an "infinitesimal library, a few French novels, an Horace, and some well-thumbed volumes of the modern English poets in the familiar edition of Tauchnitz." He was Latin by all his affinities, and that very quality of slightness, of parsimony almost, in his dealings with life and the substance of art, connects him with the artists of Latin races, who have always been so fastidious in their rejection of mere nature, when it comes too nakedly or too clamorously into sight and hearing, and so gratefully content with a few choice things faultlessly done.

And Dowson in his verse (the "Verses" of 1896, "The Pierrot of the Minute, a dramatic phantasy in one act," of 1897, the posthumous volume, "Decorations") was the same scrupulous artist as in his prose, and more felicitously at home there. He was quite Latin in his feeling for youth, and death, and "the old age of roses," and the pathos of our little hour in which to live and love; Latin in his elegance, reticence, and simple grace in the treatment of these motives; Latin, finally, in his sense of their sufficiency for the whole of one's mental attitude. He used the commonplaces of poetry frankly, making them his own by his belief in them: the Horatian Cynara or Neobule was still the natural symbol for him when he wished to be most personal. I remember his saying to me that his ideal of a line of verse was the line of Poe:

> "The viol, the violet, and the vine";

and the gracious, not remote or unreal beauty, which clings about such words and such images as these, was always to him the true poetical beauty. There never was a poet to whom verse came more naturally, for the song's sake; his theories were all æsthetic, almost technical ones, such as a theory, indicated by his preference for the line of Poe, that the letter "v" was the most beautiful of the letters, and could never be brought into verse too often. For any more abstract theories he had neither tolerance nor need. Poetry as a philosophy did not exist for him; it existed solely as the loveliest of the arts. He loved the elegance of Horace, all that was most complex in the simplicity of Poe, most bird-like in the human melodies of Verlaine. He had the pure lyric gift, unweighted or unballasted by any other quality of mind or emotion; and a song, for him, was music first, and then whatever you please afterwards, so long as it suggested, never told, some delicate sentiment, a sigh or a caress; finding words, at times, as perfect as these words of a poem headed, "O Mors! quam amara est memoria tua homini pacem habenti in substantiis suis":

"Exceeding sorrow
  Consumeth my sad heart!
Because to-morrow
  We must depart,
Now is exceeding sorrow
  All my part!

Give over playing,
  Cast thy viol away:
Merely laying
  Thine head my way:
Prithee, give over playing,
  Grave or gay.

Be no word spoken;
  Weep nothing: let a pale
Silence, unbroken
  Silence prevail!
Prithee, be no word spoken,
  Lest I fail!

Forget to-morrow!
  Weep nothing: only lay
In silent sorrow
  Thine head my way:
Let us forget to-morrow,
  This one day!"

There, surely, the music of silence speaks, if it has ever spoken. The words seem to tremble back into the silence which their whisper has interrupted, but not before they have created for us a mood, such a mood as the Venetian Pastoral of Giorgione renders in painting. Languid, half inarticulate, coming from the heart of a drowsy sorrow very conscious of itself, and not less sorrowful because it sees its own face looking mournfully back out of the water, the song seems to have been made by some fastidious amateur of grief, and it has all the sighs and tremors of the mood, wrought into a faultless strain of music. Stepping out of a paradise in which pain becomes so lovely, he can see the beauty which is the other side of madness, and, in a sonnet "To One in Bedlam," can create a more positive, a more poignant mood, with this fine subtlety:

"With delicate, mad hands, behind his sordid bars,
Surely he hath his posies, which they tear and twine;
Those scentless wisps of straw, that miserably line
His strait, caged universe, whereat the dull world stares,
Pedant and pitiful. O, how his rapt gaze wars
With their stupidity! Know they what dreams divine
Lift his long, laughing reveries like enchanted wine,
And make his melancholy germane to the stars'?

O lamentable brother! if those pity thee,
Am I not fain of all thy lone eyes promise me;
Half a fool's kingdom, far from men who sow and reap,
All their days, vanity? Better than mortal flowers,
Thy moon-kissed roses seem: better than love or sleep,
The star-crowned solitude of thine oblivious hours!"

Here, in the moment's intensity of this comradeship with madness, observe how beautiful the whole thing becomes; how instinctively the imagination of the poet turns what is sordid into a radiance, all stars and flowers and the divine part of forgetfulness! It is a symbol of the two sides of his own life: the side open to the street, and the side turned away from it, where he could "hush and bless himself with silence." No one ever worshipped beauty more devoutly, and just as we see him here transfiguring a dreadful thing with beauty, so we shall see, everywhere in his work, that he never admitted an emotion which he could not so transfigure.

He knew his limits only too well; he knew that the deeper and graver things of life were for the most part outside the circle of his magic; he passed them by, leaving much of himself unexpressed, because he would permit himself to express nothing imperfectly, or according to anything but his own conception of the dignity of poetry. In the lyric in which he has epitomised himself and his whole life, a lyric which is certainly one of the greatest lyrical poems of our time, "Non sum qualis eram bonæ sub regno Cynaræ," he has for once said everything, and he has said it to an intoxicating and perhaps immortal music:

"Last night, ah, yesternight, betwixt her lips and mine,
There fell thy shadow, Cynara! thy breath was shed
Upon my soul between the kisses and the wine;
And I was desolate and sick of an old passion,
  Yea, I was desolate and bowed my head:
I have been faithful to thee, Cynara! in my fashion.

All night upon mine heart I felt her warm heart beat,
Night-long within mine arms in love and sleep she lay;
Surely the kisses of her bought red mouth were sweet;
But I was desolate and sick of an old passion,
  When I awoke and found the dawn was grey:
I have been faithful to thee, Cynara! in my fashion.

I have forgot much, Cynara! gone with the wind,
Flung roses, roses riotously with the throng,
Dancing, to put thy pale, lost lilies out of mind;
But I was desolate and sick of an old passion,
  Yea, all the time, because the dance was long:
I have been faithful to thee, Cynara! in my fashion.

I cried for madder music and for stronger wine,
But when the feast is finished and the lamps expire,
Then falls thy shadow, Cynara! the night is thine;
And I am desolate and sick of an old passion,
  Yea, hungry for the lips of my desire:
I have been faithful to thee, Cynara! in my fashion."

Here, perpetuated by some unique energy of a temperament rarely so much the master of itself, is the song of passion and the passions, at their eternal war in the soul which they quicken or deaden, and in the body which they break down between them. In the second book, the book of "Decorations," there are a few pieces which repeat, only more faintly, this very personal note. Dowson could never have developed; he had already said, in his first book of verse, all that he had to say. Had he lived, had he gone on writing, he could only have echoed himself; and probably it would have been the less essential part of himself; his obligation to Swinburne, always evident, increasing as his own inspiration failed him. He was always without ambition, writing to please his own fastidious taste, with a kind of proud humility in his attitude towards the public, not expecting or requiring recognition. He died obscure, having ceased to care even for the delightful labour of writing. He died young, worn out by what was never really life to him, leaving a little verse which has the pathos of things too young and too frail ever to grow old.

1900.

PREFACE TO THE SECOND EDITION OF SILHOUETTES:

BEING A WORD ON BEHALF OF PATCHOULI

An ingenious reviewer once described some verses of mine as "unwholesome," because, he said, they had "a faint smell of Patchouli about them." I am a little sorry he chose Patchouli, for that is not a particularly favourite scent with me. If he had only chosen Peau d'Espagne, which has a subtle meaning, or Lily of the Valley, with which I have associations! But Patchouli will serve. Let me ask, then, in republishing, with additions, a collection of little pieces, many of which have been objected to, at one time or another, as being somewhat deliberately frivolous, why art should not, if it please, concern itself with the artificially charming, which, I suppose, is what my critic means by Patchouli? All art, surely, is a form of artifice, and thus, to the truly devout mind, condemned already, if not as actively noxious, at all events as needless. That is a point of view which I quite understand, and its conclusion I hold to be absolutely logical. I have the utmost respect for the people who refuse to read a novel, to go to the theatre, or to learn dancing. That is to have convictions and to live up to them. I understand also the point of view from which a work of art is tolerated in so far as it is actually militant on behalf of a religious or moral idea. But what I fail to understand are those delicate, invisible degrees by which a distinction is drawn between this form of art and that; the hesitations, and compromises, and timorous advances, and shocked retreats, of the Puritan conscience once emancipated and yet afraid of liberty. However you may try to convince yourself to the contrary, a work of art can be judged only from two standpoints: the standpoint from which its art is measured entirely by its morality, and the standpoint from which its morality is measured entirely by its art.

Here, for once, in connection with these "Silhouettes," I have not, if my recollection serves me, been accused of actual immorality. I am but a fair way along the "primrose path," not yet within singeing distance of the "everlasting bonfire." In other words, I have not yet written "London Nights," which, it appears (I can scarcely realise it, in my innocent abstraction in æsthetical matters), has no very salutary reputation among the blameless moralists of the press. I need not, therefore, on this occasion, concern myself with more than the curious fallacy by which there is supposed to be something inherently wrong in artistic work which deals frankly and lightly with the very real charm of the lighter emotions and the more fleeting sensations.

I do not wish to assert that the kind of verse which happened to reflect certain moods of mine at a certain period of my life is the best kind of verse in itself, or is likely to seem to me, in other years, when other moods may have made me their own, the best kind of verse for my own expression of myself. Nor do I affect to doubt that the creation of the supreme emotion is a higher form of art than the reflection of the most exquisite sensation, the evocation of the most magical impression. I claim only an equal liberty for the rendering of every mood of that variable and inexplicable and contradictory creature which we call ourselves, of every aspect under which we are gifted or condemned to apprehend the beauty and strangeness and curiosity of the visible world.

Patchouli! Well, why not Patchouli? Is there any "reason in nature" why we should write exclusively about the natural blush, if the delicately acquired blush of rouge has any attraction for us? Both exist; both, I think, are charming in their way; and the latter, as a subject, has, at all events, more novelty. If you prefer your "new-mown hay" in the hayfield, and I, it may be, in a scent-bottle, why may not my individual caprice be allowed to find expression as well as yours? Probably I enjoy the hayfield as much as you do; but I enjoy quite other scents and sensations as well, and I take the former for granted, and write my poem, for a change, about the latter. There is no necessary difference in artistic value between a good poem about a flower in the hedge and a good poem about the scent in a sachet. I am always charmed to read beautiful poems about nature in the country. Only, personally, I prefer town to country; and in the town we have to find for ourselves, as best we may, the *décor* which is the town equivalent of the great natural *décor* of fields and hills. Here it is that artificiality comes in; and if any one sees no beauty in the effects of artificial light, in all the variable, most human, and yet most factitious town landscape, I can only pity him, and go on my own way.

That is, if he will let me. But he tells me that one thing is right and the other is wrong; that one is good art and the other is bad; and I listen in amazement, sometimes not without impatience, wondering why an estimable personal prejudice should be thus exalted into a dogma, and uttered in the name of art. For in art there can be no prejudices, only results. If we are to save people's souls by the writing of verses, well and good. But if not, there is no choice but to admit absolute freedom of choice. And if Patchouli pleases one, why not Patchouli?

London, *February* 1896.

PREFACE TO THE SECOND EDITION OF LONDON NIGHTS

The publication of this book was received by the English press with a singular unanimity of abuse. In some cases the abuse was ignoble; for the most part, it was no more than unintelligent. Scarcely any critic did himself the credit of considering with any care the intention or the execution of what offended him by its substance or its subject. I had expected opposition, I was prepared for a reasonable amount of prejudice; but I must confess to some surprise at the nature of the opposition, the extent of the prejudice, which it was my fortune to encounter. Happening to be in France at the time, I reflected, with scarcely the natural satisfaction of the Englishman, that such a reception of a work of art would have been possible in no country but England.

And now, in bringing out a new edition of these poems, which I have neither taken from nor added to, and in which I have found it needful to make but little revision, it is with no hope of persuading any one not already aware of what I have to say that I make this statement on behalf of general principles and my own application of them, but rather on Blake's theory, that you should tell the truth, not to convince those who do not believe, but to confirm those who do.

I have been attacked, then, on the ground of morality, and by people who, in condemning my book, not because it is bad art, but because they think it bad morality, forget that they are confusing moral and artistic judgments, and limiting art without aiding morality. I contend on behalf of the liberty of art, and I deny that morals have any right of jurisdiction over it. Art may be served by morality; it can never be its servant. For the principles of art are eternal, while the principles of morality fluctuate with the spiritual ebb and flow of the ages. Show me any commandment of the traditional code of morals which you are at present obeying, and I will show you its opposite among the commandments of some other code of morals which your forefathers once obeyed; or, if you prefer, some righteous instance of its breaking, which you will commend in spite of yourself. Is it for such a shifting guide that I am to forsake the sure and constant leading of art, which tells me that whatever I find in humanity (passion, desire, the spirit or the senses, the hell or heaven of man's heart) is part of the eternal substance which nature weaves in the rough for art to combine cunningly into beautiful patterns? The whole visible world itself, we are told, is but a symbol, made visible in order that we may apprehend ourselves, and not be blown hither and thither like a flame in the night. How laughable is it, then, that we should busy ourselves, with such serious faces, in the commending or condemning, the permission or the exemption, of this accident or that, this or the other passing caprice of our wisdom or our folly, as a due or improper subject for the "moment's monument" of a poem! It is as if you were to say to me, here on these weedy rocks of Rosses Point, where the grey sea passes me continually, flinging a little foam at my feet, that I may write of one rather than another of these waves, which are not more infinite than the moods of men.

The moods of men! There I find my subject, there the region over which art rules; and whatever has once been a mood of mine, though it has been no more than a ripple on the sea, and had no longer than that ripple's duration, I claim the right to render, if I can, in verse; and I claim, from my critics and my readers, the primary understanding, that a mood is after all but a mood, a ripple on the sea, and perhaps with no longer than that ripple's duration. I do not profess that any poem in this book is the record of actual fact; I declare that every poem is the sincere attempt to render a particular mood which has once been mine, and to render it as if, for the moment, there were no other mood for me in the world. I have rendered, well or ill, many moods, and without disguise or preference. If it be objected to me that some of them were moods I had better never have felt, I am ready to answer, Possibly; but I must add, What of that? They have existed; and whatever has existed has achieved the right of artistic existence.

ROSSES POINT, SLIGO, *September* 2, 1896.

CONCLUSION

THE CHOICE

WITH the publication of "Pages Catholiques," a volume of selections from "En Route" and "La Cathédrale," edited with a preface by the Abbé Mugnier, Huysmans may be said to have received the imprimatur of the Church. Among many responsible Catholic testimonies, the Abbé Mugnier quotes an emphatic phrase of Dom Augustin, the Abbé of La Trappe d'Igny, the monastery described in "En Route," who rejoices that "the book will do good to those who do not usually read good books." And he himself affirms, as he presents to the world the book into which he has put so much of what is finest in Huysmans' two novels, that to receive these pages with faith is to be faithful to the spirit of Christ.

Such affirmations are of almost equal interest to those who are preoccupied with questions of religion and to those who are preoccupied with questions of art. For, after all, does not the larger part of the value of conduct, and the larger part of the value of art come from the amount of sincerity which has been put into living and working? The question itself of sincerity is certainly the most complicated question in the world; for one is not sincere, in life or in art, by intending to be. Our intentions should indeed count for very little, for an intention is not so much as the paralytic's dream of movement; it is a whisper of the reason, which may not even be heard by that deeper self, soul or instinct, which is at once what gives us our identity, and is prepared to scatter that identity into the general consciousness of the universe. I may say to myself: I will believe in such a dogma of religion, I will believe in such a theory of art. But all my saying and meaning and trying will avail me nothing if the dogma or the theory has not struck sudden fire into light, as it came startlingly upon itself, there in the darkness. Then, and then only, I shall be sincere, as I seem to discover for the first time something which I had known always. And it is this kind of sincerity, this illumination, which means so much to the man who wishes to live well and to the artist who wishes to work well.

"There are states of soul which are not to be invented," said Monseigneur d'Hulst, in reply to some doubts about the literal truth to conviction of "En Route"; and it is on this question of sincerity that the whole artistic merit of Huysmans' later work seems to me to depend. The faculty of invention, which can do so much that it seems to us sometimes as if, with Shakespeare or with Michelangelo, it could do everything, is after all never quite an absolute thing, never without its lineage, never the first word of creation. Invention is a happy way of arranging the bonfire, so that a single spark sets it all alight. That single spark is no doubt the incalculable element, which lurks everywhere in the world, but, all the same, the spark is nothing, would flicker out in an instant, if its fiery way is not prepared for it. And, when we set invention to work upon the soul, upon what is deepest in us, we must feed it with all our substance, keeping nothing back, if it is to do its work there. A man who has never been in love will never write a good love-poem; nor, if he has only loved ignobly, will he write nobly of love. And so a man who has never had the great awakening, which may bring him, in Barbey d'Aurévilly's phrase, used of Huysmans himself as long ago as 1884, "to the mouth of the pistol or to the foot of the Cross," will never be able to do what Huysmans has done: trace the itinerary of the soul, milestone by milestone, along the road of its penitence.

The conversion of Huysmans, unlike the conversion of François Coppée for instance, is a matter of some significance, apart even from the question of the influence of that change upon his work as an artist. Coppée, an amiable and charming man of letters, became ill, it appears, and fell back upon the consolations of religion, as dying men, and men who suppose themselves to be dying, often do, as after all the only consolations left. He has recovered, and he retains his piety, as we keep souvenirs, doubtless from a real sense of fidelity to an experience which has really moved us. But the experience is not everything: much depends on the man. Coppée is a sentimentalist who has written innumerable verses about the sorrows of the poor, and he has never moved us with a great emotion, or convinced us of any passionate sympathy in himself for what he is writing about. His religion leaves us equally unmoved, for it comes to us as a voice, no more, the voice of one whose opinions have no meaning for us, because they have had no deep meaning for him. But, with Huysmans, the matter is different. "His sincerity is the very form of his talent," says the Abbé Mugnier, in his excellent preface: "he owes to it his qualities and his defects, his admirers and his enemies. . . . Rarely have the man and the writer been more closely identified." And Huysmans, as we have always seen him in his books, has been an idealist *à rebours*, one so discontented with the world as it is, with what is ugly and evil in it, that he has exalted his discontent into a kind of martyrdom; and all his earlier books have been one long narrative of his martyrdom. He has avenged himself upon ugliness and evil by painting them with the exasperation of a monk of the Middle Ages, or with the angry satire of the stone-carvers who set obscene devils crawling over the devout and aspiring walls of the great cathedrals. While he has seemed to be grovelling deeper than others in the trough of Realism, he has been like a man who does penance in a devouring rage, against himself and against sin. He has seen the external world with such extraordinary vividness because he has seen it with hatred; and if love may at times blind with the shadow of too great a light, hatred is always open-eyed, with a kind of intoxication of vision. Not Swift hated the world as Huysmans has hated it. Well, he has found peace, he has become reconciled with the world, he has found his own way of living apart in it, not, as yet, in an acceptance of monastic life, but in a little hermitage of his own, "between a monastery and a wood."

That a man like Huysmans should have accepted the Church, should have found the most closely formulated theory of religion still possible, and more than a mere refuge, is certainly significant. It is significant, among other things, as a confession on the part of a great artist, that art alone, as he has conceived it, is not finally satisfying without some further defence against the world. In "A Rebours" he showed us the sterilising influence of a narrow and selfish conception of art, as he represented a particular paradise of art for art's sake turning inevitably into its corresponding hell. Des Esseintes is the symbol of all those who have tried to shut themselves in from the natural world, upon an artificial beauty which has no root there. Worshipping colour, sound, perfume, for their own sakes, and not for their ministrations to a more divine beauty, he stupefies himself on the threshold of ecstasy. And Huysmans, we can scarcely doubt, has passed through the particular kind of haschish dream which this experience really is. He has realised that the great choice, the choice between the world and something which is not visible in the world, but out of which the visible world has been made, does not lie in the mere contrast of the subtler and grosser senses. He has come to realise what the choice really is, and he has chosen. Yet perhaps the choice is not quite so narrow as Barbey d'Aurévilly thought; perhaps it is a choice between actualising this dream or actualising that dream. In his escape from the world, one man chooses religion, and seems to find himself; another, choosing love, may seem also to find himself; and may not another, coming to art as to a religion and as to a woman, seem to find himself not less effectually? The one certainty is, that society is the enemy of man, and that formal art is the enemy of the artist. We shall not find ourselves in drawing-rooms or in museums. A man who goes through a day without some fine emotion has wasted his day, whatever he has gained in it. And it is so easy to go through day after day, busily and agreeably, without ever really living for a single instant. Art begins when a man wishes to immortalise the most vivid moment he has ever lived. Life has already, to one not an artist, become art in that moment. And the making of one's life into art is after all the first duty and privilege of every man. It is to escape from material reality into whatever form of ecstasy is our own form of spiritual existence. There is the choice; and our happiness, our "success in life," will depend on our choosing rightly, each for himself, among the forms in which that choice will come to us.

1900.

Of the essays contained in this volume, those on Walter Pater, Robert Louis Stevenson, and John Addington Symonds, and the Note on Zola's Method are reprinted from my "Studies in Two Literatures" (1897), which has long since been out of print, and which I do not intend to reissue as a volume. Two prefaces are reprinted from the second editions of two volumes of verse now included in my collected "Poems" of 1902. The essay on Maupassant was published in two halves, one half by Mr Heinemann as a preface to an illustrated translation of "Boule de Suif," the other half by Messrs. G. P. Putnam's Sons as a preface to a translation of some of Maupassant's stories in their series of "Little French Masterpieces." Part of the essay on Gabriele d'Annunzio is taken from my preface to the English translation of "Il Piacere," published by Mr Heinemann; and the essay on Mérimée was originally published as a preface to the translation of "Carmen" and "Colomba" in the same publisher's "Century of French Romance." The main part of the other essays appeared in the *Quarterly Review*, the *Fortnightly Review*, the *Monthly Review*, *Harper's Magazine*, the *Lamp*, the *Bookman*, the *Saturday Review*, and the *Athenæum*. I have to thank Count Joseph Primoli for allowing me to reproduce his unpublished photograph of d'Annunzio.

BY THE SAME WRITER.

POEMS (Collected Edition in two volumes). 1902.

THE SYMBOLIST MOVEMENT IN LITERATURE. 1899.

PLAYS, ACTING, AND MUSIC. 1903.

CITIES. 1903.

IN PREPARATION.

TRISTAN AND ISEULT. A Tragedy in Verse, in Four Acts.

SPIRITUAL ADVENTURES.

STUDIES IN THE SEVEN ARTS.

A HISTORY OF ENGLISH POETRY IN THE NINETEENTH CENTURY.

Volume I. THE GEORGIAN AGE.

PRINTED BY
TURNBULL AND SPEARS,
EDINBURGH